OXFORD REVISION GU[IDE]

AS Level

AS Level

PSYCHOLOGY

through diagrams

Grahame Hill

OXFORD
UNIVERSITY PRESS

UNIVERSITY PRESS

Great Clarendon Street, Oxford OX2 6DP

Oxford University Press is a department of the University of Oxford.
It furthers the University's objective of excellence in research, scholarship,
and education by publishing worldwide in

Oxford New York

Athens Auckland Bangkok Bogotá Buenos Aires Cape Town
Chennai Dar es Salaam Delhi Florence Hong Kong Istanbul
Karachi Kolkata Kuala Lumpur Madrid Melbourne Mexico City Mumbai
Nairobi Paris São Paulo Shanghai Singapore Taipei Tokyo Toronto Warsaw

with associated companies in Berlin Ibadan

Oxford is a trade mark of Oxford University Press

First published 2001
Reprinted 2001
ISBN 0 19 832833 8

For Valérie Férec – it would not have been possible without you!
I would also like to thank all the following for their support:
my family, my friends at the Sixth Form College Colchester
(especially David, Morag, Rosemary, and Sue), and my students.

Illustrated by Oxford Illustrators
Typeset and designed by Hardlines, Charlbury, Oxford
Printed in Great Britain

Contents

AS = Content relevant to AS Level specifications
BR = Content suitable for AS Level background reading
A2 = Content only covered in year 2 (A Level) of specification

The above content is relevant to the AQA Specification A (**AQAa**), Edexcel (**EDX**) and **OCR** AS level specifications (syllabi). *Some* content may apply to AQA specification B.

Introduction. What is psychology?

DEFINITIONS

The word 'Psychology' is derived from two Greek roots: 'Psyche', meaning 'mind' or 'soul' and 'Logos', meaning 'study of'. Psychology, therefore, literally means 'study of the mind'. However, a more recent definition by Atkinson et al (1991) suggests that psychology is:

'The scientific study of behaviour and mental processes'
Just giving this simple definition, however, is a bit misleading, since psychologists now and throughout their history have not only disagreed about the definition of psychology, but have also strongly disagreed about *what* should be studied in the subject and *how* it should be studied.

THE HISTORY OF PSYCHOLOGY

WHERE DID PSYCHOLOGY COME FROM?
Psychology developed from three main areas of study:

PHILOSOPHY
- Many of the problems which psychology has investigated were first most clearly outlined by Greek philosophers such as Socrates, Plato, and Aristotle in the 5th century BC. Two more recent philosophical influences on the development of psychology as a science were:
1 **Empiricism** - which argued that humans should only measure data that is *objectively observable,* such as behaviour.
2 **Positivism** - which argued that the *methods* and principles of *science* should be applied to human behaviour.

BIOLOGY
Biology has had two important influences:
1 Evolution - Darwin's suggestion that humans have *evolved* from other animals. The discoveries in *genetics* that followed from his evolutionary theory have had many important implications for the study and understanding of behaviour.
2 Physiology - the discoveries, mostly by the medical profession, of the structure and function of the brain, nervous, and endocrine systems have significantly contributed to the understanding of behaviour.

PHYSICS
- A subject that because of its great success has been adopted as the ideal model by scientists in psychology, who have borrowed its *scientific methods* and *principles.*
- Physicists, such as Fechner, started applying their subject to human behaviour and experience (psychophysics) in the nineteenth century, with some success.

WHEN DID PSYCHOLOGY START?
The date **1879** is usually said to be the start of psychology as a **separate scientific discipline**, since it was when Wilhelm Wundt created the first psychology laboratory in Leipzig. Wundt is, therefore, regarded as the 'founding father' of psychology, although Americans tend to suggest that William James should have this honour since his 1890 book (which took 12 years to write) entitled *Principles of Psychology* was a major landmark in psychology's literature and he began teaching a course on the relationship between physiology and psychology at Harvard University in 1875.

HOW DID PSYCHOLOGY DEVELOP?
- **Structuralism** - was the first approach to investigating psychology, pioneered by Wundt himself, who thought that the object of psychological investigation should be the *conscious mind,* and that it should be studied by *introspection* (looking inwards at one's own mental experience) in order to *break it down* into its component parts (such as images, sensations and feelings) like the science of chemistry had done with chemicals. One structuralist, Titchener, claimed there were a total of 46,708 basic sensations that combined to form the structure of the human mind, but the approach was very limited in its ability to explain and was replaced by functionalism.
- **Functionalism** - the approach William James advocated. James was influenced by Darwin's views and argued that the workings of the mind are functional, to survive and adapt, so we should investigate *what behaviour and thoughts are for.* Many of James's insights remain valid today, but functionalism was superseded by the next two very powerful approaches that both started around the turn of the century.
- **Psychoanalysis** - was in fact a method of *therapy* developed by Sigmund Freud in Austria, but in many major books, such as *The interpretation of dreams* (1900), Freud began describing in detail an underlying theory of the human mind and behaviour that has had an enormous (and controversial) impact on psychology. Freud argued that the proper object of psychological investigation should be the *unconscious mind*, and that our behaviour is determined by processes of which we are not aware.
- **Behaviourism** - Behaviourists, such as John Watson, were extremely critical of all the approaches that concerned themselves with 'minds', and proposed that psychology should only investigate *observable behaviour* if it wanted to be an objective science. This approach dominated experimental psychology until the 1950s, when a strong resurgence of interest in the 'mind' developed in the form of the cognitive and the humanistic approaches, which suggested that behaviourism ignored all the most important and interesting things that go on in our heads.
- **Cognitive psychology** - aims to investigate the mind by using *computer information processing* ideas to arrive at testable *models* of how the brain works, and then applying *scientific methods* to confirm these models. The cognitive approach has enjoyed much success and is a very dominant one in psychology today.
- The **Humanistic approach**, however, has had less of an impact on psychology, since it has deliberately adopted a *less scientific* view of the human mind by arguing that psychology should focus on each *individual's conscious experience* and *aims* in life.
- The **Biological approach** has advanced *evolutionary, physiological,* and *genetic* explanations for human behaviour throughout the history of psychology.

The cognitive approach to psychology

ORIGINS AND HISTORY

- The cognitive approach began to revolutionise psychology in the late 1950s and early 1960s, to become the dominant paradigm in the subject by the 1970s. Interest in mental processes had been gradually resurrected through the work of people like Tolman and Piaget, but it was the arrival of the **computer** that gave cognitive psychology the terminology and metaphor it needed to investigate human minds.
- Cognitive psychology compares the human mind to a computer, suggesting that we too are **information processors** and that it is possible and desirable to study the **internal mental processes** that lie between the stimuli we receive and the responses we make. Cognition means 'knowing' and cognitive processes refer to the ways in which knowledge is gained, used and retained. Therefore, cognitive psychologists have studied perception, attention, memory, thinking, language, and problem solving.
- Cognitive psychologists believe these internal mental processes (our programming) can be investigated scientifically by proposing models of psychological functions and then conducting research to see, when people are given an input of information, whether their output of behaviour/verbal report matches what the models would predict.

E. Loftus

'...cognition refers to all those processes by which sensory input is transformed, reduced, elaborated, stored, recovered and used... cognition is involved in everything a human being might possibly do.'
Neisser (1966)

ASSUMPTIONS

Cognitive psychologists assume that:

1. The study of **internal mental processes is important in understanding behaviour** - cognitive processes **actively** organise and manipulate the information we receive - humans do not just passively respond to their environment.
2. Humans, like computers, are **information processors** - regardless of our hardware (brains or circuits) both receive, interpret and respond to information - and these processes can be modelled and tested **scientifically**.

METHODS OF INVESTIGATION

Cognitive psychologists mostly use:

- **Experimentation** - usually conducted in the laboratory, e.g. memory experiments conducted under strictly controlled conditions, where independent variables such as the time delay before recall are manipulated to find the effect on the amount of information retained.
- **Case studies** - for example the study of brain damaged patients such as those with anterograde amnesia in memory research.

CONTRIBUTION TO PSYCHOLOGY

Cognitive psychologists have sought to explain:

- **memory,** e.g. Atkinson and Shiffrin's multi-store model of the input, storage and loss of information, etc.
- **perception,** e.g. Gregory's theory on the role of mental processes in influencing/organising visual stimuli
- **attention,** e.g. Broadbent's filter model
- **artificial intelligence,** e.g. Rumelhart and McClelland's parallel distributed network models
- **social cognition,** e.g. the effects of stereotypes on interpersonal perception
- **abnormality,** e.g. Beck's ideas on the errors of logic and negative thinking of depressed patients

CONTRIBUTION TO SOCIETY

Cognitive psychology has had a broad range of applications, for example to

- **memory** - to help improve memory through mnemonic devices or to aid the police in eyewitness testimony
- **education** - Information processing theory has been applied to improve educational techniques
- **therapy** - such as the use of Ellis's rational emotive therapy to restructure faulty thinking and perceptions in depression, for example. When combined to form cognitive-behavioural techniques, effectiveness is improved
- **health promotion** - e.g. the health belief model and the following (or not) of health advice

STRENGTHS

Cognitive psychology is probably the most dominant approach today:

- It investigates many areas of interest in psychology that had been neglected by behaviourism; yet, unlike psychoanalysis and humanism, it investigates them using more rigorous scientific methods.
- In contrast to the biological approach, it bases its explanations firmly at a functional, psychological level, rather than resorting to reductionism to explain human behaviour.
- The approach has provided explanations of many aspects of human behaviour and has had useful practical applications.
- Cognitive psychology has influenced and integrated with many other approaches and areas of study to produce, for example, social learning theory, cognitive neuropsychology, social cognition, and artificial intelligence.

WEAKNESSES

Cognitive models have been accused of being

- over simplistic - ignoring the huge complexity of human functioning compared to computer functioning
- unrealistic and over hypothetical - ignoring the biological influences and grounding of mental processes
- too cold - ignoring the emotional life of humans, their conscious experience and possible use of freewill

Types of memory

ENCODING TYPES OF MEMORY

The human sensory systems, such as our eyes and ears, receive many different forms of stimulation, ranging from sound waves to photons of light. Obviously the information reaching our senses is transformed in nature when it is represented in our brains, and encoding refers to the process of representing knowledge in different forms.

IMAGERY MEMORY

- Some memory representations appear to closely resemble the raw, unabstracted data containing original material from our senses, such as the extremely brief iconic (visual) and echoic (auditory) after images that rapidly fade from our eyes and ears. Yet even after these have gone, we retain the ability to recall fairly vivid visual images of what we have seen and to hear again tunes we have experienced.
- Baddeley and Hitch (1974) have investigated this sort of short term imagery ability by suggesting that we have a 'visuospatial scratchpad' for summoning up and examining our visual imagery.
- Photographic (eidetic) memory is an extremely rare ultra enhanced form of imagery memory, shown in a weak form by perhaps 5% of young children (Haber, 1979).

PROCEDURAL MEMORY

- Also known as implicit memory, this is the memory for **knowing how** to do things such as talk, walk, juggle, etc. Although we retain these skills and abilities, we are often completely **unable to consciously introspect upon or describe** how we do them. Procedural memory is similar to Bruner's enactive mode.
- Procedural knowledge is very resistant to forgetting (we never forget how to ride a bicycle) and is also resistant to brain damage that eradicates other forms of memory - anterograde amnesiac patients, who forget simple events or verbal instructions after a few moments, are often able to learn new procedural skills such as playing table-tennis.

DECLARATIVE MEMORY

- Sometimes termed explicit memory, this type concerns all the information that we can **describe or report**, and as such has been the focus of the *majority* of research on memory. Declarative memory includes:
  a **semantic memory** - this concerns memory for meaning, the storage of abstract, general facts regardless of when those facts were acquired e.g. *knowing what* a word means.
  b **episodic** - this is 'knowing when' memory based upon personal experience and linked to a particular time and place in our lives. Episodic memory can be quite precise - Lindsay and Norman (1977) asked students "what were you doing on a Monday afternoon in the 3rd week of September, 2 years ago?", and found many actually knew. Very vivid episodic memories have been termed 'flashbulb' memories (Brown and Kulik, 1977) which involve recalling exactly what you were doing and where you were when a particularly important, exciting or emotional event happened.

DURATION TYPES OF MEMORY

Ever since William James (1890) distinguished between *primary* memory which feels like our present conscious experience, and *secondary* memory which seems like we are 'fishing out' information from the past, cognitive psychologists have been very interested in the possibility of different types of memory store based on the duration of time memories last for. Cognitive psychologists have proposed ***three types*** of time based store, each with differences in duration, capacity, coding and function.

SENSORY MEMORY
(sometimes called the short term sensory store or sensory register)

- The sense organs have a limited ability to store information about the world in a fairly unprocessed way for less than a second, rather like an afterimage. The visual system possesses *iconic* memory for visual stimuli such as shape, size, colour and location (but not meaning), whereas the hearing system has *echoic* memory for auditory stimuli.
- Coltheart et al (1974) have argued that the momentary freezing of visual input allows us to select which aspects of the input should go on for further memory processing. The existence of sensory memory has been experimentally demonstrated by Sperling (1960) using a tachistoscope.

SHORT-TERM MEMORY

- Information selected by attention from sensory memory, may pass into short-term memory (STM).
- STM allows us to retain information long enough to **use** it, e.g. looking up a telephone number and remembering it long enough to dial it. Peterson and Peterson (1959) have demonstrated that STM lasts approximately **between 15 and 30 seconds,** unless people rehearse the material, while Miller (1956) has found that STM has a **limited capacity** of around **7 'chunks'** of information.
- STM also appears to mostly **encode** memory **acoustically** (in terms of sound) as Conrad (1964) has demonstrated, but can also retain visuospatial images.

LONG-TERM MEMORY

- Long-term memory provides the lasting retention of information and skills, from **minutes** to a **lifetime**.
- Long-term memory appears to have an almost **limitless capacity** to retain information, but of course its capacity could never be measured - it would take too long!
- Long-term information seems to be encoded mainly in terms of **meaning** (semantic memory), as Baddeley has shown, but also retains procedural skills and imagery.

Research on sensory memory, short-term and long-term memory

SENSORY MEMORY

- Since sensory memory lasts less than a second, most of the material in it will have been forgotten before it can be reported! *Sperling* studied the sensory memory for vision (the iconic store) by using a *tachistoscope* - a device that can flash pictoral stimuli onto a blank screen for very brief instances. Using this device, Sperling was able to ask subjects to remember as many letters as they could from a **grid of 12 symbols** that he was going to display for just **one twentieth of a second**, and found that while they could only recall around **four** of the symbols before the grid faded from their sensory memory, they typically reported seeing a lot more than they had time to report.
- **Capacity** - Sperling presented the 12 symbol grid for 1/20th of a second, followed immediately by a **high, medium** or **low tone,** which indicated which of the three rows of four symbols the subject had to attend to from their iconic memory of the grid. In this partial report condition, recall was on average just over 3 out of the 4 symbols from any row they attended to, suggesting that the iconic store can retain **approximately 76%** of all the data received.

	Step 1	Step 2	Step 3
	Show grid	Ring tone	Recall letters
7 1 V F			? ? ? ?
X L 5 3		Medium tone	X L 5 3
B 4 W 7			? ? ? ?

- **Duration** - If there was a delay between the presentation of the grid and the sounding of the tone, Sperling found that more and more information was lost (only 50% was available after a 0.3 second delay and only 33% was available after a 1 second delay).

SHORT-TERM MEMORY

- **Duration** - Peterson and Peterson (1959) investigated the duration of short-term memory with their **trigram experiment**. They achieved this by
  1. asking subjects to remember a single nonsense syllable of three consonants (a *trigram* of letters such as FJT or KPD).
  2. giving them an *interpolated task* to stop them rehearsing the trigram (such as counting backwards in threes from one hundred).
  3. testing their *recall after* 3, 6, 9, 12, 15 or 18 seconds (recall had to be perfect and in the correct order to count). While average recall was very good (about 80%) after 3 seconds, this average dropped dramatically to around 10% after 18 seconds.

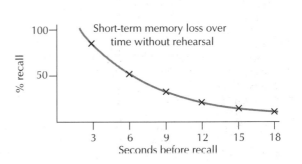

- **Capacity** - Many early researchers in the area of memory, including Ebbinghaus, noted that short term memory appears to have a limited storage capacity. *Miller* (1956) investigated this limited capacity experimentally, refering to it as '**The magical number seven, plus or minus two'**. Miller found that the amount of information retained could be increased by **chunking** the information - packaging it into larger items or units, although the STM can still only retain 7 + or - 2 of these chunks. Chunking is greatly improved if the chunks already have **meaning** from LTM.

Unchunked items
0 1 0 3 3 8 9 8 2 1 8 6 5 7
M P I B M I T V A A F B I R A F
Chunked items
0 1 0   3 3   8 9 8   2 1   8 6 5 7
M P   I B M   I T V   A A   F B I   R A F

- **Encoding** - It has been argued that the main way information is encoded or retained in STM is through sound - an **acoustic code**. Regardless of whether we see or hear material, we tend to find ourselves repeating the information verbally to ourselves to keep it in mind (STM), and hopefully pass it on to long term storage. Conrad (1964) demonstrated acoustic STM encoding, finding that rhyming letters were significantly harder to recall properly than non rhyming letters, mostly due to acoustic confusion errors, e.g. recalling 'B' instead of 'P'. Baddeley found similar effects for rhyming vs. non-rhyming words.
Den Heyer and Barrett (1971) showed that STM stores visual information too.

1) B T C P G E D
2) F T Z Q W R N
3) MAT, CAT, SAT, BAT, HAT, RAT, FAT
4) PIE, SIX, TRY, BIG, GUN, HEN, MAN

Acoustic confusion errors are made when recalling lists 1 & 3, even though the letters are visually presented. This shows the material is retained acoustically in STM.

LONG-TERM MEMORY

- **Duration** - Ebbinghaus tested his memory using nonsense syllables after delays ranging from 20 minutes to 31 days later and found that a large proportion of information in LTM was lost comparatively quickly (within the first hour) and thereafter stabilised to a much slower rate of loss.
Linton used a diary to record at least 2 'every day' events from her life each day over 6 years, and randomly tested her later recall of them. She found a much more even and gradual loss of data over time (approx. 6 % per year).
- **Capacity** - Enormous but impossible to measure.
- **Encoding** - Baddeley (1966) showed that LTM stores information in terms of meaning (semantic memory), by giving subjects four lists to remember.
If recall was given immediately, list A was recalled worse than list B, but there was little difference between the recall of lists C and D, indicating acoustic STM encoding.
After 20 minutes, however, it was list C that was recalled worse than D since words with similar meanings were confused, indicating semantic LTM encoding.

Baddeley's (1966) lists:

List A - Similar sounding words
e.g. man, map, can, cap.

List B - Non similar sounding words
e.g. try, pig, hut, pen.

List C - Similar meaning words
e.g. great, big, huge, wide.

List D - Non similar meaning words
e.g. run, easy, bright.

Multi-store model of memory

- Much research was devoted to identifying the properties of sensory, short-term, and long-term memory, and cognitive psychologists such as Atkinson and Shiffrin (1968) began to regard them as **stores** - hypothetical holding structures.
- Atkinson and Shiffrin proposed the two-process model of memory, which showed how information flowed through the two stores of short-term and long-term memory, but like many of the models, they assumed the existence of a sensory memory that precedes the short-term memory, and so it is sometimes termed the multi-store model.

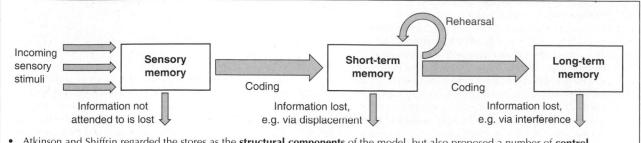

- Atkinson and Shiffrin regarded the stores as the **structural components** of the model, but also proposed a number of **control processes**, such as attention, coding and rehearsal, which operate in conjunction with the stores.

In addition to the research on the differing durations, capacities etc. of the memory stores there are two main lines of evidence that support the model's assumptions about the way information flows through the system and the distinct existence of short-term and long-term memory stores - free recall experiments and studies of brain damaged patients.

FREE RECALL EXPERIMENTS

- In free recall experiments, subjects are given a number of words (for example 20) in succession to remember and are then asked to recall them in any order ('free recall'). The results reliably fall into a pattern known as the **serial position curve**. This curve consists of

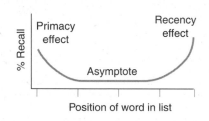

  a a **primacy effect** - Subjects tend to recall the first words of the list well, which indicates that the first words entered short-term memory and had time to be rehearsed and passed on to long-term memory before the STM capacity was reached. The primacy effect, therefore, involves recall from long term memory.
  b an **asymptote** - The middle portion items of the list are remembered far less well than those at the beginning and the end. This is probably because the increasing number of items fills the limited capacity of the STM and these later items are unable to be properly rehearsed and transferred to LTM before they are displaced.
  c a **recency effect** - Subjects usually recall those items from the end of the list first, and tend to get more of these correct on average than all the earlier items. This effect persists even if the list is lengthened (Murdock, 1962), and is thought to be due to recall from the short-term memory store - since the items at the end of the list were the last to enter STM and were not displaced by further items.
- Further evidence for the primacy/recency effects comes from two other findings:
  a Slower rates of presentation can improve the primacy effect perhaps due to more rehearsal time, but have little or no influence on the recency effect.
  b The recency effect disappears if the last words are not recalled straight away. Glanzer and Cunitz (1966) gave subjects an interference task immediately after the last word of the list and found a primacy but no recency effect.

STUDIES OF BRAIN DAMAGED PATIENTS

Cases of **anterograde amnesia** such as H.M. (Milner et al, 1978) or Clive Wearing (reported in Blakemore, 1988) provide strong evidence for the distinction between STM and LTM. Anterograde amnesia is often caused by brain damage to the hippocampus and those suffering from it seem incapable of transferring new factual information between STM and LTM. With this inability, they are essentially trapped in a world of experience that only lasts as long as their short-term memory does. Patients afflicted by anterograde amnesia often retain most of their long term memory for events up until the moment of brain damage and maintain their procedural memories. While they seem incapable of gaining new long-term declarative memory for semantic or episodic information most are able to learn new procedural skills (like playing table-tennis).
If these people are given free recall experiments, they show good recency effects but extremely poor primacy effects (Baddeley and Warrington, 1970).

CRITICISMS OF THE MULTI-STORE MODEL

It is too simplistic, in that:
a It under-emphasises interaction between the stores, for example the way information from LTM influences what is regarded as important and relevant to show attention to in sensory memory and helps the meaningful chunking of information in STM.
b STM and LTM are more complex and less unitary than the model assumes. This criticism is dealt with by the Working Memory model of STM by Baddeley and Hitch (1974) and by research into the semantic, episodic, imagery and procedural encoding of LTM.

c Mere rehearsal is too simple a process to account for the transfer of information from STM to LTM - the model ignores factors such as the effort and strategy subjects may use when learning (**elaborative** rehearsal leads to better recall than just maintenance rehearsal) and the model does not account for the type of information taken into memory (some items, e.g. distinctive ones, seem to flow into LTM far more readily than others). These criticisms are dealt with by the Levels of Processing approach of Craik and Lockhart (1972)

Levels of processing and working memory

LEVELS OF PROCESSING APPROACH TO MEMORY - CRAIK AND LOCKHART (1972)

THE APPROACH
- Craik and Lockhart's important article countered the predominant view of fixed memory **stores**, arguing that it is what the person **does** with information when it is received, i.e. how much attention is paid to it or how deeply it is considered, that determines how long the memory lasts.
- They suggested that information is more readily transferred to LTM if it is *considered*, *understood* and related to past memories to gain *meaning* than if it is merely *repeated* (maintenance rehearsal). This degree of consideration was termed the '**depth of processing**' - the deeper information was processed, the longer the **memory trace** would last.
- Craik and Lockhart gave three examples of **levels** at which verbal information could be processed:
  1 **Structural** level - e.g. merely paying attention to what the words *look* like (very shallow processing).
  2 **Phonetic** level - processing the *sound* of the words.
  3 **Semantic** level - considering the **meaning** of words (deep processing).

EVIDENCE
- Craik and Tulving (1975) tested the effect of depth of processing on memory by giving subjects words with questions that required different levels of processing, e.g.
  'table'
  Structural - 'Is the word in capital letters?'
  Phonetic - 'Does it rhyme with "able"?'
  Semantic - 'Does it fit in the sentence "the man sat at the _____"?'
- Subjects thought that they were just being tested on reaction speed to answer yes or no to each question, but when they were given an unexpected test of recognition words processed at the semantic level were recognised more often than those processed phonetically and structurally.

MODIFICATIONS
Many researchers became interested in exactly what produced **deep** processing:
- **Elaboration** - Craik and Tulving (1975) found complex semantic processing (e.g. 'The great bird swooped down and carried off the struggling __') produced better cued recall than simple semantic processing (e.g. 'She cooked the __').
- **Distinctiveness** - Eysenck and Eysenck (1980) found even words processed phonetically were better recalled if they were distinctive or unusual.
- **Effort** - Tyler et al (1979) found better recall for words presented as difficult anagrams (e.g. 'OCDTRO') than simple anagrams (e.g. 'DOCTRO').
- **Personal relevance** - Rogers et al (1977) found better recall for personal relevance questions (e.g. 'Describes you?') than general semantic ones (e.g. 'Means?').

EVALUATION
- **Strengths** - good contribution to understanding the processes that take place at the time of learning.
- **Weaknesses** - There are many problems with defining 'deep' processing and why it is effective.
- Semantic processing does not always lead to better retrieval (Morris et al, 1977).
- It describes rather than explains.

THE WORKING MEMORY MODEL - BADDELEY AND HITCH (1974)

THE MODEL (AS OF 1990)
The working memory model challenged the unitary and passive view of the multi-store model's short term memory store.
Working memory is an **active** store to hold and manipulate information that is currently being consciously thought about. It consists of 3 separate **components:**
- **The central executive** - a modality-free controlling attentional mechanism with a limited capacity, which monitors and co-ordinates the operation of the other two components or slave systems.
- **The phonological loop** - which itself consists of two subsystems,
  a The *articulatory control system* or 'inner voice' which is a verbal rehearsal system with a time-based capacity. It holds information by articulating sub-vocally material we want to maintain or are preparing to speak.
  b The *phonological store* or 'inner ear' which holds speech in a phonological memory trace that lasts 1.5 to 2 seconds if it does not refresh itself via the articulatory control system. It can also receive information directly from the sensory register (echoic) or from long term memory.
- **The visuospatial sketchpad** - or 'inner eye' which holds visual and spatial information from either the sensory register (iconic) or from long term memory.

EVIDENCE
- The existence of separate systems in working memory has been shown experimentally by using concurrent tasks (performing two tasks at the same time) - if one task interferes with the other, then they are probably using the same component.
- Thus, if articulatory suppression (continually repeating a word) uses up the phonological loop, another task involving reading and checking a difficult text would be interfered with, but not a spatial task.

EVALUATION
- Working memory provides a more thorough explanation of storage and processing than the multi-store model's STM.
- It can be applied to reading, mental arithmetic and verbal reasoning.
- It explains many STM deficits shown by brain-damaged patients.
- However, the nature and role of the central executive is still unclear.

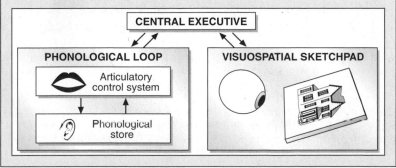

Forgetting in short-term memory

Short-term memory contains information that is present in our minds and is currently being thought about at any one time, but which soon slips into the past - hopefully to long-term memory so that we can access it again.

Peterson and Peterson (1959) found 90% of STM information was forgotten after just 18 seconds without rehearsal, while memory span studies reveal that forgetting starts once more than 7+/- 2 items enter STM.

We have all been caught out by STM forgetting, e.g. when we forget some of the names of a large group of people we have only just been introduced to, or forget what we were about to say or do next. Cognitive psychologists have provided theoretical explanations of STM's limited duration and capacity.

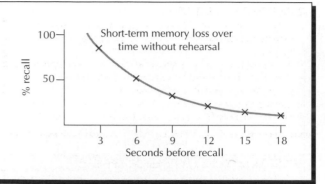

TRACE DECAY THEORY

- Trace decay theory seems to focus on explaining STM forgetting in terms of its limited duration.
- Donald Hebb (1949) suggested that information in STM created an active trace or engram in the form of a brief excitation of nerve cells that, unless refreshed by rehearsal, would spontaneously fade away or decay over time.
- Peterson and Peterson originally argued that the forgetting they found over their 3 to 18 second time delays occurred through trace decay.

Evaluation

- Pure trace decay is very difficult to test. Ideally no new information should be presented in the time between when the trace is acquired and when it is recalled to prevent confounding variables like displacement, yet Peterson and Peterson asked subjects to count backwards to stop them rehearsing.
- Reitman (1974) asked subjects to detect tones between presenting and recalling information, thinking this would hopefully prevent rehearsal without providing any new displacing material. Only about a quarter of information was forgotten after a 15 second delay which was more likely to be due to spontaneous trace decay than the Petersons' result.
- Baddeley and Scott (1971) concluded that 'something like trace decay occurs in the Peterson task, but is complete within five seconds, and is certainly not sufficiently large to explain the substantial forgetting that occurs in the standard paradigm' (quoted from Baddeley, 1997).

DISPLACEMENT THEORY

- Displacement theory seems to focus on explaining STM forgetting in terms of its limited capacity.
- Miller (1956) argued that the capacity of STM is approximately 7+/-2 items of information. Despite the fact that these items can be chunked to increase their capacity, displacement theory suggests that there are only a fixed number of 'slots' for such information and that once they are full (capacity is reached) new information will push out or displace old material (which may be lost unless it was processed sufficiently to pass into LTM).
- In Peterson and Peterson's experiment, therefore, the increase of forgetting over time may have been a result of the counting backwards task increasingly displacing the original trigrams.

Evaluation

- Waugh and Norman (1965) used the **serial probe technique** where 16 digits are rapidly presented to subjects who are then given one of those digits (the probe) and have to report the digit which followed it. It was found that the nearer the end of the 16 digit sequence the probe was presented, the better was the recall of the following digit. This seems to support displacement theory since digits nearer the end of the sequence have fewer following digits to displace them.

> Order of Sequence presented **3 7 2 9 0 4 5 6 3 1 9 0 7 8 2 6**
>
> If probe = 8 then recall of digit (2) is good (little displacement)
> If probe = 4 then recall of digit (5) is poor (greater displacement)

- The poorer recall (asymptote) shown in the middle of the serial position curve that results from free recall studies could similarly be attributed to displacement.

EVALUATION OF STM THEORIES OF FORGETTING

- In some of the research it is unclear what the relative influences of displacement and trace decay are on STM forgetting. Researchers such as Shallice (1967) have found that presenting digits at faster speeds in serial probe tests increases the ability to recall the digits presented earlier in the sequence. Thus trace decay may be responsible for some of the STM forgetting, since the faster presentation means the digits nearer the beginning of the sequence have less time to decay before being tested.
- It is also unclear how distinct the concepts of displacement and trace decay really are. For example displacement in STM works on the assumption that it has a limited capacity, which is measured in terms of memory span (usually 7+/-2 items or chunks). However Baddeley et al (1975) have shown that fewer words can be retained in STM if they take *longer* to pronounce. It seems STM capacity for words depends on the *duration* of pronunciation (how long it takes to say them) rather than the *number* of meaningfully chunked items - in this case words.
- Finally it is also unclear what is actually happening in trace decay and displacement to cause the forgetting. Is the trace really fading or, because it is so fragile, is it being degraded by other incoming information? Similarly with displacement, is the new material nudging aside, overwriting or distracting attention from the old material (or just making it harder to discriminate)? While **interference theory** has some of the same kinds of questions to answer, it has been more successful in explaining STM forgetting by showing how the **similarity** of competing information from the interpolated task used (as well as from previous trials) can affect the recall of the Petersons' trigrams (see interference theory).

Forgetting in long-term memory

INTERFERENCE THEORY
- One explanation of LTM forgetting is that over time more and more material will be stored and become confused together.
- Interference is most likely to occur between similar material.
- **Proactive interference** is where material learnt first interferes with material learnt later.
- **Retroactive interference** is where material learnt at a later time interferes with material learnt earlier.

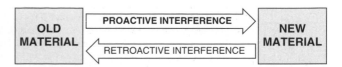

OLD MATERIAL	PROACTIVE INTERFERENCE →	NEW MATERIAL
	← RETROACTIVE INTERFERENCE	

RESEARCH ON INTERFERENCE EFFECTS
- *Proactive interference* - Underwood (1957) found that the more nonsense syllable lists his students had previously learned, the greater their forgetting of new nonsense syllables was after a 24 hour delay. This was because the new nonsense syllables became increasingly confused with those from the old lists. Wickens et al (1963) found subjects could be released from proactive interference effects by changing the nature (and thus reducing the similarity) of the new items to be learned, e.g. from nonsense syllables to numbers.
- *Retroactive interference* - McGeoch and Macdonald (1931) presented subjects who had learnt a list of words with various types of interference list to learn for ten minutes afterwards. Recall of the original words was then tested and those students given an interference list of *similar meaning* words recalled on average far less (12.5%) than those given unrelated words (21.7%) or nonsense syllables (25.8%). Best recall (45%) was gained for subjects who were given no interference test at all.

EVALUATION
1 **Artificiality** - Some of the research has been conducted using nonsense syllables often learned under artificially compressed laboratory conditions (rather than the more everyday distributed learning over time) and so interference theory has declined in popularity as an explanation of forgetting. However, many interference studies have been conducted with greater ecological validity, e.g. Baddeley and Hitch (1977) found rugby players' forgetting of the names of teams they had played depended more on interference from the number of rugby matches played since than on the passage of time.
2 **Applications** - Release from proactive interference has been applied by Gunter et al (1981) to increase recall of news items by ensuring dissimilar items followed each other. Retroactive interference has been applied, e.g. by Loftus, to understand the effect of post-event information such as leading questions on the recall of eyewitness testimony.
3 **Reason for interference** - Some believe interference occurs when information is unlearned (Underwood, 1957) or over-written (Loftus, 1979) by other information. Tulving however, argues that interference of retrieval cues rather than stored material is responsible. Tulving and Pstoka (1971) found that the retroactive interference effect on a word list disappeared if cues (e.g. category headings of the words) were given for it.

CUE DEPENDENT RETRIEVAL FAILURE
Information may be *available* to recall but *temporarily inaccessible*, for example:
- Tulving (1968) found that different items from a list might be recalled if people are tested on it on three separate occasions, probably because of the different cues present in each test.
- The tip of the tongue phenomenon. Brown and McNeill (1966) induced this "state in which one cannot quite recall a familiar word" by reading definitions of infrequently encountered words and found the first letter and number of syllables could be identified before complete recall.

Memory **cues** or **prompts** may therefore be necessary to access information.

WHAT CUES AID RETRIEVAL?
Much research has investigated the type of cues that, depending upon their presence or absence, will determine retrieval failure.
- Tulving and Pearlstone (1966) studied intrinsic cues (those meaningfully related to the material to be remembered) by asking subjects to memorise lists of words from different categories. Subjects given the category headings as retrieval cues recalled more of the words than those who were not. Tulving proposed the *encoding specificity principle* to account for this - items committed to memory are encoded with the precise semantic context present at the time of learning.

Evaluation - Thomson and Tulving (1970) confirmed this, but later research found cues not around at the time of learning can help too.
- **Context-dependent forgetting** is caused by the absence of *external* environmental cues that were present at the time of learning. Godden and Baddeley (1975) asked divers to learn word lists either on land or under water and found they recalled about 40% less in the opposite environmental context than in the same one. However, no effect was seen if a recognition test was used. Smith (1979) found more forgetting occurred a day later if subjects who had learnt 80 words in a distinctive basement room were then asked to recall them in a very differently furnished 5th floor room (12 words) compared to the original room (18 words). Interestingly, almost as many words were recalled (17.2) by a third group who sat in the 5th floor room but were asked to remember as much as they could about the basement room before recall.

Evaluation - Differences in environmental contexts have to be quite large before they significantly affect memory. However, imaginative context recreation can be applied to improve recall in eye-witness testimony.
- **State-dependent forgetting** is caused by the absence of *internal* bodily cues that were experienced at the time of learning. Bower (1981) found that his subjects recalled more memories learnt when sad if he tested them when hypnotised to be in a sad mood than a happy one. State-dependent effects have been found for alcohol (Goodwin et al, 1969) and other state-altering substances.

Evaluation – However, true state-dependent memory involving mood has not always been found for emotionally neutral information.

The role of emotion in forgetting

What effect do emotions have on forgetting?
Cognitive psychologists have sometimes neglected emotions in their models of memory, perhaps because of their focus on the information processing comparison with computers - who do not have them (yet!). However two concepts, repression and flashbulb memory, have created interest in the effect of emotion on memory - the first suggesting it could increase forgetting, the second that it could prevent it. Cognitive psychologists have tried to use their theories (e.g. of rehearsal, interference and cue dependency) to explain such emotional effects.

REPRESSION

- Repression is a concept from *psychodynamic* psychology which focuses heavily on emotion. Freud proposed that forgetting is *motivated* by the desire to *avoid displeasure*, so embarrassing, unpleasant or anxiety-producing experiences are repressed - pushed down into the *unconscious*.
- Repression is a protective *defence mechanism* that involves the ego actively blocking the conscious recall of memories - which become *inaccessible*. Direct recall attempts will either fail, lead to distorted recall or digression from the topic. Psychoanalytic techniques, such as dream interpretation, free association etc., are necessary to access repressed memories.
- Freud argued that repression was the most important of defence mechanisms and that it not only accounted for his patients' anxiety disorders (the result of repressing more traumatic experiences) but was a common cause of everyday forgetting.

Evaluation

- Theoretically, forgetting more unpleasant than pleasant memories could just mean that people rehearse upsetting material less because they do not want to think, or talk to others, about it. It is also difficult to tell to what extent the repressor chooses not to search their memory or is unable to.
- Experimental evidence is difficult to gather due to the ethical problems of probing for traumatic memories or creating them by exposing subjects to unpleasant, anxiety-provoking experiences.
- Those studies that have been conducted show mixed results and, where negative emotions have been found to increase forgetting, there has been debate over the cause - emotion can affect memory without the need for an ego.
- Mild anxiety has been produced in the laboratory by giving false 'failure feedback', which does impair memory. However rather than causing repression, Holmes (1990) argues that it causes people to think about the failure which distracts attention away from the memory test (*interference theory*), since giving 'success feedback' also impairs recall.
- Higher anxiety was produced by Loftus and Burns (1982) who showed two groups a film of a bank robbery, but exposed one of the groups to a far more violent version where a young boy was shot in the face. The group that saw this version later showed far poorer recall of detail than the control group. Freud might have suggested repression, but Loftus (1987) could explain the forgetting with the *weapons focus* effect, where fearful or stressful aspects of a scene (e.g. the gun) channel attention towards the source of distress and away from other details. Alternatively people may need to be in the same state (i.e. anxious) to recall properly - this is a *cue-dependent* explanation.

FLASHBULB MEMORY

- Brown and Kulik (1977) suggested some events can be remembered in almost photographic detail - as if they are imprinted upon the mind. They called this type of recall 'flashbulb memory' and found it was most likely to occur when the event was not only surprising to the person but also had consequences for their own life.
- Thus they found around 90% of people reported flashbulb memories associated with personal shocking events, but whether they had such memories for public shocking events like assassinations depended upon how personally relevant the event was for them - 75% of black participants in their research had a flashbulb memory for the assassination of black-rights activist Martin Luther King, compared to 33% of white participants.
- Brown and Kulik (1977) argued that flashbulb memory was a *special* and *distinct* form of memory since:
1 The emotionally important event triggers a neural mechanism which causes it to be especially well imprinted into memory.
2 The memories were more detailed and accurate than most.
3 The structural form of the memory was very similar - people nearly always tended to recall where they were, what they were doing, who gave them the information, what they and others felt about it and what the immediate aftermath was, when they first knew of the event.

Evaluation

- Neisser (1982) however, disagrees that flashbulb memories are distinct from other episodic memories, since:
1 The long-lasting nature of the memory is probably due to it being frequently *rehearsed* (thought about and discussed afterwards) rather than being due to any special neural activity at the time. Existing memory theory, e.g. levels of processing, would explain meaningful and distinctive events lasting longer.
2 The accuracy of such memories has often been shown to be no different from most other events, e.g. McCloskey et al's (1988) study of memory after the Challenger space shuttle explosion and Wright's (1993) of the Hillsborough football tragedy.
3 The similar form of 'flashbulb memories' may just reflect the normal way people relate information about events to others.
Despite such criticisms some research still supports the notion of flashbulb memory. Conway et al (1994) argue that studies that use events that are really relevant to peoples' lives (e.g. their own on Margaret Thatcher's resignation) find more accurate flashbulb memories over time. Cahill and McGaugh (1998) think that because it is adaptive to remember emotionally important events animals have evolved arousing hormones that help respond in the short term and aid storage of the event in the long term.

SO ARE THE EFFECTS OF EMOTION POSITIVE OR NEGATIVE ON MEMORY?

- Research findings are mixed, e.g. Levinger and Clark (1961) found free associations to emotional words (e.g. 'quarrel' and 'angry') harder to immediately recall. However, other researchers found that after a longer delay the effect reversed and the emotional words were recalled better. Generally positive long-term effects on memory are found for slightly above average levels of arousal (perhaps supporting flashbulb memory), but negative effects for very high levels of arousal. Typical laboratory studies only produce lower arousal levels and have not provided much support for everyday repression, whereas profound amnesia might result from very traumatic or long-term negative emotional arousal which cannot be laboratory-generated.

Reconstructive memory

WHAT IS THE RECONSTRUCTIVE APPROACH TO MEMORY?

- In contrast to much cognitive research on memory, which focuses on quantitative tests of how many randomly selected digits, words or nonsense syllables can be remembered under strictly controlled conditions, the reconstructive memory approach has tended to concentrate more on *qualitative changes* in what is remembered, often of more *everyday material* such as stories, pictures or witnessed events under more *natural conditions*.
- The pioneer of reconstructive memory research was **Bartlett** (1932) who argued that people do not passively record memories as exact copies of new information they receive, but *actively* try and *make sense* of it *in terms of what they already know* – a process he called *'effort after meaning'*. Bartlett therefore proposed that information may be remembered in a distorted way since memories are essentially 'imaginative reconstructions' of the original information in the light of each individual's past experiences and expectations; rather than remembering what actually happened we may remember what we think should or could have occurred. Bartlett termed the mental structures, that held past experiences and expectations and could influence memory so much, **schemas**.

SCHEMA THEORY

More recent research by cognitive psychologists in the 1970's aimed to specify in more detail the properties of schemas and how they affect memory. Rumelhart and Norman (1983), for example, described how schemas:

1 *represent* both simple and complex *knowledge of all kinds* (e.g. semantic, procedural etc.)
2 *link together* to form larger systems of related schemas (e.g. a restaurant schema links to other 'eating location' schemas) or smaller systems of sub-schemas (e.g. a restaurant schema consists of sub-schemas of ordering, eating and paying schemas)
3 have slots with *fixed values* (defining, unchangeable characteristics), *optional values* (characteristics that may vary according to the specific memory the schema is storing) and *default values* (the most typical or probable characteristic a schema is likely to encounter)
4 acquire their content through generalised personal *experience* or the taught beliefs and stereotypes of a group or society.
5 operate as *active recognition devices* - all schemas constantly try to make sense of new information by making the best fit with it.

An example of a picnic schema is given by Cohen (1993) below. Notice that if the food eaten at a particular picnic was forgotten, then it may be assumed that sandwiches were eaten by default. Cohen also points out five ways in which schemas may influence memory – by providing or aiding selection and storage, abstraction, integration and interpretation, normalisation and retrieval. These properties mean that there are both advantages and disadvantages of schemas for memory:

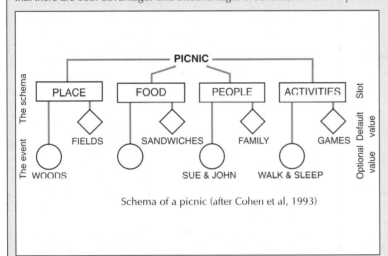

Schema of a picnic (after Cohen et al, 1993)

Advantages - schemas enable us to store the central meaning or gist of new information without necessarily remembering the precise details (abstraction, selection and storage), unless perhaps the details were particularly unusual. This saves memory resources. Schemas also help us understand new information more readily (integration and interpretation, normalisation) and fill in or guess missing aspects of it through the default values (retrieval). This makes the world more coherent and predictable.

Disadvantages – information that does not quite fit our schemas, especially the minor details, may be ignored and forgotten (selection and storage) or distorted (normalisation) so as to make better sense to us, while the guesses/filling-in of memory by the default values (integration and interpretation, retrieval) may be completely inaccurate. This may cause inaccurate, stereotyped and prejudiced remembering.

EVIDENCE FOR SCHEMAS RECONSTRUCTING MEMORY

- Bartlett (1932) found strong evidence for reconstructive memory by asking people to reproduce stories and pictures either serially (by remembering another person's reproduction) or by testing the same person on a number of occasions. When testing English subjects with an unfamiliar North American folk story, 'The War of the Ghosts', Bartlett found their recall became shorter (indicating the gist of the story had been removed) and also distorted by their culture (they omitted unfamiliar details and 'rationalised' the story to make it more coherent and familiar, e.g. recalling the ghosts in 'boats' not 'canoes').
- Brewer and Treyens (1981) tested memory for objects in an office that 30 subjects had waited in individually for 35 seconds. Their 'office schema' seemed to strongly affect their recall. *Expected* objects (e.g. a desk) that were in the room were recalled well but *unexpected* objects (e.g. a pair of pliers) were usually not. Some subjects *falsely* recalled *expected* objects that were not actually in the room (e.g. books and pens).
- Bransford and Johnson (1972, 1973) showed how schemas help to encode and store difficult to understand or ambiguous information.

EVALUATION OF RECONSTRUCTIVE MEMORY

- Bartlett's original research was more ecologically valid than most, but was criticised for its informal nature and lack of experimental controls. However, many recent and well-controlled experiments have consistently shown the reconstructive effect of schemas on memory.
- Bartlett and other reconstructive memory researchers have been accused of over-emphasising the inaccuracy of memory and using unfamiliar material to support the reconstructive effect of schemas on memory. Even quite complex real life material can often be accurately recalled.
- Often unusual information that cannot be easily incorporated into existing schemas (like a skull in the office of the Brewer and Treyens study) is well remembered. This distinctiveness effect has long been noticed and can be accounted for by the schema-plus-tag model of Graesser and Nakamure (1982).
- The concept of a schema and its action is still a little vague.

Key application - of memory research to eyewitness testimony

THE NATURE OF THE WITNESS AFFECTING EYEWITNESS TESTIMONY

RECONSTRUCTIVE MEMORY e.g. Bartlett's work on how schemas, expectations and stereotypes change memory has been applied to explain the effects of:

- **Prejudice** - Allport and Postman (1947) found that prejudice influenced the recall of whether a black or white person was holding a cut throat razor in a picture.
- **Inferences** - Harris (1978) found that over 60% of subjects would infer information not present in testimony based on their expectations, even when trained not to. For example if given the testimony 'I ran up to the burglar alarm in the hall' many would later assert that the burglar alarm had been rung.
- **Expectations** - List (1986) found subjects who had watched videos of shop-lifting incidents a week earlier recalled more of the actions that had a high probability of occurring during shoplifting than a low probability. They even falsely remembered high probability actions they had not witnessed on the video.
- **Stereotypes and face recognition** - Bull (1982) revealed people were willing to identify strangers as criminals just by their appearance. Yarmey (1982, 1993) found people readily stereotype faces as 'good guys' and 'bad guys' and discovered that the elderly were more likely to misidentify innocents as criminals based on their stereotypes of what they thought a criminal looked like. Racial stereotypes may also influence eyewitness testimony since Shepherd et al (1974) found cross-racial face recognition is poor.

THE NATURE OF THE EVENT AFFECTING EYEWITNESS TESTIMONY

CUE-DEPENDENT MEMORY e.g. state- and context-dependent retrieval have been applied to explain the effects of:

- **Stress** - Clark et al (1987) suggest that recall of violent crime may be more difficult because it occurs in a less aroused state.
- **Face recognition and context** - Shapiro and Penrod (1986) suggest matching witnessed faces to mug shots, photo-fits or line-ups may be difficult because of the different contexts on witnessing and recall; mug-shots and photo-fits being 2-dimensional and without expressive movement may provide insufficient cues, while line-ups involve different locations and clothing. Crime re-enactments may help by recreating context.

MEMORY PROCESSING MODELS e.g. rehearsal and depth of processing have been applied to explain the effects of:

- **Timing** - Clifford and Richards (1977) found better recall of details for a person who had approached police officers for 30 rather than 15 seconds. Potential jurors rated crime duration, and thus time to get a good look at the suspect, the 4th most important influence on eyewitness accuracy out of 25 variables (Lindsay, 1994). Greater exposure may allow more processing.
- **Processing and face recognition** -Shapiro and Penrod (1986) found subjects asked to make judgements about a face rather than just look at it showed more accurate later recall. Research shows that more familiar and distinctive faces are remembered better after long delays, as processing models would predict.

HOW ACCURATE IS EYEWITNESS TESIMONY?

Cognitive research has been applied to answer this question...

EYEWITNESS TESTIMONY

POST EVENT INFORMATION AFFECTING EYEWITNESS TESTIMONY

INTERFERENCE THEORY and **RECONSTRUCTIVE MEMORY THEORY** have been applied to the following:

- Loftus has shown how information received after a witnessed event (especially in the form of leading questions) can have a retroactive interference effect on the memory of that event. Information can be:

1 **Added to an account** - Loftus and Zanni (1975) showed subjects a film of a car accident, and got more subjects to incorrectly recall seeing a broken headlight by asking "did you see *the* broken headlight?" than asking "did you see *a* broken headlight?". Loftus (1975) even got subjects to recall seeing a non-existent barn in a picture by using a similar technique of adding post-event information.

2 **Distorted** - Loftus and Palmer (1974) received higher estimates of speed when asking "how fast were the cars going when they *smashed* into each other?" than when the verb '*hit*' was used.

3 **Substituted** - Loftus et al (1978) changed the recognition of a 'stop' sign to a 'yield' sign with misleading questions.

However there are many debatable issues involved in this area:

1 **Artificiality** - Yuille and Cutshall (1986) found the eyewitness testimony of a **real life** and quite traumatic event was very accurate and resistant to leading questions. This was only a single case study however.

2 **Demand characteristics** - McCloskey and Zaragoza (1985) suggest that subjects may just be following the expectations to recall the (misleading) information that was last given to them. However warnings that incorrect post event information has been given does not appear to stop incorrect information being recalled (Lindsay, 1990).

3 **Degree of interference possible** - Loftus (1979) has shown that *obviously* incorrect post event information has little or no effect on accurate recall. Interference is most likely to occur with minor details and if post event information is given after a long time delay.

4 **Nature of interference** - Loftus (1979) is convinced that post event information replaces the original information - which cannot be recalled even if money is offered for accurate information. McCloskey and Zaragoza (1985) disagree - they showed that if subjects are given misleading information and are later offered a choice of the original or a neutral alternative, they tend to choose the original, indicating that the original material is not 'overwritten' or permanently distorted.

- **Interference and face recognition** - Davis and Jenkins (1985) found the accuracy of face recognition is significantly reduced if subjects are shown composite photo-fit pictures of other faces beforehand. Gorenstein and Ellsworth (1980) found witnesses are more likely to identify (correctly or otherwise) a person from a line-up if they had appeared in mug shots the witness had searched beforehand.

'Reconstruction of automobile destruction' Loftus and Palmer (1974)

BACKGROUND

There is much support for the idea that most people, when they are witnesses to a complex event, such as a traffic accident, are very inaccurate when reporting numerical details like time, distance, and especially speed, even when they know that they will be questioned on them (e.g. Marshall, 1969). As a consequence, there can sometimes be large variations in estimates between witnesses and so it seems likely that such inaccurate testimony could easily be influenced by variables such as the phrasing of questions or 'leading' questions.

AIM

Loftus and Palmer, therefore, aimed to investigate the effect of leading questions on the accuracy of speed estimates in, and perceived consequences of, a car crash.

EXPERIMENT ONE

Subjects: 45 students, tested in groups of different sizes.

Design: Laboratory experiment.

Procedure:

7 films of traffic accidents, ranging in duration from 5 to 30 seconds, were presented in a random order to each group.

After each film, the subjects had to give a general account of what they had just seen and then answer more specific questions about the accident. The critical question, 'About how fast were the cars going when they hit each other?' acted as the independent variable, since it was manipulated in five conditions. Nine subjects heard the sentence with the verb 'hit' in it, and then an equal number of the remaining subjects were asked the same question but with the verb 'smashed', 'collided', 'bumped' or 'contacted' instead of 'hit'. The estimated speed was the dependent variable.

Results

Speed estimates for the verbs of experiment one		Significance of result	Accuracy of subjects' speed estimates		
Verb	Mean speed estimate	Results were significant at the $P < .005$ level, according to analysis of variance of the data.	In 4 of the 7 films the speed of the cars was known.		
				Actual speed of collision	Mean speed estimate
Smashed	40.8		Film 1	20 mph	37.7 mph
Collided	39.3		Film 2	30 mph	36.2 mph
Bumped	38.1		Film 3	40 mph	39.7 mph
Hit	34.0		Film 4	40 mph	36.1 mph
Contacted	31.8				

Discussion

The results indicate that not only are people poor judges of speed, but they are systematically and significantly affected by the wording of a question. However, this finding could be attributed to either response-bias (the subject remembers accurately but is pressured by the word to increase or decrease the estimate) or a genuine change in the subject's memory of the event (the word makes the subject recall the event as worse than it was). If the latter explanation is true, then the subject might be led into recalling details that did not occur. The second experiment was designed to determine which explanation of different speed estimates was correct.

EXPERIMENT TWO

Subjects: 150 students, tested in groups of different sizes.

Design: Laboratory experiment.

Procedure:

A film lasting just less than a minute was presented to each group which featured four seconds of a multiple traffic accident. After the film, the subjects had to give a general account of what they had just seen and then answer more specific questions about the accident. The critical question concerning the speed of the cars was the independent variable, and it was manipulated by asking 50 subjects 'About how fast were the cars going when they hit each other?', another 50 'About how fast were the cars going when they smashed into each other?' and another 50 acted as a control group who were not asked the question at all. One week later the dependent variable was measured - without seeing the film again they answered ten questions, one of which was a critical one randomly positioned in amongst the ten questions, asking 'Did you see any broken glass? Yes or no?'. Although there was no broken glass it was expected that some might be falsely remembered if the leading question of a week ago had changed the memory of the event to seem worse than it was.

Results

Verb	Mean estimate	Response	Smashed	Hit	Control	Probability of seeing broken glass with speed estimate			
						Verb	1-5 mph	6-10 mph	11-15 mph 16-20 mph
Smashed	10.46 mph	Saw broken glass	16	7	6	Smashed	.09	.27	.41 .62
Hit	8.00 mph	Did not see glass	34	43	44	Hit	.06	.09	.25 .50

Discussion

The authors conclude that the results show that the verb 'smashed' not only increases the estimates of speed, but also the likelihood of seeing broken glass that was not present. This indicates that information from the original memory is merged with information after the fact, producing one distorted memory. This shift in memory representations in line with verbal cues has received support from other research.

EVALUATION

Methodological: A well operationalised and controlled experiment, but lacked the ecological validity of having real life events and involved witnesses.

Theoretical: The research supports the idea that memory is easily distorted and has implications for eyewitness testimony in court.

Links: Interference and forgetting in memory, practical applications of memory, laboratory experimentation.

Contemporary issue - does hypnosis recover accurate memories?

WHAT IS HYPNOSIS?

The word 'hypnotism' is derived from the Greek for sleep - 'hypnos', however there are distinct differences between the two phenomena. Hypnosis is characterised by:

1 **Relaxation and suspension of planning** - hypnotised subjects sit quietly and do not seem to plan or initiate activity. Control is given over to the hypnotist.
2 **Suggestibility** - hypnotised subjects will respond to suggestions and obey instructions with little sign of inhibition, even if the request is unusual or seemingly impossible to do.
3 **Atypical behaviour** - hypnotised subjects can apparently perform behaviours that they would not normally be willing or able to do, such as controlling severe pain, experiencing hallucinations and, of course, retrieving forgotten memories.

Depth of hypnosis can be measured, e.g. by the Stanford Hypnotic Susceptibility Scale - a list of 12 hypnotic suggestions that are increasingly difficult to follow. About 15% of people are highly hypnotisable, 15% are very resistant to it, and the rest are somewhere in between.

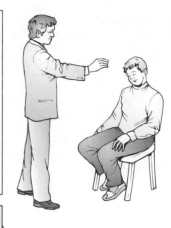

Cognitive psychological research on repression, interference, reconstructive memory and cue dependent memory can be used to help understand the accuracy of memories retrieved through hypnosis in two main situations - during therapy and police investigation. The former tends to focus on the victim's memory, while the latter has been applied to both victim and eyewitness recall.

CLINICAL HYPNOSIS AND MEMORY

Much debate has been generated over the accuracy of memories of childhood abuse, satanic abuse and even alien abduction retrieved using hypnosis during therapy that had not been remembered up until that point. It is often assumed that such *recovered memories* are due to the *repression* of these traumatic events and that *hypnotic regression* was required to retrieve them. Victims frequently find that the recovered memories help them make sense of disturbances in their behaviour, beliefs or emotions.

Evaluation of hypnosis for recovering repressed memory

For - there may be many genuine cases, since:
- child abuse is disturbingly common and amnesia for such traumatic events does occur - Herman and Schatzow (1987) found 28% of female incest victims reported severe childhood memory losses, especially the more violent the abuse.
- hypnotic age regression is an established technique (it is item 7 on the Stanford Hypnotic Susceptibility Scale) and may work through reducing recall inhibitions, overcoming memory blocks through accessing a different level of consciousness or even aiding context recreation of the time (*cue-dependent memory*).

Against - given the sensitivity and implications of such claims, many researchers think hypnotically recovered memories should not be relied upon without objective corroborative evidence, since:
- The concept of psychoanalytic repression and the extent of the unavailability it claims to produce has been criticised.
- Hypnosis may lead to *false memory syndrome*. Therapists may give *leading suggestions* before or during hypnosis which may distort original memories by acting as *retroactive interference* or encourage confabulation of fictitious memories by aiding *imaginative reconstruction*. Support for this is that:
1 Hypnosis increases the ability to imagine and even hallucinate.
2 Very hypnotisable people may be even more imaginative and/or have a 'fantasy-prone personality' (Wilson and Barber, 1983)
3 Hypnosis can produce experiences of future or even past lives.
4 Certain therapists tend to retrieve certain types of recovered memory - some frequently find abuse, others alien abduction (a more recent culture-bound and less credible phenomena).
5 Clients want to find causes for their problems and, being unaware of them, may readily believe they forgot others were to blame.
6 Independent corroboration has refuted many recovered memories.

POLICE HYPNOSIS AND MEMORY

In contrast to the clinical use of hypnosis to recover memories the client did not know they had, forensic or investigative hypnosis is usually employed in criminal investigations to try and access consciously forgotten information that victims or witnesses think they do, or might, possess.

The information gained can be used as forensic evidence or for investigative purposes to create leads that can be corroborated. Far more objection is raised to the former use than the latter.

Evaluation of hypnosis for victim and witness testimony

For - Police officials hope that the relaxed and focused state of hypnosis, as well as the more specific hypnotic techniques such as context recreation (based on *cue-dependent memory* theory) and the 'freeze-framing' of mental scenes to focus on detail, will greatly increase the amount and accuracy of previously inaccessible material recalled (a property termed hypermnesia).
- Geiselman and Machlowitz (1987) reviewed 38 experimental studies on hypnosis; 21 found significantly more correct information recalled, 4 significantly less and 13 no difference. However 8 experiments found an increase in errors while 10 showed no effect on error rate. Hypnosis was most effective in the studies using interactive interviews (not fixed questions), on more realistic material, after longer time delays.

Against - Gudjonsson (1992) suggests the highly suggestible, compliant and imaginative state of hypnosis may lead witnesses to greater *confabulation* and vulnerability to *leading questions*, as well as overconfidence in the accuracy of their recall.
- Putnam (1979) revealed that hypnotised subjects made more errors and were more likely to follow misleading information when answering questions on a videotape of an accident.
- Sanders and Simmons (1983) discovered hypnotised subjects who had witnessed a pick-pocket on video were less accurate in their interview answers (although just as confident) and identity parade identification (which they were more likely to be misled on) compared to non-hypnotised subjects.
- Geiselman et al (1985) found American law enforcers using the Cognitive Interview technique (which involves context recreation and different recall perspectives) produced greater correct recall of a violent crime video (41.2 items) than a standard interview conducted under hypnosis (38 items).

Culture and perception

WHY STUDY CROSS-CULTURAL DIFFERENCES IN PERCEPTION?

A major assumption of cross-cultural research is that differences between cultures are more likely to be caused by the differing physical and social environments experienced by the members of those cultures, whereas similarities across cultures are more likely to reflect biological, inherited abilities common to the whole species. Cross-cultural differences in perception might therefore be caused by differing experiences influencing perceptual set.

Many studies have shown individual experience can affect perceptual set and thus perception. Bugeleski and Alampay for example (1961) discovered that subjects presented with pictures of animals and then the ambiguous 'rat-man' figure were more likely to see the rat than a control group who were more likely to see the man. The culture a person is raised in may therefore affect not only object recognition but also the more basic perceptual processes such as size constancy and depth perception.

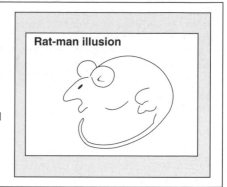

Rat-man illusion

CROSS-CULTURAL DIFFERENCES

ILLUSION STUDIES

- Rivers (1901) in a very early study discovered that Murray Islanders, both adults and children, were more susceptible to the vertical - horizontal illusion but less susceptible to the Muller-Lyer illusion than English subjects.

- Allport and Pettigrew (1957) found that a rotating trapezoid was more likely to be seen as a swaying rectangle by western cultures and urban Zulus who are used to seeing rectangular windows but more likely to be seen for what it was by non-urban Zulus.

- Segall et al (1963) conducted a very large scale study, testing around 1,900 subjects over a six year period, and argued that Africans and Filipinos were less susceptible than European subjects to the Muller-Lyer illusion because they did not live in such a 'carpentered world' where right angles are so frequently encountered that they are readily learnt as depth cues.
  However the 'carpentered world hypothesis' cannot account for findings that some groups of subjects living in rectangular constructed environments also fail to show susceptibility to the Muller-Lyer illusion (Mundy-Castle and Nelson, 1962) or that no difference has been found in its perception between urbanised and non-urbanised aborigines (Gregor and McPherson, 1965).

SIZE CONSTANCY

- Turnbull (1961) suggested that size constancy may be lacking in pygmies living in dense rain forests without the open space required to develop the ability. When taken to an open plain to see a herd of buffalo in the distance one pygmy reported being unable to identify such 'strange insects' and was amazed at what happened as they drove closer to the herd and the insects appeared to grow into buffalo. This was not a rigorously controlled experiment however.

OBJECT RECOGNITION IN PICTURES

- Western missionaries and anthropologists have often reported that the non-western cultures they made contact with had difficulty in recognising western pictures of objects. However, differences in the materials and artistic styles used in the pictures may have influenced their recognition ability.

DEPTH PERCEPTION IN PICTURES

- Hudson (1960) discovered that people from African cultures have difficulty perceiving two-dimensional pictures as 3 dimensional objects. However, the unnatural materials and lack of natural depth cues such as texture gradient may have influenced the African subjects' perception.

Vertical-horizontal illusion the vertical line is perceived as longer than the horizontal line but is not

Muller-Lyer illusion the right-hand side vertical line is perceived as longer but is not

Carpentered world

Non-carpentered world

EVALUATION

Cross-cultural differences in perception are often regarded as evidence for the idea that perception is flexible and so influenced by learning. However, the evidence:

- is not always conclusive and does not always show very large differences,
- ignores the vast similarity in perceptual ability across cultures,
- may only reflect the artificial methodologies and un-ecological materials used
- may even be due to biological factors since, for example, there is evidence that physiological differences in the eye can account for differences in susceptibility to the Muller-Lyer illusion in different subjects.

'Pictorial perception and culture' Deregowski (1972)

AIM
To present studies to show that different cultures perceive pictures in different ways. Cross-cultural studies of picture perception:
1 provide an insight into how perception works (indicating the role played by learning in perception) and
2 investigate the possibility of a universal cross-cultural means of communication (a 'lingua franca').

EVIDENCE
Pictorial object recognition studies

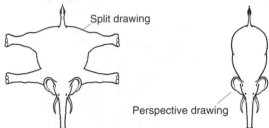

Split drawing

Perspective drawing

Pictorial depth recognition studies

What is the man doing?

2-dimensional picture   3-dimensional model   2-dimensional model

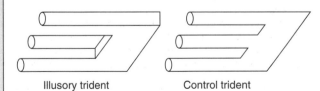

Illusory trident   Control trident

- Anecdotal reports from missionaries and anthropologists living among remote cultures have shown these cultures to have difficulties recognising objects from pictures, especially from accurate perspective drawings which do not represent all aspects of an object. Some studies have shown that African subjects from remote villages can pick out the correct toy from pictures of familiar animals (e.g. lions) though not unfamiliar ones (e.g. kangaroos).
- Hudson showed that African children and adults prefer split drawings to correct perspective drawings.

Hudson tested South African Bantu workers to see whether they could interpret a combination of three pictorial depth cues as a three dimensional representation:
- Familiar size - where the larger of two objects is drawn further away,
- Overlap - where nearer parts of a picture obscure farther away parts, and
- Perspective - where lines known to be parallel converge at the horizon.

The subjects were asked questions about the relationship between objects in the picture to see whether they had two- or three-dimensional vision. For example in the picture opposite, a three-dimensional viewer would say that the man is about to throw his spear at the antelope, a two-dimensional perceiver would say that the man is about to throw his spear at the elephant.

Hudson found two-dimensional perception in African tribal subjects across all ages, educational and social levels, and this finding was confirmed by pictorial depth measuring apparatus developed by Gregory.

Hudson showed Zambian subjects a drawing of two squares (arranged so that western subjects perceive them as a three-dimensional cube) and asked them to build a model of it out of modelling clay and sticks. Most of the Zambians built two-dimensional models, whereas the few who showed three-dimensional perception built a three-dimensional cube.

A group of Zambian school children, having been divided into two- and three-dimensional perceivers, were shown a picture illusion which three-dimensional western perceivers become confused by (since they attempt to see it as a three-dimensional picture of a trident). Three-dimensional perceivers spent longer looking at the illusory trident than a normal control trident, compared to the two-dimensional perceivers who showed no significant difference in viewing the two, when asked to copy the tridents.

EVALUATION
Methodological:

Design -   A wide range of methods used in the subject's own environment. However, most involve natural experiments, with a consequent lack of experimenter control over the independent variable (culture) and extraneous variables during testing.

Apparatus -   Pictures lacked important depth cues, such as texture gradient, and were presented on paper rather than on ecologically natural materials.

Theoretical: Three explanatory theories are given, but little evidence is used to support or decide between them. There is an ethnocentric assumption that western methods of pictorially representing objects especially involving depth cues are more correct than others and should be universally recognised.

Links: Nature-nurture debate in perception. Cross-cultural psychology.

The social psychological approach to psychology

ORIGINS AND HISTORY

- Researchers can be said to adopt a social psychological approach when they focus their research on **social behaviour** (between individuals and groups) and tend to regard **other people** and **social contexts** as just as, if not more, important as influences upon people as their dispositions and personality characteristics.
- Social behaviours include those most important to us such as attraction, helping, prejudice and aggression, while the influences studied include those of individuals (e.g. leadership and obedience), groups (e.g. conformity and crowding), societies (e.g. social norms and expectations) and culture (e.g. history, politics and language).
- Social psychology has a long history within scientific psychology, e.g. Triplett's (1898) social facilitation experiment. Like most psychological research, social psychologists began by investigating social processes and influence as they applied to the *individual*. Most of this research came from America and dominated social psychology, but a more sociological and European approach was gradually incorporated to take more account of social, historical and political contexts and collective/shared representations and identities.
- Social constructionism has taken the social approach one step further by suggesting our society, culture and language affect the very way we define psychological concepts and the process of scientific investigation itself - making unbiased study difficult if not impossible.

Stanley Milgram
Social psychology can be defined as 'the scientific investigation of how the thoughts, feelings and behaviours of individuals are influenced by the actual, imagined or implied presence of others' G. Allport (1935)

ASSUMPTIONS

Social psychologists assume that, for anyone who has been raised in a society:

1 All behaviour occurs in a social context, even when nobody else is physically present.
2 A major influence on people's behaviour, thought processes and emotions are other people and the society they have created.

METHODS OF INVESTIGATION

Social psychologists have used a very wide range of methods, e.g.
- Field experiments - e.g. Piliavin and others changed the type of victim requiring help in the everyday environment of a subway.
- Laboratory experiments - e.g. Milgram changed various social variables to affect obedience under controlled conditions.
- Surveys - e.g. questionnaires have been used on many people to measure the frequency and reasons for prejudiced attitudes.
- Observation / content analysis - e.g. to record discrimination.

CONTRIBUTION TO PSYCHOLOGY

Social psychologists have sought to explain:
- **Social influence** e.g. conformity, obedience, leadership, social facilitation and crowd behaviour.
- **Social cognition** e.g. social identity / categorisation, attitudes, attribution, stereotyping and emotion.
- **Social behaviour** e.g. inter-personal and inter-group aggression, discrimination, attraction and helping.
- **Social development** e.g. gender, self, attachment and intellectual development over time as a result of changing roles, social expectations, social circumstances and cultural influences.

CONTRIBUTION TO SOCIETY

Social psychology has had a broad range of applications, for example to:
- **Criminology** - e.g. attribution theory and jury decision-making.
- **Education** - e.g. the labelling and stereotyping of students' educational performance.
- **Industry** - e.g. in leadership/management selection and group productivity.
- **Sport** - e.g. team and audience effects on performance.
- **The Environment** - e.g. the effects of architecture and crowding on behaviour or attitude change towards the environment
- **Health** - e.g. social factors affecting the exposure and reaction to stress.

STRENGTHS

Social psychology is still an important approach today.
- Social influences have been shown to be involved in, and have a strong effect upon, people's behaviour, thinking and emotions – often stronger than dispositional influences.
- The approach has provided explanations for a great many phenomena.
- The approach has had many useful practical applications in a wide range of areas.
- The approach has provided evidence for its concepts and theories using a wide range of methods, often conducted in a scientifically objective manner.

WEAKNESSES

At times the social psychological approach has:
- Underestimated what people bring with them into social situations - individual differences (whether inherited or learnt) do affect the results of social psychological studies but are sometimes explored less.
- Provided only 'superficial snapshots of social processes' (Hayes, 1995), ignoring their development over time and the broader social, political, historical and cultural context that the research takes place in. For example American researchers measuring what their students find attractive in a photograph of a face in laboratory conditions at a particular time in history.

Social power

DEFINITION
Social power refers to the influence a person has to change another's thoughts, feelings, or behaviour. There are many sources of power, many ways in which it can work and many effects it can have on those who have it and those who yield to it.

NORMS OF POWER
Power relations are embedded in the hierarchical nature of society. Zimbardo et al's (1973) prison simulation experiment showed how the role of prison guard and the power that went with it could be readily assumed by subjects selected on the basis of their normality. Clearly, the norms of guard power (operating from coercive and legitimate power bases) can be readily understood (although exaggerated by media portrayal) and conformed to by anyone.

THE IMPACT OF POWER.
According to **social impact theory** (Latane, 1981), the strength of influence felt by a target is determined by three factors:
- The **strength** (or importance) of the influencer,
- The **number** of influencers,
- The **immediacy** (or closeness) of the influencer/s.

Increases in each of the above factors will cause the power of influence to increase, while decreases in these factors (or an increase in the target's strength or number) will have the opposite effect. For example, you are more likely to be influenced by several very important people standing in front of you, than by one unimportant person talking over the telephone.

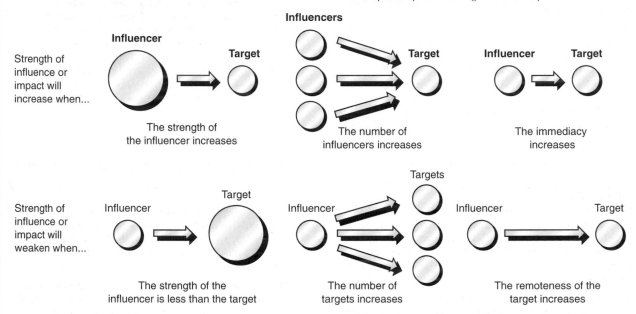

Strength of influence or impact will increase when...

The strength of the influencer increases

The number of influencers increases

The immediacy increases

Strength of influence or impact will weaken when...

The strength of the influencer is less than the target

The number of targets increases

The remoteness of the target increases

TYPES OF POWER
Raven and others have identified six different (although they can operate simultaneously) sources or *bases of power*:

1 Reward power
This influence is based on the ability to provide what others **want** or to remove what they do not want. Many people possess this source of power (e.g. parents, employers, friends), but note that they offer many different types of reward (e.g. love, money, approval). This power only works as long as the rewards can be given by the influencer and are wanted by the receiver.

2 Coercive power
This involves the ability to **punish**, by inflicting some form of negative stimulus (e.g. disapproval, ridicule, pain) or by removing pleasant stimuli (e.g. affection, wages). This power base requires constant supervision, since it produces negative feelings and attitudes in its victims who only tend to comply behaviourally to demands rather than really accepting them.

3 Referent power
This is the influence a person has because they are **respected** or admired. The target wishes to identify with (be like) the influencer and is more likely to follow their wishes. Role models and idols have this power, but only maintain it as long as they are liked or respected.

4 Legitimate power
This is where the target accepts the **norms** (probably internalised) that the influencer should have (has the right to) influence over them. The legitimacy of the power obviously depends on the situation - we accept that a referee can tell us what to do in a football match, but not outside of that situation.

5 Expert power
The power an influencer has because the target believes they possess **superior knowledge** in a desired area. We are thus at the mercy of our doctor's advice in matters of health, and at the mercy of garage mechanics when our cars need servicing.

6 Informational power
One person or a group of people, expert or otherwise, can have power if they provide socially accepted **information**. This ties in with the social reality hypothesis and Festinger's social comparison theory (we look to others to know how to react in certain situations).

'A study of prisoners and guards in a simulated prison' Haney, Banks, and Zimbardo (1973)

AIM
To demonstrate the situational rather than the dispositional causes of negative behaviour and thought patterns found in prison settings by conducting a prison simulation with 'normal' subjects playing the roles of guard and prisoner.

METHOD
Subjects: 22 male subjects selected (through personality assessment) from an initial pool of 75 volunteers based on their stability, maturity and lack of involvement in anti-social behaviour. They were mostly Caucasian, middle class, college students, who were strangers to each other and were randomly allocated to either prisoner or guard roles. Prisoners signed a consent document which specified that some of their human rights would be suspended and all subjects were to receive $15 a day for up to 2 weeks.

Apparatus: Prison - a basement corridor in Stanford University Psychology department converted into a set of 2 x 3 metre prison cells with a solitary confinement room (a tiny unlit closet), a 'yard' room and an observation screen (through which covert video and audiotape data recording could take place).
Uniforms - to facilitate role identification, guards were given khaki shirts and trousers, batons and reflecting sunglasses. Prisoners wore loose fitting smocks with identification numbers, no underwear, a lock and chain around one ankle, and a nylon stocking cap to cover their hair.

Procedure: The procedure, as with the apparatus, was designed to establish 'functional equivalents' for the experience of prison life.
- Prisoners were arrested by real police outside their houses by surprise, taken to a real police station for finger-printing and processing, and were then driven blindfolded to the mock prison (where they were stripped naked, 'deloused', and dressed in prisoner's uniform). Prisoners remained in the 'prison' 24 hours a day and followed a schedule of work assignments, rest periods, and meal/toilet visits.
- Guards worked only 8 hour shifts, and were given no specific instructions apart from to 'maintain a reasonable degree of order within the prison necessary for its effective functioning' and a prohibition against the use of physical violence.

RESULTS
The effects of imprisonment were assessed by video and audio tape observation of behaviour and dialogue, self-report questionnaires, and interviews. The experiment had to be terminated after 6 days, instead of the intended 14, because of the pathological (abnormal) reactions shown by both prisoners and guards.

- **Effects on prisoners** - subjects showed what was termed the 'Pathological Prisoner Syndrome' - disbelief was followed by rebellion which, after failure, was followed by a range of negative emotions and behaviours. All showed passivity (some becoming excessively obedient) and dependence (initiating very little activity without instruction). Half the prisoners showed signs of depression, crying, fits of rage, and acute anxiety, and had to be released early. All but two of those who remained said they would forfeit the money if they could be released early.

The experimenters proposed that these reactions were caused by a loss of personal identity, emasculation, dependency, and learned helplessness brought about by the arbitrary and unpredictable control, and the norms and structures of the prison system.

- **Effects on guards** - subjects showed what was termed the 'Pathology of Power' - huge enjoyment of the power at their disposal (some worked extra time for no pay, and were disappointed when the study was over) led to the guards abusing it and dehumanising the prisoners. All prisoners' rights were redefined as privileges (going to the toilet, eating, and wearing eye-glasses became rewards), and punishment with little or no justification was applied with verbal insults. Although not all guards initiated aggressive action, none contradicted its use in others.
The experimenters proposed that these reactions were caused by a sense of empowerment legitimised by the role of 'guard' in the prison system.

EVALUATION
Methodological: Lack of ecological validity - A role play simulation lacks 'mundane realism' and may produce artificial results. The experimenters admit factors, such as the lack of physical violence and minimum duration of the sentence, limit the generalisability of the simulation, but point out that most of the functional equivalents of the prison system were implemented and that most of the subjects' excessive reactions went beyond the demands of the role play (prisoners called each other by their ID numbers in private, and guards showed aggression even when they thought they were not being observed).

Data analysis - Was mostly qualitative rather than quantitative.

Ethical problems - 1 The study was ethically approved beforehand - perhaps the dramatic and disturbing results cause the ethical objections, but these came from the subjects not the experimenters.

2 The subjects had signed an informed consent document, but were unaware that they would be arrested in public and of exactly how realistic their imprisonment would be.

3 The experiment was terminated early and debriefing and assessment of the subjects took place weeks, months and years afterwards.

Theoretical: The research provides support for social psychological explanations of behaviour, has wide ranging implications for the usefulness and ethics of existing penal systems, and has been used to facilitate our understanding of the psychological effects of imprisonment.

Links: Social influence - particularly power, leadership, obedience (see Milgram) and conformity.

Studies of conformity

CONFORMITY DEFINITIONS AND TYPES
Definition: 'Yielding to group pressure' Crutchfield (1962).
According to Aronson (1976) the pressure can be real (involving the physical presence of others) or imagined (involving the pressure of social norms/expectations). Kelman (1958) suggests that the yielding can take the form of

- compliance - A change in behaviour without a change in opinion (just going along with the group),
- internalisation - A change in both behaviour and opinion (the group's and your own opinions coincide), or
- identification - The individual changes their behaviour and opinions to identify with the influencing group.

CONFORMITY STUDIES

JENNESS (1932)
Asked subjects to estimate the number of beans in a bottle, first individually and then as a group. When asked individually again, the subjects showed a shift towards the group's estimate rather than their own.
This was rather a simple experiment, however.

SHERIF (1935)
Asked subjects to estimate how far a spot of light in a completely dark room moved. Sherif kept the point of light stable, but due to the autokinetic effect illusion (caused by small eye movements) each individual reported fairly consistent estimates that often differed from other subjects.
However, when subjects were put in groups, their estimates converged towards a central mean, despite not being told to arrive at a group estimate and despite denying that they had been influenced by the others in post experimental interviews.

ASCH (1951, 1952, 1956)
Asch wanted to test conformity under non ambiguous conditions and, therefore, devised a very simple perceptual task of matching the length of a line to one of three other comparison lines. The task was so easy that control subjects made almost no errors. In the experimental condition only one real (naive) subject was tested at a time, but was surrounded by seven confederates of the experimenter, who were also supposed to be subjects but had been told beforehand to all give the same wrong estimate on 12 out of the 18 trials. The only real subject was second to last to give their estimate, and was, therefore, faced with either giving their own opinion or conforming to the group opinion on the critical trials.

The average rate of conformity was 32%. 74% conformed at least once and 26% never conformed.
Asch conducted variations to identify factors influencing conformity, such as:

- increasing the group size - Asch found little increase above 3 or 4, although other studies have found that larger groups will increase conformity but at a decreasing rate.
- providing support for the subject - when Asch provided an ally that agreed with the naive subject's estimates, conformity dropped to 5.5%. It seems that the unanimity of the group is important. If the ally changed to the group's estimates, then the naive subject would often follow suit.
- increasing the difficulty of the task - when the comparison lines were made closer in length, the rate of conformity increased.
- when the naive subject could write down their response, conformity dropped.

Even subjects that did not conform, felt strong social pressure to do so. One was heard to exclaim 'I always disagree - darn it!', and on being debriefed, commented 'I do not deny that at times I had the feeling "to heck with it, I'll go along with the rest"'.

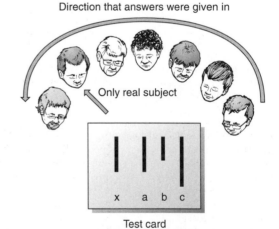

Direction that answers were given in

Only real subject

x a b c

Test card

CRUTCHFIELD (1954)
Crutchfield tested for conformity without physical presence by placing subjects in individual cubicles with electronic display boards which supposedly let each subject know what the others had answered. In fact, he allowed each subject to believe they were the last to answer and presented them with uniformly wrong group answers on half the tasks.
With this more efficient and standardised procedure Crutchfield tested over 600 subjects using a variety of stimuli such as Asch's line comparison tests, obviously incorrect factual statements, and personal opinions. He found 30% conformity in Asch's line test, 46% conformity to the suggestion that a picture of a star had a larger surface area than a circle (when it was a third smaller), and 37% agreement to the statement 'I doubt that I would make a good leader' (which none agreed to when asked on their own).

CRITICISMS OF CONFORMITY STUDIES
- Artificiality - the above studies used well controlled and standardised procedures but mostly reflect conformity under laboratory conditions, with meaningless stimuli.
- The high conformity found may only reflect the norms prevalent in the USA in the 1950s. Replications have found widely varying rates of conformity in more recent times and when the studies have been conducted cross culturally.
- Ethics - subjects were deceived.

Theories of conformity

CRUTCHFIELD'S CONFORMING PERSONALITY THEORY (1955)

After Crutchfield had tested his subjects for conformity, he also gave them a number of personality and I.Q. type tests, and found, for example, that those subjects who conformed the most typically

- were less intellectually competent - perhaps they were more open to the expert power of others
- had less ego strength - perhaps making them less confident in their own opinion
- had less leadership ability - perhaps making them less able to assert their own opinion
- were more narrow minded / authoritarian - perhaps inclining them to stick to the majority answer

However, if conforming personalities exist, then they should conform in a variety of situations, but McGuire (1968a) has found inconsistency of conformity across different situations.

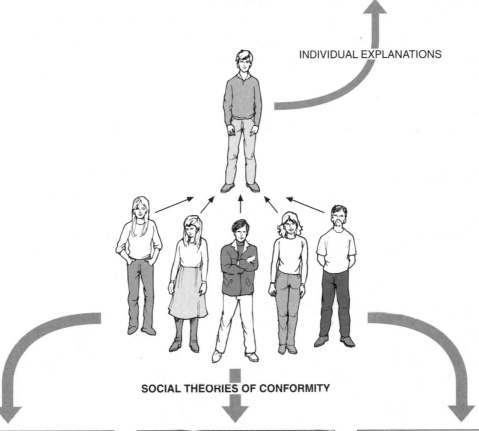

INDIVIDUAL EXPLANATIONS

SOCIAL THEORIES OF CONFORMITY

INFORMATIONAL SOCIAL INFLUENCE

Deutsch and Gerard (1955) have suggested that one motive for conformity is based on the **need** that everyone has **for certainty**.

When individuals are placed in ambiguous/**uncertain conditions**, they are more likely to refer to others to know how to react (Festinger called this **social comparison**).

Under these conditions, other people possess informational or **expert power** and individuals may show **internalisation** conformity - both their behaviour and opinions coincide with the group's.

Informational influence explains the conformity found in Sherif's study and much of the conformity in Asch's tasks - especially when the difficulty of the task was increased. A few of Asch's subjects seemingly experienced perceptual distortion, but the majority believed that the group's judgement was superior.

NORMATIVE SOCIAL INFLUENCE

Deutsch and Gerard (1955) have proposed that another motive for conformity is based upon the **need** for **social acceptance** and **approval**.

When individuals are put into a potentially **embarrassing situation**, such as disagreeing with the majority, they are faced with a **conflict** between their own and others' opinions.

Under these conditions other people have **reward** or **coercive power** which may lead individuals into **compliance** - publicly agreeing with the group, but privately maintaining their own opinions.

Normative influence explains some of Asch's conformity results, especially in the private answer variation. Some of his subjects reported private disagreement with the group's answers, commenting 'If I'd been the first I probably would have responded differently'.

REFERENT SOCIAL INFLUENCE

Turner (1991) suggests that people have a tendency to categorise themselves as members of different groups (Social Identity Theory) and argues that we are most likely to conform to the norms of those groups that we feel we are members of.

This occurs because people expect to agree with the members of such groups, but do not necessarily expect their views to coincide with those of other groups and are therefore less likely to conform to out-group than in-group pressure.

Under these conditions, members of the in-group possess **informational**, and perhaps also **reward** and **referent power**, which may lead the individual to **identification** conformity - their behaviour and beliefs coinciding with the group's, while they feel they are members of that group.

Milgram's (1963) study of obedience

AIM
To investigate how far people will go in obeying an authority figure .

PROCEDURE
Subjects were led to believe that the experiment was investigating the effects of punishment on learning. The subjects were tested one at a time and were always given the role of teacher (through a fixed lottery). The subject saw his apparent co-subject (in reality an actor) strapped into a chair with electrodes attached to him, since he was to be the 'learner'. The subject ('teacher') was told the shocks would cause no permanent tissue damage and was given a trial shock of 45 volts.

The subject then started the experiment in the shock generator room next door by testing the learner over an intercom, and was told by the experimenter (the authority figure) to administer increasing levels of electric shock for each wrong answer (which the actor gave often). In the basic set-up of the experiment the subject received feedback reactions from the learner he was 'electrocuting' only by a thump on the wall at 300 volts followed by no further reply. The experiment finished when either the subject refused to continue (disobeyed the experimenter's request), or had reached the maximum shock on the scale (450 volts). The subject was then fully debriefed as to the real nature of the experiment, re-introduced to the learner in a friendly way and reassured that no damage had been done since the learner had not really received any shocks at all!

SUBJECTS
They were 40 males between the ages of 20 and 50 from a range of occupations and were drawn from the New Haven area. They were obtained by newspaper ad's for participation in a study of learning at Yale University and were paid $4.50 just for turning up.

THE LEARNER
An actor was required to play the role of the learner - an Irish-American, 47-year-old accountant who appeared mild-mannered and likeable.

APPARATUS
Two rooms in the Yale Interaction Laboratory were used - one for the learner containing an 'electric chair' and an answering device, the other for the teacher and experimenter with an electric shock generator. The generator did not actually give shocks to the learner, and was used to measure the dependent variable of obedience. It was a convincing machine with a row of 30 switches ranging from 15 to 450 volts in increments of 15 volts, and was marked with descriptive terms of the shock effects - ranging from 'slight shock' through to 'Danger: severe shock' and 'XXX'.

THE EXPERIMENTER
He was 31 years old, dressed in a grey laboratory coat, and appeared somewhat stern and impassive through the experiment. If at any point the subject showed reluctance to administer the shock, he would command them to continue with standardised prompts ranging from "please continue" to "You have no other choice, you *must* go on".

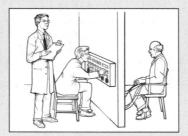

RESULTS
Levels of obedience expected
Psychology students and professional colleagues were asked what percentage of subjects would administer the highest degree of shock (450 volts) - the answers ranged from 1 to 3, with a mean of 1.2.

Levels of obedience obtained
65% of subjects continued to the maximum shock level of 450 volts. No subject stopped before 300 volts.

Subjects' realisation of shock effects
In the post-experimental interview the subjects were asked "How painful to the learner were the last few shocks that you administered to him?". The mean response was 13.42 out of 14 - 'extremely painful' on the scale.

Behavioural reactions to the study
"In a large number of cases the degree of tension reached extremes that are rarely seen in sociopsychological laboratory studies. Subjects were observed to sweat, tremble, stutter, bite their lips, groan and dig their fingers into their flesh. These were characteristic rather than exceptional responses to the experiment.... One sign of tension was the regular occurrence of nervous laughing fits.... Full-blown, uncontrollable seizures were observed for 3 subjects. On one occasion we observed a fit so violently convulsive that it was necessary to call a halt to the experiment. In the post experimental interviews subjects took pains to point out that they were not sadistic types, and that the laughter did not mean they enjoyed shocking the victim". Milgram (1963).

EVALUATION OF METHODOLOGY
Experimental validity
The procedure was well standardised and obedience was accurately operationalised as the amount of voltage given. Orne and Holland (1968) however, have argued that the subjects did not really think that the learner would come to harm. They suggested that the subjects were involved in a *'pact of ignorance'* with the experimenter and obeyed in much the same way as a member of a magician's audience will comply and put their head under a guillotine which has just split a cabbage head in two! The genuine distress of the subjects, their ratings of the shock pain and their comments during debriefing count against this criticism, as does the study by Sheridan and King (1972).

Ecological validity
Some psychologists have suggested that the experiment is an artificial test of obedience and therefore **lacks 'mundane realism'** or ecological validity. Milgram argues that while there are important differences between experimental and real life obedience, there is a fundamental similarity in the psychological processes at work - especially the process of agency.

The subjects were also American, male and volunteers – an unrepresentative sample that may have already been more obedient and helpful, but later studies have found similarly high rates of obedience using other samples and more everyday tasks and contexts (see replications and field studies of obedience). The methodology also caused numerous ethical problems (see ethics and obedience studies).

Studies of obedience

MILGRAM'S VARIATIONS ON THE BASIC STUDY

Milgram decided to conduct many **variations** of the study to determine the key factors that were responsible for the obedience (overall 636 subjects were tested during the 18 different variation studies). In the basic set-up of the experiment the subject received feedback reactions from the learner he was 'electrocuting' only by a thump on the wall at 300 volts followed by no further reply, but in a later condition vocal feedback was given (this was standardised by the use of a tape recording).
The table below shows some of the different variables that were carefully manipulated to see the effect on obedience (measured by the percentage that gave the maximum 450 volt shock).

Vocal feedback condition	
At **75 volts**	moans / groans.
At **150 volts**	requests to be excused from the experiment.
At **195 volts**	yelled "Let me out! My heart's bothering me"
At **285 volts**	agonised scream
At **300 volt**	kicked the wall and begged to be released.
At **315 volts**	no further responses.

65%	Remote - victim condition.	The victim in a separate room and no feedback until a bang on the wall at 300 volts. No subject stopped before 300 volts.
62.5%	Vocal - feedback condition.	With the verbal protestations, screams, wall pounding and ominous silence after 300 volts. Only a few stopped before 300 volts.
92.5%	Two teacher condition.	The subject was paired with another teacher (a confederate) who actually delivered the shocks while the subject only read out the words.
47.5%	Shift of setting condition.	The experiment was moved to a set of run down offices rather than the impressive Yale University.
40%	Proximity condition.	Learner moved into the same room so the teacher could see his agonised reactions .
30%	Touch proximity condition.	The teacher had to force the learner's hand down onto a shock plate when he refused to participate after 150 volts.
20%	Absent experimenter condition.	The experimenter has to leave and give instructions over the telephone. Many subjects cheated and missed out shocks or gave less voltage than ordered to.
10%	Social support condition.	Two other subjects (confederates) were also teachers but soon refused to obey. Most subjects stopped very soon after the others.

REPLICATIONS OF MILGRAM'S STUDY

Varying the subjects **Gender** - women were found to show similar levels of obedience by Milgram, but other studies have found both lower levels (when asked to electrocute another woman) and higher levels (when asked to electrocute a puppy).
Nationality - cross-cultural studies have found varying obedience levels - higher in Holland, Austria and Germany, but lower in Britain and Australia. The different procedures used in these studies make proper comparison difficult.

Varying the victim **Gender** - a female victim has occasionally reduced obedience
Species - Sheridan and King (1972) found 75% obedience when real electric shocks were used on puppies.

Varying the setting See field experiments…

FIELD EXPERIMENTS ON OBEDIENCE

High levels of obedience have been shown many times under real life conditions.

Hofling et al (1966) investigated obedience in American hospitals. They found that 95.5% (21 out of 22) of the nurses tested obeyed an unknown doctor's telephone instructions to administer twice the maximum allowed dose of a drug (in fact a harmless placebo) that was clearly labelled with warnings against such an action and that was not on the ward stock list for the day. This was in contrast to 21 out of 22 nurses who replied that they would not have obeyed the doctor and broken the hospital regulations for medication when asked how they would have reacted in the same situation. This study was conducted under slightly unusual conditions however (although in a natural environment it still lacked ecological validity), and the results have not been replicated when the procedure was changed to make it more realistic, i.e. a drug known to the nurses, and with others around to consult.

Bickman (1974) investigated obedience on the streets of New York. He revealed that when an experimenter was dressed in a guard's uniform and told passers-by to pick up paper bags or give a coin to a stranger there was 80% obedience, compared to 40% when the experimenter was dressed more 'normally'. A milkman's uniform, however, did not have the same effect as the guard's on obedience.

Meeus and Raaijmakers (1986) investigated obedience in a business setting in Holland. They had an experimenter ask subjects to act as interviewers, supposedly in order to test the effects of stress on job applicants by delivering 15 increasingly distressing and insulting remarks to applicants (in fact confederates) at a time of high unemployment. 91.5% of their subjects obeyed the experimenter and made all 15 remarks despite the psychological distress shown by the applicants.

Explanations and ethics of obedience studies

EXPLANATIONS OF OBEDIENCE STUDIES

SOCIAL POWER EXPLANATIONS

THE IMPACT OF POWER - *Social impact theory* (Latane and Wolf) explains factors that affected obedience in Milgram's studies

1 The impact of the **experimenter's power on the subject** - The experimenter was close (immediacy of influence was high) and important (strength of influence was high) to the subject. When the experimenter gave instructions over the telephone obedience decreased (as immediacy decreased). When there were a number of (confederate) teachers who disobeyed in the social support condition, the subjects' obedience decreased as the experimenter's power and authority was spread amongst many teachers, having less impact on each one (diffusion of impact).

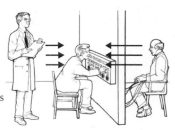

2 The impact of the **learner's distress on the subject** - The subject was not in close proximity to the learner (low immediacy of influence). When the consequences of the shocks were made more immediate (when the learner was brought into the same room) the impact of the learner's distress increased and obedience decreased. When there were two teachers, and the naive subject only had to read out the questions, he felt even less individually responsible for his actions (diffusion of impact) and obedience increased.

TYPES OF POWER USED

- The location of respectable Yale university added **legitimate power** to the situation (obedience decreased when the location changed).
- The experimenter represented scientific authority and possessed expert and legitimate power (obedience decreased when he was absent), especially with his grey laboratory coat which represents the power that uniform has in our society - see studies by Haney, Banks and Zimbardo (1973) and Bickman (1974).

MILGRAM'S AGENCY THEORY

- Milgram (1974) suggests that when faced with commands from legitimate authority figures we lose our sense of responsibility for our own actions and become the agents of others' wishes (the state of agency). Thus the high levels of obedience found in Milgram's studies resulted from the experimenter as the authority figure **taking responsibility** for the consequences of the obedience.
- According to Milgram (1974) agency involves a **cognitive shift in viewpoint** that results in people switching from their normal **autonomous state** (where they feel in control of, and responsible for, their actions) to the **agentic state** (where they regard themselves as "the instrument for carrying out another person's wishes").
- The purpose of the agentic state is to allow human hierarchical social systems to function properly – if people did not automatically yield to those of higher status then society would be disorganised and unable to achieve its collective goals efficiently (or at all) and disobedient, lower ranking individuals would constantly risk punishment from those above them in the hierarchy.
- Milgram proposed the agentic state was a product of evolution and pointed out that we grow up in a society where we constantly submit to those in authority from the moment we are born, e.g. to parents, teachers and employers.
- The agentic state can account for the horrific acts committed in the name of obedience – for example soldiers who have committed atrocities arguing they were only following orders and were not responsible for their actions.

EVALUATION OF THE ETHICS OF OBEDIENCE STUDIES

MILGRAM

Against the study

Baumrind (1964) criticised the study as being unethical since:

a It caused distress to the subjects. One had a violent seizure and all of the subjects could have suffered psychological damage, e.g. guilt or loss of self-esteem.

b Milgram deceived the subjects as to the true nature of the experiment, and therefore did not receive their informed consent.

c Milgram's study abused the right of subjects to withdraw from a psychology study - those wishing to leave were told to continue.

For the study

Milgram defended himself on ethical grounds by pointing out:

a The methodology was not unethical since the results obtained were completely unexpected, and although the subjects appeared uncomfortable with their obedience, Milgram concluded "momentary excitement is not the same as harm".

b Subjects could have left, they were not physically restrained. Indeed Milgram designed many variations to increase refusal/disobedience.

c All subjects were fully debriefed and reassured. They were shown that the learner was completely unharmed and had not received any shocks. A follow up opinion survey conducted a year later found that 84% were "glad to have been in the experiment", 15% were neutral, and only 1.3% were "sorry or very sorry to have been in the experiment". Around 80% of the respondents said there should be more experiments like Milgram's conducted, and about 75% said they had learnt something of personal value from their experience. The subjects were also examined by a psychiatrist one year after the study who found no signs of harm.

OTHER OBEDIENCE STUDIES

In a similar way to Milgram's studies virtually every later study of obedience has broken some ethical guidelines, ranging from deception and lack of fully informed consent over the true nature of the experiment to causing psychological distress, embarrassment and even physical harm to animals (the real electric shocks given to Sheridan and King's puppy).

Resisting influence

EXAMPLES OF RESISTING SOCIAL INFLUENCE
- **Independence in conformity and obedience experiments** - Although disobedience in Milgram's (1963) experiment was low (35% refused to give the maximum shock), Asch's (1951) conformity experiment showed higher rates of resistance (26% did not conform at all and all 50 were resistant at least once in the original test). Resistance was significantly increased by having social support - just one ally in Asch's study lowered conformity from an average of 32% to 5%, two other teachers disobeying in Milgram's study lowered obedience to 10%.
- **Rebellion** - Gamson et al (1982) found 97% of groups showed dissent and 50% completely rebelled to unfair requests from authority figures - probably because groups provide a greater opportunity for dissent to be expressed and discussed, and social support to justify and implement rebellion. However, although resisting authority, many participants were just *conforming* to others in the group who were rebelling.

TYPES OF RESISTANCE
Independent behaviour - involves the true rejection of social influence to behave in accord with one's own internal attitudes, regardless of whether they coincide with the influencer's.
Anti-conformity - involves resisting social influence by deliberately opposing the majority and refusing to behave like them. This behaviour is still affected by society however.

REASONS FOR RESISTING SOCIAL INFLUENCE
- **Group identity** – Different social groups have different goals and so may not want to follow other group norms.
- **Psychological reactance** - Brehm (1966) argued that perceived constraints on freedom lead some to resist in order to assert their freedom - telling people they are not allowed to do something is often a good way of getting them to do it!
- **Socialisation** – Individual experience and the society that one is raised in can affect the level of independence. Berry (1966, 1967) discovered that Eskimos, who live in an individualistic hunting society where self reliance is highly valued, showed more independent behaviour than members of the Temmi of Africa whose collectivist agricultural society is more dependent upon co-operation, agreement and conformity.

MINORITY INFLUENCE

At times minority groups may not only resist, but actually influence majority groups in society. Throughout history minorities (often defined in terms of political power rather than just number) such as scientific, religious, women's and black rights groups have changed the majority viewpoint (Kuhn called this a 'paradigm shift'). In fact, without minorities to introduce change and innovation, conformity to the majority status quo would stagnate progress in society.

STUDIES OF MINORITY INFLUENCE

Moscovici et al (1969) tested subjects in groups of 6 on their ability to judge the colour of 36 blue slides of varying brightness. Unknown to the rest of the subjects, 2 in each group were confederates who acted as a minority group. They found that when the minority:
1 *Consistently* judged the slides to be green rather than blue, the majority followed them on 8.42% of trials
2 *Inconsistently* judged the slides to be green rather than blue (on 2 in every 3 trials), the majority followed them on only 1.25% of trials
Furthermore, in later individual tests the subjects exposed to the minority were more likely (than control groups with no minority) to report ambiguous green/blue slides as green, *especially* if they had previously resisted the minority view, indicating a longer term influence.

- Nemeth et al (1974) replicated Moscovici et al's study but had their 2 confederates:
1 Randomly say green on half the trials and green/blue on the other half. This caused no minority influence because of the inconsistency.
2 Consistently say green or green/blue depending on the brightness of the slides. This consistency led to 21% minority influence.
3 Say green on every trial. This consistency caused no minority influence, perhaps because it was seen as being rigid and unrealistic.

- Maass and Clark (1983) studied majority and minority influence on attitudes to gay rights. Regardless of whether the majority view was for or against gay rights they found that their subjects' publicly expressed views followed the majority but their privately expressed views shifted towards the minority viewpoint. This indicates minorities cause a change in private opinions / attitudes *before* a change in public behaviour.

THEORIES OF MINORITY INFLUENCE

Dual Process theory – Moscovici (1980) argued that since minorities do not have the informational and normative influence of the majority (in fact they are often ridiculed by them), they must exert their influence through their ***behavioural style – how*** they express their views. ***Consistency*** of viewpoint, both over time and between members of the minority group, is the most important aspect of this style since this not only draws attention to the minority view and gives the impression of certainty and coherence, but also causes doubt about majority norms. Other important features of behavioural style are ***investment*** (the minority has made sacrifices for the view), ***autonomy*** (the view is made on principle without ulterior motives) and ***flexibility*** (the consistent viewpoint must not be seen as too rigid and dogmatic).
This behavioural style means that minorities and majorities exert their influence through 2 different processes (thus *dual* process theory)
- Majorities influence minorities quickly through ***compliance*** (the minority often changes their public behaviour but not private opinions)
- Minorities influence majorities more slowly through ***conversion*** (the majority gradually change their private opinions before their public behaviour). This conversion will hopefully lead to majority internalisation (both public and private acceptance of the minority view).
Moscovici argues that conversion occurs because minority views encourage ***cognitive conflict*** and therefore greater processing in the long term which may cause the restructuring of the majority group's attitudes.
Attribution theory - e.g. Kelley (1967) suggests consistency encourages the attribution of minority behaviour to internal causes (i.e. real belief) rather than situational ones (i.e. just a social fad).
Social Identity Theory - suggests opinion change is more likely if in-group rather than out-group members express the minority views.
Social impact theory – suggests minority views have increasing impact when high profile (greater immediacy) and when advanced by many people (increasing number of influencers) of higher status (increasing strength of influence).

Contemporary issue - Is hypnosis just role-playing?

WHAT IS THE TRADITIONAL VIEW OF HYPNOSIS?

Hypnosis has long fascinated both psychologists and the general public because of the dramatic changes in behaviour it produces. Hypnotised subjects can apparently experience the world in a different way - showing distortions of perception like tasting an onion as an apple or smelling ammonia as water and even hallucinations, such as seeing things that are not there or not seeing things that are. In addition they seem able to perform behaviours that they would not normally be willing or able to do - such as controlling severe pain, showing increased strength, retrieving forgotten memories or acting like a chicken.

The traditional view of hypnosis is known as the altered state or special process approach to hypnosis, which proposes that:

1 Hypnosis represents an altered state of consciousness, distinct from both waking and sleep states. Hilgard proposes the neo-dissociation theory, which suggests that hypnosis divides consciousness into separate channels of awareness.

2 Hypnosis is a special state since phenomena can be produced during it (like pain resistance) that cannot be shown under normal conditions.

SOCIAL INFLUENCE AND HYPNOSIS

In contrast to the traditional altered state view of hypnosis, some social psychologists support the non-state or social psychological approach to hypnosis, which argues that:

1 Hypnosis is really only a form of social influence, **not** an altered state.

2 All phenomena produced under hypnosis can be produced without it (by people motivated to simulate hypnosis).

It has therefore been suggested that the following social psychological concepts and research can account for the behaviour and experiences produced under hypnosis, without the need for a special state or division of consciousness:

CONFORMITY AND ROLE PLAYING

* Social psychologists suggest that people play a variety of **roles** in society (e.g. son, brother, student, football supporter, shop assistant etc.) and each role has a different set of **norms** (expected ways of behaving) that are **conformed** to in each role. We readily shift from one role to the next depending upon the social context and may thus behave very differently in various situations (we may not behave the same way at home as at work or at a football match). People are very aware of how those who are 'hypnotised' behave and may therefore, deliberately or not, conform to the norms of the role of 'hypnotised subject' in situations where it is expected. One could compare such behaviour to **demand characteristics** in research situations. Pressure to conform to the hypnotic role and its norms is often increased by the presence of people other than the hypnotist, such as audiences at hypnosis stage shows - where especially dramatic behaviour may be expected.

* Conformity could occur for two main reasons which might produce different kinds of role playing:

1 **Normative social influence** - not following suggestions in hypnotic situations is potentially very embarrassing, which may lead people to behave as expected but not believe they are really hypnotised (a kind of conformity known as compliance).

2 **Informational social influence** - people being hypnotised want to understand or justify what happens to them when hypnotised but may be uncertain as to how else to do so other than accept the traditional and socially accepted view that being in an altered state enables you to perform in extraordinary ways without being able to refuse. This may lead them to behave as expected, even if they do not want to, and really believe they are hypnotised (a kind of conformity known as internalisation).

OBEDIENCE TO AUTHORITY

* Studies of obedience such as Milgram's have consistently shown that we should not underestimate the ability of (non-hypnotised) people to follow the commands of an authority figure, even if reluctant to do, especially if close in proximity to them. It can be argued that the hypnotist is essentially an authority figure whose suggestions are obeyed and whose influence works at close proximity.

* Hypnotists who are perceived as legitimate and credible authority figures can thus produce extreme behaviour in their subjects through mere obedience since, by the very nature of the hypnotic situation, they take all responsibility for the actions produced. According to Milgram this causes a state of 'agency' which reduces the 'hypnotised' person's inhibitions. At the same time an increase in motivation may result from a fear of embarrassment or punishment if they disobey commands.

EVALUATION -Social psychologists who argue that social influence can account for hypnotic phenomena provide support for their view by either criticising altered state research or showing that motivated people can simulate (pretend) the same phenomena without hypnosis.

* **'Lie' detecting** - Coe and Yashinski (1985) found that people with post hypnotic amnesia increase their recall if led to believe that a lie detector test will find out if they are lying. Pattie (1937) showed that hypnotised subjects given the suggestion that they could not feel anything in one hand reported sensations administered to the fingers of both their hands if they were inter-linked (making it difficult to tell which was which). Subjects under the hypnotic suggestion of deafness have failed delayed auditory feedback tests that real deaf people pass. This suggests that the subjects were merely behaving *as if* they were hypnotised.

* **Physiological evidence** - Altered state researchers have found differences in brain activity levels between low and highly susceptible subjects when hypnosis is attempted. However critics suggest this finding may just reflect a state of relaxation rather than hypnotic trance.

* **Task performance** - Motivated simulators have performed many tasks in the same way as hypnotised subjects, e.g. eating onions while pretending they are apples or following an instruction to throw 'acid' at another person. Barber and Hahn showed that motivated subjects could reduce their experience of cold pressor pain (caused by immersing the hand in icy water) to a similar degree to hypnotised subjects. However, Orne et al (1968) found that hypnotised subjects responded to a suggestion to touch their forehead (when they heard the word 'experiment' mentioned throughout a 2 day period) more often than simulators. Colman (1987) argues that the fact that simulators can imitate many aspects of the hypnotic state does not mean that the state does not exist.

* **Trance logic** - Trance logic refers to the ability of hypnotised subjects to tolerate logical inconsistency. Orne showed hypnotised subjects can hallucinate a transparent image of a person sitting in a chair, even if that person was also seen standing next to them, without being perturbed by the inconsistency. Simulators asked to fake this hypnotic situation often do not behave in the same way.

Social theories of prejudice - social group explanations

STEREOTYPING

- As Pennington (1986) notes, stereotyping involves
  a **categorising** people into groups based on visible **cues**, such as gender, nationality, race, religion, bodily appearance, etc.
  b assuming **all** members of a group share the **same characteristics**.
  c **assigning individuals to these groups** and presuming they possess the same characteristics based on little information other than their possession of the noticeable trait or cue.
- While stereotyping is an **in-built cognitive process**, it is important to realise that the **cues** seen as important to categorise (e.g. gender, skin colour, religion, etc.) and the **content** of the stereotype itself (e.g. personality traits) are not fixed, but historically determined and **changeable** over time.
- Stereotypes serve to **exaggerate** the **similarities within groups** ('those people are all the same') and exaggerate the **differences between groups** ('they are not like us').
- Stereotyping, therefore, literally involves **pre-judging** an individual, and, although it serves the important **functions** of categorising and generalising knowledge, it can lead to **unrealistic perceptions**, and **inter-group hostility**.

Evidence
- Karlins et al (1969) showed how the content of stereotypes concerning 'Americans' and 'Jews' changed over a 40 year period - the former seeming to become more 'materialistic' and the latter appearing to be less 'mercenary', for example.
- Many studies have shown how stereotyping can lead to prejudice, e.g. Buckhout (1974) and Duncan (1976).

Evaluation
- McCauley & Stitt (1978) propose that stereotypes are now best regarded as **probabilistic beliefs**. People are asked to estimate what percentage of a group would possess certain characteristics, and this is compared to the estimate for people in general, to arrive at a diagnostic ratio.
- Although the contents of stereotypes are usually derogatory, and stereotyping accounts for the **thinking** in prejudice, it does **not** explain the **strong negative emotions** nor all the discriminatory **behaviour** shown in society.

INTERGROUP CONFLICT THEORY

- According to Sherif, the prejudice in society is caused by:
  a The existence of groups
  b **Competition** between those groups
- Conflict exists between groups because each group will struggle to obtain limited resources. Sherif argued that competition will always provoke prejudice, and conducted a field study to investigate this idea.

Evidence
- Sherif et al (1961) conducted a field study in Robbers' Cave State Park in America. Two groups of 11 boys were created and a tournament was set up between them that was sufficient to produce fighting and name calling.
- The basis of many wars has been resource competition.

Evaluation
- Tyerman and Spencer's (1983) study on groups of boy scouts showed that competition is not always sufficient to cause conflict and discrimination.
- Sherif's study was ethically dubious given that its goal was to deliberately create prejudice and fighting over penknives was involved.

THE PROCESS OF STEREOTYPING

Intra group similarities in characteristics are exaggerated

Inter group differences are exaggerated

Intra group similarities in characteristics are exaggerated

Individual allocated to group based on visible cues

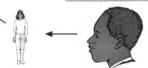

MINIMAL GROUP THEORY

- Minimal group theory suggests that merely dividing people into groups is sufficient to cause prejudice to occur between them. Tajfel and Turner (1979) explain this phenomena in terms of their social identity theory (SIT), which proposes that
  a people allocate themselves to groups and gain their identity from those groups
  b people need to feel good about themselves and, therefore, seek positive self-esteem
  c people will want to feel they are in the best group and will, therefore, act to make it so, even if that means putting other groups down

Evidence
- Tajfel et al (1971) conducted a study on Bristol schoolboys, who they assigned to meaningless groups, in some cases completely randomly by the toss of a coin. Tajfel found that the individual members would not only allocate more points to their own group members but would often maximise the difference between the groups - even if it meant their own group receiving fewer points overall.

Evaluation
- Tajfel's results have received cross-cultural confirmation, but his experiments have been accused of artificiality and demand characteristics. The study may only reflect the norms of competition found in many societies - co-operative societies may not show the minimal group effect (Wetherall, 1982).

SCAPEGOATING THEORY

- Scapegoating theory has its roots in Dollard et al's frustration-aggression theory, which argues that socially **frustrating conditions** such as economic depression and unemployment **leads to aggression**.
- According to the theory, this aggression needs to be **displaced** and **blame** allocated, so a **scapegoat** is found - usually a **minority** 'out-group' which is in a less powerful position to defend itself.

Evidence
- Weatherley (1961) found that anti-Semitic subjects (those prejudiced against Jews), who were frustrated by being insulted, were later more aggressive in their descriptions of people with Jewish sounding names. However, it should be noted that verbal prejudice does not always show itself in discriminatory behaviour as LaPiere (1934) found.
- The scapegoating of minorities in times of economic hardship has been historically documented world-wide.

Evaluation
- This theory links well with intergroup conflict theory by elaborating on another effect of competition, the frustration it can provoke.
- The theory accounts for the fluctuations of prejudice and discrimination over time, reflecting changing economic conditions.

'Experiments in intergroup discrimination' Tajfel (1970)

AIM

To illustrate a fundamental cause of intergroup discrimination - the mere categorisation of people into groups. Tajfel proposed that because of the frequent competitive behaviour shown by groups in our society, individuals do **not** just learn to conform to **specific** prejudices, but learn a **general** tendency (a '**generic norm**') to categorise people into ingroups and outgroups ('us' versus 'them') and to act in favour of their own ingroups. This generic norm of discriminating against the outgroup soon comes to operate automatically in any group situation, **without**

- any individual interest reasons for the discrimination
- any previous attitudes of hostility or dislike towards the outgroup
- any need for negative attitudes to develop before the discrimination occurs

Tajfel aimed to support the above theory that people will automatically discriminate without any prior prejudice merely by being put into groups, by testing the effect of categorisation on children's behaviour without the effect of any pre-existing attitudes or self interest.

EXPERIMENT ONE
METHOD

Subjects: sixty-four, 14 and 15 year old schoolboys, previously acquainted with each other, tested in groups of eight at a time.

Procedure: All subjects took part in a study that they were told tested visual judgement, involving estimating the number of dots on a screen. The boys were then informed that they would be divided into groups such as 'over-estimators' or 'under-estimators' (supposedly based on their performance, but in fact at random) and were asked to participate in a task where they had to allocate reward and penalty points (that would later be translated into real money at a rate of 1 tenth of a penny per point) to other boys.

Each boy was then individually told which group they were in and tested in isolation from the others. Each received a booklet of matrices that showed how they could allocate different combinations of rewards and penalties to boys from the groups, but it was made clear that

- they would **not know** the **identities** of the boys they were allocating points to, **only** whether they were members of the **same group** as themselves (ingroup) or of the **other group** (outgroup)
- they would **never** be **allocating** points **to themselves** - their points would be determined by the actions of every other boy in the same way

Each matrix consisted of 14 combinations of rewards or penalties, with the top and bottom row points always going to the member of one of the groups. Six types of matrix, with differing combinations of rewards and penalties, were each presented with three different group choices, e.g.

1 Between **two** **ingroup** members:

| Rewards for member 36 of 'overestimators' | 1 | 2 | 3 | 4 | 5 | 6 | 7 | 8 | 9 | 10 | 11 | 12 | 13 | 14 | Choice | 8 |
| Rewards for member 23 of 'overestimators' | 14 | 13 | 12 | 11 | 10 | 9 | 8 | 7 | 6 | 5 | 4 | 3 | 2 | 1 | example | 7 |

2 Between **two** **outgroup** members:

| Rewards for member 42 of 'underestimators' | 1 | 2 | 3 | 4 | 5 | 6 | 7 | 8 | 9 | 10 | 11 | 12 | 13 | 14 | Choice | 7 |
| Rewards for member 15 of 'underestimators' | 14 | 13 | 12 | 11 | 10 | 9 | 8 | 7 | 6 | 5 | 4 | 3 | 2 | 1 | example | 8 |

3 Between an **ingroup** and an **outgroup** member:

| Rewards for member 36 of 'overestimators' | 1 | 2 | 3 | 4 | 5 | 6 | 7 | 8 | 9 | 10 | 11 | 12 | 13 | 14 | Choice | 14 |
| Rewards for member 42 of 'underestimators' | 14 | 13 | 12 | 11 | 10 | 9 | 8 | 7 | 6 | 5 | 4 | 3 | 2 | 1 | example | 1 |

In each matrix, subjects had to choose just one of the two point combinations for the group members (typical example choices are shown above).

RESULTS

Subjects could adopt one of three strategies: maximum ingroup profit, maximum fairness, or maximum generosity to outgroup. It was found that

- in choices between two ingroup members, or two outgroup members, the strategy of maximum fairness was usually adopted, but
- in choices between a member of the ingroup and outgroup a strategy nearer maximum ingroup profit was significantly shown.

EXPERIMENT TWO
METHOD

Subjects: forty-eight, 14 and 15 year old schoolboys, previously acquainted with each other, tested in three groups of sixteen at a time.

Procedure: Subjects were again randomly divided into two groups, supposedly based upon their preferences for the paintings of Klee and Kandinsky, and were given new matrices consisting of 13 combinations of rewards or penalties to further test ingroup favouritism choices.

Between an **ingroup** and **outgroup** member:

| Rewards for member 17 of 'Klee group' | 7 | 8 | 9 | 10 | 11 | 12 | 13 | 14 | 15 | 16 | 17 | 18 | 19 | Choice | 19 | 19 | 7 |
| Rewards for member 25 of 'Kandinsky group' | 1 | 3 | 5 | 7 | 9 | 11 | 13 | 15 | 17 | 19 | 21 | 23 | 25 | example | 25 | 25 | 1 |

RESULTS

Subjects could adopt one of three intergroup strategies: maximum ingroup profit, maximum joint profit, or maximum difference in favour of the ingroup. Subjects significantly tended to adopt the strategy of **maximum difference in favour of the ingroup** e.g. 7 / 1 at the expense of maximum ingroup profit, e.g. 19 / 25

EVALUATION

Methodological:
Artificiality - Groups are rarely meaningless.

Theoretical: The research opposes previous beliefs that competition was necessary and sufficient to produce prejudice.

Links: Prejudice. Self identity and self-esteem

Key application - The reduction of prejudice

METHOD OF REDUCTION

EDUCATION
Educating children with notions of tolerance and providing them with an insight into the causes and effects of prejudice can help reduce prejudice and discrimination according to a number of theories. **Conformity to norms theory** would argue that education is necessary to prevent a 'non-conscious ideology' forming in communities where prejudice is so accepted it becomes an unquestioned norm.
Social learning theory suggests prejudice should be seen to be punished and tolerance rewarded if imitation in children is to be produced.

EXAMPLES

EXAMPLES
Jane Elliot conducted the 'blue eyes-brown eyes' study on her classes to teach them what it felt like to be the victim of prejudice (just based on eye colour). Interviews with the children as adults revealed that the study had inoculated them against discriminatory behaviour.
Public campaigns by minority groups, such as the 'Black is Beautiful' movement, had lasting effects on public awareness of racial issues in the USA.

EVALUATION

EVALUATION
Education can reduce prejudice if it is carried out at a social level and is seen to be unacceptable by the majority in society.
Education has its greatest effect on the young. If adults 'are compelled to listen to information uncongenial to their deep-seated attitudes, they will reject it, distort it, or ignore it' (Aronson, 1992).

EQUAL STATUS CONTACT
Meeting members of other social groups can reduce prejudice by reducing **the effect of stereotypes**. This occurs as
- intergroup similarities are perceived (they are like us)
- outgroup differences are noted (they are not all the same)

Contact only changes group stereotypes if
- it is between individuals of equal status
- individuals are seen as representative of their group

EXAMPLES
Racial de-segregation studies have had some success.
Deutsch and Collins (1951) - found desegregated public housing increased inter-racial 'neighbourly activities' which were shown by 39% and 72% of the white housewives in the two desegregated housing projects but by only 1% and 4% of those in the two segregated projects. There was evidence that racial group perceptions changed dramatically for some, as one white housewife commented 'I started to cry when my husband told me we were coming to live here. I cried for three weeks… Well all that's changed… I see that they're just as human as we are… I've come to like them a great deal'.
Star et al (in Stouffer et al, 1949) found that 93% of white officers and 60% of enlisted men reported getting along 'very well' with the black troops they were fighting with in World War Two (everyone else said 'fairly well').

EVALUATION
Sherif, in the Robber's Cave study, found inter-group contact alone was insufficient to reduce prejudice between competing groups. Equal status contact only acts to reduce prejudice at an interpersonal level and does not counter the prejudice of group stereotypes (individuals are seen as 'exceptions to the rule'), if inequality at a social level makes true equal status contact impossible.
Stephan (1978) reviewed desegregation studies and found no significant reduction in prejudice or increase in black children's self esteem (but see Hraba and Grant, 1970).
Star et al's study revealed that improved racial relationships in desegregated troops were not always generalised to interactions outside of fighting conditions, for example one white soldier commented 'they fought and I think more of them for it, but I still don't want to soldier with them in garrison'.

SUPER-ORDINATE GOALS
Star et al concluded that 'efforts at integration of white and coloured troops into the same units may well be more successful when attention is focused on concrete tasks or goals requiring common effort'. Making groups work together to achieve 'super-ordinate goals' (goals that cannot be achieved by groups working separately) is likely to reduce prejudice according to
- **intergroup conflict theory** - super-ordinate goals reduce the competition that causes prejudice.
- **social identity theory** - working together may merge 'in' and 'out' groups to one whole in-group identity.

EXAMPLES
Sherif et al (1961) significantly reduced intergroup hostility between two groups of children, the 'Eagles' and the 'Rattlers', by providing 'super-ordinate goals' in the last phase of their 'Robber's Cave' experiment.
Aronson et al (1978) used the 'jigsaw technique' with mixed race classroom groups. Each child received a part of the whole assignment and was dependent on the other children in the group to perform well in it. Inter-racial liking and the performance of ethnic minorities was increased.

EVALUATION
Inter-personal liking in these studies is not always generalised to social groups as a whole. When children leave their jigsaw classrooms they may return to a prejudiced family or society.
Superordinate goals cannot always be set up between all groups and failure to achieve them may result in worse prejudice.

SOCIAL POLICY
Political and social measures can act to reduce institutionalised discrimination through
- ensuring political power sharing
- providing equal opportunities legislation
- affecting the media (which maintains and perpetuates unequal **stereotypes**)
- encouraging 'one-nation' in-group perception (**social identity theory**)
- targeting areas of economic frustration

EXAMPLES
The Supreme Court case of Brown vs. Board of Education in 1954 started the desegregation of public schools in the USA. Power sharing in South Africa ended Apartheid policies there.
Bogatz & Ball (1971) found that white children in the USA who watched mixed race TV programs like 'Sesame Street' developed more positive attitudes towards blacks and Hispanics.

EVALUATION
Policies like desegregation must be equally applied and regarded as inevitable and socially supported - half-hearted measures often cause more disruption.
There is a danger that discrimination will just shift to more subtle forms.

'Black is Beautiful: A Re-examination of Racial Preference and Identification' Hraba & Grant (1970)

AIM
A study by Clark and Clark (1947) conducted in 1939 reported that black children preferred white dolls and rejected black dolls when asked to choose which were nice, which looked bad, which they would like to play with, and which were a nice colour. This implied that they thought black is not beautiful and was interpreted as meaning they would rather be white. Later research tended to support the idea that for black children inter-racial contact with white children resulted in white preference, although some research indicated the opposite or no effect. Conclusions are difficult to draw, however, because the studies were not only conducted at different times, but also used different techniques, samples and settings. Hraba and Grant aimed to closely replicate the original Clark and Clark study to test their findings.

METHOD
Subjects: The sample was drawn from 5 public schools in Lincoln, Nebraska in May 1969 (where 1.4% of the population were black) that between them accounted for 73% of the black population of the correct age group of 4-8 year olds. The sample was 160 children, 89 were black (of whom 70% had white friends) and 71 were white (drawn randomly from the same classrooms).

Apparatus: 4 dolls – 2 black, 2 white that were identical in all other respects.

Procedure: Clark and Clark's procedure was followed as closely as possible. Children were individually interviewed with the dolls as part of a natural experiment (lack of experimenter control over the independent variables). The main independent variables were:
Race – operationalised by skin colour in 2 main conditions – black (later divided into light, medium and dark black) and white.
Time – the 1969 Hraba & Grant results were compared with the 1939 Clark & Clark results for black children.
The effect of the children's *age* was also investigated and the race of the interviewer was controlled for.
The dependent variables were *racial preference* and *racial identification* (operationalised by the children's answers to Clark and Clark's original 8 questions – see below) plus the *behavioural consequences* of racial preference and identification (operationalised by an additional question on the race of the children's best friend given to the children and their teachers).

RESULTS
Hraba & Grant found many differences in the doll choices of the black and white children in their study and many significant differences at P< .02 level or better between their results and those of Clark & Clark. Children mostly preferred same-race dolls.

DEPENDENT VARIABLES	INDEPENDENT VARIABLES		
	Clark & Clark (1939) **Black children**	**Hraba & Grant (1969)** **Black children**	**Hraba & Grant (1969)** **White children**
Racial preference Give me the doll that....	white doll / black doll	white doll / black doll	white doll / black doll
1 you want to play with	67% 32%	30% 70%	83% 16%
2 is a nice doll	59% 38%	46% 54%	70% 30%
3 looks bad	17% 59%	61% 36%	34% 63%
4 is a nice colour	60% 38%	31% 69%	48% 49%
Where percentages do not add up to 100% children failed to make a choice.	The black children's preference for the white doll occurred at all ages, and this *increased* with their *skin lightness* and *decreased* with *age*.	Black children preferred the black doll at all ages (*regardless* of *skin lightness* this tendency *increased* with *age*) and were more ethnocentric on question 4 than white children.	White children preferred the white doll and this trend also *increased* with *age* (except on question 4). They were more ethnocentric on questions 1& 2 than black children.
Racial identification Give me the doll that.... 5 looks like a white child 6 looks like a coloured child 7 looks like a Negro child **Racial self-identification** Give me the doll that.... 8 Looks like you	Correct identification for white dolls was 94%, coloured dolls 93% and Negro dolls 72%. Misidentification was more likely with younger and lighter skinned black children (80% of whom misidentified themselves as white)	Correct identification for white dolls was similar to Clark and Clark's - 90% for white dolls, 94% for coloured dolls and 86% for Negro dolls. Younger children misidentified themselves more but only 15% of lighter skinned children did.	White children were also more likely to misidentify themselves at younger ages.
Behavioural consequences What race is your best friend?		There was no relationship between doll preference and race of best friend by black or white children, even in those who always preferred same race dolls.	

DISCUSSION
Doll preference - 4 possible interpretations are proposed for the black children not being white-orientated in their interracial setting:
1 'Negroes are becoming Blacks proud of their race' - times may be changing, although not at the same rate across the country.
2 Black children in Lincoln, unlike in other cities, would have chosen black dolls 30 years ago. This cannot be tested now.
3 The black pride campaign organised by the 'Black Movement' in Lincoln may have modelled positive attitudes towards being black.
4 Interracial contact and acceptance may increase black pride - 70% of black and 59% of white children had opposite colour friends.
Doll preference and friendship – 3 reasons are given for why doll preference did not always reflect the children's friendship choices:
1 If 'Black is beautiful' means rejection of white, the black children should all have had black friends, but despite their preferences this may have been impractical because they were in predominately white schools.
2 The 'Black is beautiful' pride that caused the black children to choose black dolls may have been caused by contact with white friends; more black children who had friends of both races preferred black dolls on all questions (except question 4).
3 Doll choice may not be a valid measure of friendship choice since factors other than colour may be more important when making friends.

EVALUATION OF STUDY
Methodological - A forced 2-doll choice ignores the intensity of preference and may *lack validity* as a measure of race and self-liking.
Theoretical   - Social Identity Theory is supported (the perception of groups we identify with affects our self perception).
Links   - Social Identity Theory. Reduction of discrimination through contact and changing norms. Ethnocentrism.

'Good Samaritanism: an underground phenomenon?' Piliavin, Rodin, and Piliavin (1969)

BACKGROUND

Social psychologists were prompted into investigating helping behaviour by the case of Kitty Genovese (a woman stabbed to death over a period of 30 minutes in front of 38 unresponsive witnesses). Most studies were conducted under strict laboratory conditions, using non-visual emergency situations. The main theories of helping behaviour involved diffusion of responsibility and the economic analysis of costs and rewards for helping.

AIM

To investigate, under real life conditions, the effect on the speed and frequency of helping, and the race of the helper, of
- the type of victim (drunk or ill)
- the race of the victim (black or white)
- the presence of helping models (present or absent)
- the size of the witnessing group

METHOD

Design

Field experiment

Independent variables (4):
- Type of victim (drunk or ill)
- Race of victim (black or white)
- Presence of helping models (present or absent)
- Size of the witnessing group

Dependent variables recorded:
- Frequency of help
- Speed of help
- Race of helper
- Sex of helper
- Movement out of area
- Verbal comments

Subjects

New York subway travellers between 11am and 3 pm, approximately 45% black, 55% white, mean of 8.5 bystanders in critical area, opportunity sample.

Situation

Non stop 7.5 minute journey in subway carriage

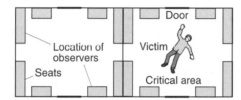

Location of observers · Seats · Door · Victim · Critical area

Procedure

4 teams of 4 researchers
- 2 female who recorded reactions
- 2 male, one acting victim, one model

Victims - 3 white, 1 black, all aged between 26-35, dressed and acted identically. Instructed to collapse after 70 seconds and remain on floor until helped.
Model instructed to help 70 seconds after collapse until end if no other help.

103 trials conducted in total, of which: 38 involved drunk victim (smelt of alcohol and carried a bottle in paper bag). 65 involved sober victim carrying a cane.

RESULTS

1	Frequency of help was impressive - overall 93% helped spontaneously (before the model), 60% of which involved more than one helper. Help was so spontaneous that the model's effect could not be properly studied.	Unlike earlier studies of helping behaviour, bystanders were continuously and visually presented with the emergency situation, making it difficult to ignore.
2	No diffusion of responsibility was found with group size.	Immediate situations decrease diffusion of impact.
3	A victim who appeared ill was more likely to receive help than one who appeared drunk. There was 100% help for the cane victim (of which 63 out of 65 trials involved spontaneous help) but 81% help for the drunk victim (of which 19 out of 38 trials involved spontaneous help). Help was also offered more quickly for the cane victim (a median of 5 seconds compared to 109 second delay with the drunk victim).	The Arousal: Cost-Reward Model proposes that the decision to help depends upon the costs and rewards of helping versus not helping. Therefore, less help for drunk victim since costs of helping are high (perhaps dangerous), costs of not helping are low (no blame), and rewards are low (probably less gratitude).
4	There was a tendency for same race helping to be more frequent, especially in the drunk condition.	Less costs of helping same race in terms of public censure, more witness arousal empathy with victim.
5	Men were significantly more likely to help the victim than women.	Less cost for men in terms of ability to physically help.
6	The longer the emergency continued without help being given: **a** The less impact the model had on the other bystanders. **b** The more likely bystanders were to leave the area. **c** The more likely it was that observers would discuss their behaviour.	Arousal: Cost-Reward Model argues that bystander arousal produced by the plight of others can be reduced by leaving the area or rationalising the decision not to help (e.g. by regarding the victim as undeserving) if help is not given.

The above table has the following column headers:

RESULTS | DISCUSSION OF RESULTS

STRENGTHS OF STUDY
- High ecological validity - study took place under naturally occurring conditions.
- Highly standardised procedure
- Yielded a lot of detailed data.
- Proposed a theoretical explanation to account for levels of helping in all conditions of the experiment.

WEAKNESSES OF STUDY
- Methodological weaknesses - conditions are under less strict control in field experiments than laboratory experiments. Insufficient trials conducted in some conditions of the experiment to yield reliable data, e.g. there were fewer drunk victims, only 8 black cane carriers.
- Ethical weaknesses - deception, lack of consent, no debriefing, and the production of anxiety and/or inconvenience for the bystanders are all ethically problematic.

The cognitive developmental approach to psychology

ORIGINS AND HISTORY

- Researchers can be said to adopt a cognitive developmental approach when they not only focus their research on the **inner mental processes of thinking and reasoning** (as do cognitive psychologists in general) but are also interested in how these **change over time** and **can account for behaviour** shown at different ages.
- The study of the development of knowledge and understanding (epistemology) has long interested philosophers and a variety of psychologists have also attempted to explain cognitive development, but have differed in their views on **why** cognitive abilities change over time – whether it is more due to nature (e.g. biology, genetics) or nurture (e.g. environment, social instruction). There has also been some debate as to **how** the changes occur over time – whether qualitatively (in discrete stages) as most suggest or quantitatively (gradually in degree rather than type).
- Piaget is probably the best known cognitive developmental researcher who suggested thinking progressed through qualitative changes (in stages) due to the increasing biological maturity of mental structures with age and environmental interaction. He applied his stage theory to explain a wide variety of children's comments, judgements and actions, for example how their morality developed over time.
- Other researchers have disagreed with Piaget, for example over the cause of cognitive development (e.g. Vygotsky and Bruner believe society plays a more important role) or over the cognitive structures that are changing (e.g. information-processing theorists).
- Most cognitive developmental research has focused on the changes of mental abilities in childhood, however the approach has been applied throughout the life span, for example to the changes of old age.

Jean Piaget

'What makes their [cognitive] theories 'developmental' is the belief that the ways in which we process experience – be it physical, mathematical, or moral experience – normally change in an orderly, increasingly adaptive, species-specific fashion.' Flanagan (1984)

ASSUMPTIONS

Cognitive developmental psychologists assume that:

1 It is necessary to refer to **inner mental concepts** such as thoughts, beliefs and cognitive structures in order to understand behaviour.
2 These mental concepts **change in important ways** over time, particularly in childhood, and these changes have a major influence on people's behaviour, judgement and attitudes at different ages.

METHODS OF INVESTIGATION

Cognitive developmental psychologists have used methods such as:

- Observation - e.g. Piaget's naturalistic observations of children's everyday statements and play.
- Longitudinal study - e.g. Piaget's study of changes in his own children over the course of their childhood or Kohlberg's study of moral reasoning in the same adults over many years.
- Experimentation – e.g. cross-sectional experiments comparing the ability of two different age groups to pass conservation tests.

CONTRIBUTION TO PSYCHOLOGY

Cognitive developmental psychologists have sought to explain:

- **Cognitive changes** - e.g. in the intellectual abilities of children and older adults.
- **Social cognition** - e.g. moral behaviour and reasoning about moral situations at different ages.
- **Social behaviour** - e.g. play and helping behaviour.
- **Socialisation** - e.g. gender and self-development.

CONTRIBUTION TO SOCIETY

The cognitive developmental approach has had a fairly specialised range of applications, for example to:

- **Education** - e.g. the application of cognitive developmental theory to improve classroom practice and aid student progression.
- **Child care** - e.g. to facilitate care in play and peer relations.
- **Criminology** - e.g. children's ability to understand and be held responsible for their crimes, or the link between moral development and criminal behaviour in adolescence and adulthood.

STRENGTHS

The cognitive developmental approach has:

- Overcome the rather static view of mental processes that has dominated traditional cognitive psychology, and has tried to account for the origin of such processes.
- Shown that a straightforward link between age and behaviour cannot be fully made or understood without considering the changing nature of underlying mental structures.
- Had useful practical applications and implications for society.
- Usually conducted scientific and objective research to support its theories.

WEAKNESSES

Unfortunately the cognitive developmental approach has:

- Had a fairly specialised and thus limited contribution to psychology and society.
- Tended at times to underestimate the discrepancies between cognition and behaviour, e.g. between what people say and do about moral situations, and between the ability a child possesses and shows (e.g. due to demand characteristics).
- Not always justified whether cognitive changes are best viewed as occurring in qualitatively different stages rather than in a more gradual quantitative manner.
- Neglected individual differences in cognitive development.

Piaget's theory of cognitive development

BACKGROUND

Jean Piaget

- Jean Piaget, although a zoologist by training, was involved in the early development of intelligence tests. He became dissatisfied with the idea that intelligence was a fixed trait, and came to regard it as a process which developed over time due to biological maturation and interactive experience with the world, which adapted the child to its environment.
- Piaget was interested in the kind of mistakes that children make at different ages, thinking that these would reflect the cognitive progress they had made, and so spent many years studying children (especially his own) via the clinical interview method, informal experiments, and naturalistic observation.

Intellectual development occurs through <u>active interaction</u> with the world
Increased understanding only happens as the child actively interacts with and *discovers* the world, children do not passively receive their knowledge, they are *curious* and *self-motivated*.

Intellectual development occurs as a <u>process</u>
Piaget thought that children think in *qualitatively* different ways from the adult, we are not born with all our knowledge and understanding 'ready-made', but have to develop our intelligence in **stages**.

Individuals <u>construct</u> their understanding of the world
Through interaction, each individual has to **build** their own mental framework for understanding and interacting with their environment.

WHAT DOES THE CHILD BUILD?

HOW DOES THE CHILD BUILD?

SCHEMATA
A schema is an internal representation of a specific physical or mental action. It is a basic building block or unit of intelligent behaviour which enables the individual to interact with and understand the world. The infant is born with certain reflexive action schemata, such as sucking or gripping, and later acquires symbolic mental schemata. The schemata continue to develop and increase in their complexity and ability to let their owners function well in the world.

ASSIMILATION
This is the process whereby new objects, situations or ideas are understood in terms of the schemata the child already possesses. The world is 'fitted in' to what the child already knows.

ACCOMMODATION
This is the process whereby the existing schemata have to be modified to fit new situations, objects or information. The existing schemata are expanded or new ones are created.

OPERATIONS
In middle childhood, **operations** are acquired - these are higher order mental structures which enable the child to understand more complex rules about how the environment works. Operations are logical manipulations dealing with the relationships between schemata.

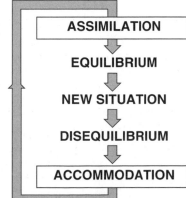

ASSIMILATION

↓

EQUILIBRIUM

↓

NEW SITUATION

↓

DISEQUILIBRIUM

↓

ACCOMMODATION

A baby uses its innate feeding schema to suck on all nipples (mother's or baby bottle's).

The child can deal with the world.

The baby encounters a drinking beaker for the first time.

The baby's sucking schema is not appropriate - a big mess is made!

The baby has to modify its feeding schema so it can use all beakers (ie return to assimilation).

(Adapted from Gross, 1996)

Piaget's stages of cognitive development 1

Piaget proposed four stages of cognitive development which reflect the increasing sophistication of children's thought. Every child moves through the stages in a sequence dictated by biological maturation and interaction with the environment.

1 THE SENSORIMOTOR STAGE
(0 to 2 Years)

The infant at first only knows the world via its immediate senses and the actions it performs. The infant's lack of internal mental schemata is illustrated by;

- profound *egocentrism* - the infant cannot at first distinguish between itself and its environment.
- lack of *object permanence* - when the infant cannot see or act on objects, they cease to exist for the child.

Throughout this stage internal representations are gradually acquired until the *general symbolic function* allows both object permanence and language to occur.

Evidence for
Piaget investigated his children's lack of object permanence during this stage by hiding an object from them under a cover. At 0 to 5 months, an object visibly hidden will not be searched for, even if the child was reaching for it. At 8 months the child will search for a completely hidden object.

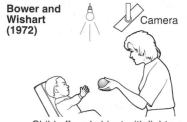

Bower and Wishart (1972) Camera

Child offered object with lights on. Child begins to reach for object.

Evidence against
Bower and Wishart (1972) offered an object to babies aged between 1 to 4 months, and then turned off the lights as they were about to reach for it. When observed by infra-red camera, the babies were seen to continue reaching for the object despite not seeing it.
Bower (1977) tested month old babies who were shown a toy and then had a screen placed in front of it. The toy was secretly removed from behind the screen, and when the screen itself was taken away, Bower claimed that the babies showed surprise that the toy was not there.

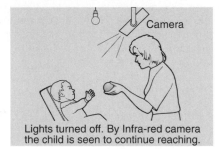

Camera

Lights turned off. By Infra-red camera the child is seen to continue reaching.

2 THE PRE-OPERATIONAL STAGE
(2 to 7 Years)

The child's internal mental world continues to develop, but

- is still **dominated by** the external world and the **appearance** of things.
- shows **centration** - the child only focuses on one aspect of an object or situation at a time.
- **lacks** the mental sophistication necessary to carry out logical **operations** on the world.

The pre-operational child, therefore, shows
- *class-inclusion problems* - difficulty in understanding the relationship between whole classes and sub-classes. The child focuses on the most visibly obvious classes and disregards less obvious ones.
- *egocentrism* - the difficulty of understanding that others do not see, think and feel things like you do.
- *lack of conservation* - the inability to realise that some things remain constant or unchanged despite changes in visible appearance. By only focusing on the most visible changes, the child fails to conserve a whole host of properties, such as number, liquid and substance.

Evidence for
Class-inclusion tests - if a child is shown a set of beads, most of which are brown but with a few white ones, and is asked 'are there more brown beads or more beads', the child will say more brown beads.

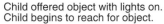

Piaget and Inhelder (1956) - demonstrated the egocentrism of pre-operational children with their 'Three Mountain Experiment'. Four year olds, when shown a mountain scene and tested to see if they could correctly describe it from different viewpoints, failed and tended to choose their own view. Six year olds were more aware of other viewpoints but still tended to choose the wrong one.

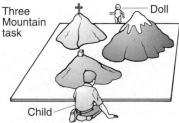

Three Mountain task

Doll

Child

Conservation experiments - Piaget tested for many different types of conservation. The child would fail in each case, since it lacked the necessary operations.

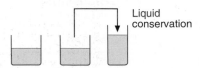

Liquid conservation

Evidence against
McGarrigle et al modified Piaget's class inclusion tasks to make them more understandable and appropriate. They first asked pre-operational children (with an average age of 6) a Piagetian type question - 'Are there more black cows or more cows?' They then turned all of the cows on their sides (as if asleep) and asked 'Are there more black cows or more sleeping cows?' The percentage of correct answers increased from 25% to 48%.

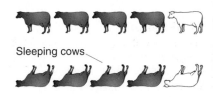

Sleeping cows

Hughes demonstrated that 3.5 to 5 year olds could de-centrate and overcome their egocentrism, if the task made more 'human sense' to them. When these children had to hide a boy doll from two policemen dolls (a task that required them to take into account the perspectives of others but had a good and understandable reason for doing so) they could do this successfully 90% of the time.

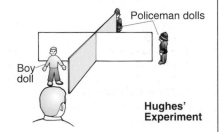

Policeman dolls

Boy doll

Hughes' Experiment

'Asking only one question in the conservation experiment' Samuel and Bryant (1984)

AIM

To support, using a more detailed procedure and a wider age range of subjects, Rose and Blank's experimental criticism of Piaget's conservation studies. Piaget and Szeminska (1952) found pre-operational children (below the age of seven) could not conserve (realise that some properties, such as number, volume, and mass, remain the same despite changes in their physical appearance) by conducting experiments, whereby:

1 They showed 2 rows of counters and asked a pre-transformation question 'are there the same number in each row?' The answer was usually '**yes**'.

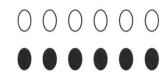

2 They then lengthened one of the rows and asked the (same) post-transformation question 'are there the same number in each row?' The answer given was then usually '**no**'.

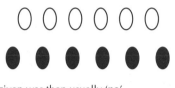

Piaget took the 'no' answer to mean that the children thought there were now a greater number of counters in the lengthened row and that these children could not conserve. However, Rose and Blank (1974) disagreed with this conclusion. They argued that Piaget had made a methodological error by imposing **demand characteristics** - when an adult deliberately changes something and asks the same question twice, children think that a different answer is **expected**, even though they may well be able to conserve. Rose and Blank (1974) conducted a study where they only asked one question (the post transformation one) to reduce these misleading expectations, and found that more children were able to conserve when they only had to make one judgement than when they had to make two in the standard Piagetian presentation.

Samuel and Bryant (1984) wanted to replicate this study on a larger scale using

- four age groups (5, 6, 7 and 8 year olds),
- three types of conservation test (number, mass, and liquid volume), and
- three ways of presenting the tests (standard Piagetian way, one judgement/question way, and fixed array with no visible transformation).

METHOD

Subjects: Independent measures design was used. 252 boys and girls were divided into 4 age groups (of 5, 6, 7 and 8 year olds).

Procedure: In each age group every child was tested 4 times each for conservation of number, mass, and liquid volume in one of three ways:

- The standard Piagetian way: (asking the pre- and post-transformation questions)

- The one judgement way: (asking only the post-transformation question)

- The fixed array way: (asking only the post-transformation question, **without seeing** the transformation)

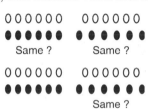

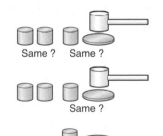

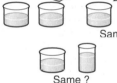

In all three methods of presentation, the 12 conservation tests each child experienced were systematically varied to prevent order effects. Two different versions of each type of conservation test were given to ensure the child could show a proper understanding of the concepts involved.

RESULTS

Mixed design analysis of variance and Newman-Kreuls tests showed that

- Children were significantly more able to conserve in the one judgement task.
  This supports Rose and Blank's (1974) experiment and criticism of Piaget's methods.
- Older children did significantly better than younger children in conservation.
  This supports Piaget's theory of cognitive development in general.
- The conservation of number task was significantly easier than the other tasks.
  Indicating support for Piaget's notion of decalage.

MEAN ERRORS OUT OF 12 CONSERVATION TESTS

Age	Standard	One judgement	Fixed Array
5	8.5	7.3	8.6
6	5.7	4.3	6.4
7	3.2	2.6	4.9
8	1.7	1.3	3.3

EVALUATION

Methodological: *Good methods* - The study used a control group, different tests of conservation, and different aged subjects.
Good data analysis - The data was extensively analysed to reveal its significance.

Theoretical: *Implications* - The study supports some of Piaget's notions and some of those of his critics.

Links: Child cognitive development. Research methods – demand characteristics.

Bruner's theory of cognitive development

BRUNER'S ASSUMPTIONS

Jerome Bruner was a cognitive scientist who agreed with Piaget that active interaction with the world could increase a child's underlying cognitive capacity to understand the world in more complex ways. Bruner differed from Piaget, however, in that he:

- Was more concerned with **how** knowledge was **represented** and organised as the child developed, and therefore proposed different **modes** of representation.
- Emphasised the importance of **social** factors in cognitive development, in particular the role of language, social interaction and experience, which could pull the child towards better understanding. Cognitive growth depends upon the mastery of 'skills transmitted with varying efficiency and success by the culture' and occurs 'from the outside in as well as from the inside out' Bruner (1971).

MODES OF REPRESENTATION

Bruner's theory is concerned with **ways** of **representing** or thinking about knowledge at different ages, not stages as such. Bruner proposed **three modes** of representation that develop in order and allow the child to think about the world in more sophisticated ways, but all exist in the adult (we do not lose these ways of thinking like in Piaget's stages). The modes are:

- The enactive mode (0 - 1 years) - this mode of representation is dominant in babies, who first represent or interact with the world through their actions. Knowledge is therefore stored in '**muscle memory**'.
- The iconic mode (1 - 6 years) - this mode represents knowledge through visual or auditory **likenesses** or **images**. Children dominated by their iconic mode have **difficulty** thinking beyond the images, to categorise the knowledge or understand relationships between objects.
- The symbolic mode (7 years onwards) - this mode enables children to encode the world in terms of information storing symbols such as the words of our language or the numbers of mathematics. This allows information to be **categorised** and summarised so that it can be more readily **manipulated** and considered. The symbolic mode allows children to think beyond the physical images of the iconic mode.

THE ROLE OF LANGUAGE AND EDUCATION

Like Vygotsky, Bruner stressed education and social interaction as major influences upon cognitive development, and in particular proposed that society provides our language which gives us symbolic thought. Unlike Piaget, who thought that language was merely a useful tool which reflects and describes the underlying symbolic cognitive structures such as operations,

Bruner believed that language is symbolic/logical/operational thought - the two are inseparable. According to Bruner therefore, **language training** can speed up cognitive development, a suggestion that Piaget's theory rejects (since he believed that cognitive structures could only be developed through the child's individual maturation and interaction with the world).

LANGUAGE ACCELERATING DEVELOPMENT

- Francoise Frank (reported by Bruner, 1964) showed how the ability of pre-operational children to give the correct answer in liquid conservation tasks could be improved if they were encouraged to use and rely upon their linguistic descriptions (i.e. their symbolic mode) of the task.
- Frank reduced the visual (iconic mode) effect of the conservation changes by screening most of the beakers during the experiment. Once the children were less dominated by their iconic mode, they could concentrate on their verbal (symbolic mode) descriptions of what was happening, and were more able to conserve.
- Once the 5 and 6 year olds had used their language to solve the conservation task, they showed an increased ability to pass other non-screened conservation tasks. 5 year olds showed an increase from 20 to 70%.
  6-7 year olds increased from 50 to 90%.

Step 1 Show standard beakers with equal water and a wider beaker of the same height.

Step 2 Screen the beakers so the water level is hidden, but mark the level of the water on screen.

Step 3 Pour water from the standard beaker into the screened wider beaker.

Step 4 Ask the child, without it seeing the water 'which has more to drink or do they have the same?'
Result - in comparison with an unscreened pre-test there is an increase in correct answers:
4 year olds - increase from 0% to 50%
5 year olds - increase from 20% to 90%
6 year olds - increase from 50% to 100%
Children justify their response linguistically by saying for example 'You only poured it'.

Step 5 The screen is removed and:
4 year olds - all revert to the pre-test answer of less water in the wider beaker, overwhelmed by the appearance of the water (iconic mode).
5-6 year olds - virtually all stick to the right answer, relying on their previous verbal justification (symbolic mode) 'You only poured it from there to there'.

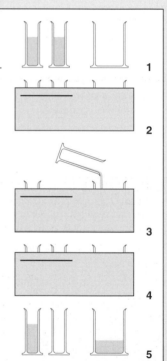

Sonstroem et al (1966) encouraged children who failed conservation of substance tests to use all of their modes of representation to increase their ability to conserve. The children who rolled the plasticine into a ball themselves (enactive mode) while watching their own actions (iconic mode) and verbally describing what was happening, e.g. 'it's getting longer but thinner' (symbolic mode) showed the greatest improvement in conservation.

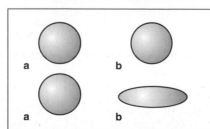

When the ball 'b' is rolled into a sausage, pre-operational children think there is more plasticine.

Vygotsky's theory of cognitive development

VYGOTSKY'S APPROACH
- Vygotsky was a Russian psychologist whose ideas on cognitive development were very similar to Bruner's. Vygotsky focused on the importance of *social interaction* and *language* as major influences on children's development of understanding.

SOCIAL INTERACTION

- Vygotsky sees the whole process of cognitive development as being social in nature - *'we become ourselves through others'*.
- At first the child responds to the world only through its actions, but society provides the *meaning* of those actions through social interaction.
- Vygotsky illustrates this with the example of pointing - the child may reach towards an object and fail to grasp it, but the parent will *interpret* this as a pointing gesture.
- 'The original meaning to this unsuccessful grasping movement is thus imparted by others. And only afterwards, on the basis of the fact that the child associates the unsuccessful grasping movement with the entire objective situation, does the child himself begin to treat the movement as a pointing gesture. Here the function of the movement itself changes: from a movement directed towards an object, it becomes a movement directed towards another person, a means of communication, the grasping is transformed into pointing.' Vygotsky (1978)

INTERNALISATION AND LANGUAGE

- Cognitive development, therefore, proceeds, according to Vygotsky, as the child gradually *internalises* the meanings provided by these social interactions. The child's thinking and reasoning abilities are at first primitive, crude and do not involve the use of language, and so the greatest advance comes when we internalise *language*.
- Speech starts off as communication behaviour that produces changes in others, but when language becomes internalised, it converges with thought - *'thought becomes verbal and speech rational'* Vygotsky (1962). Language allows us to 'turn around and reflect on our thoughts' - directing and *controlling* our thinking, as well as communicating our thoughts to others.
- Eventually, language splits between these two functions as we develop an abbreviated inner voice for thinking with, and a more articulate vocabulary for communicating with others. Internal language vastly increases our powers of problem solving.
- The use of language can be said to progress in three stages:
1 Pre-intellectual social speech (0-3 years), where thinking does not occur in language and speech is used to provoke social change.
2 Egocentric speech (3-7 years), where language helps the child control behaviour but is spoken out loud.
3 Inner speech (7 years +), where the child uses speech silently to control their own behaviour and publicly for social communication.

ZONE OF PROXIMAL DEVELOPMENT

- Because cognitive development is achieved by the *joint* construction of knowledge between the child and society, it follows that any one child's potential intellectual ability is greater if working in *conjunction* with a more expert person / other than alone. Vygotsky defines the *zone of proximal development* (ZPD) as

'the distance between the actual developmental level as determined by individual problem solving and the level of potential development as determined through problem solving under adult guidance or in collaboration with more capable peers. The zone of proximal development defines those functions that have not yet matured but are in the process of maturation, functions that will mature tomorrow but are currently in an embryonic state. These functions could be termed the "buds" or "flowers" of development rather than the "fruits" of development'.

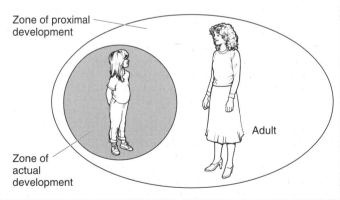

Zone of proximal development

Zone of actual development

Adult

EVALUATION OF VYGOTSKY'S THEORY

Vygotsky's ideas have:
- become increasingly popular as it became clear that Piaget had under emphasised the role of social factors in cognitive development.
- been developed by others such as Bruner who have conducted more research to provide evidence for them than Vygotsky himself did.
- been successfully applied to education.

Key application - of cognitive developmental theories to education

APPLICATIONS OF PIAGET'S THEORY TO EDUCATION

Piaget did not apply his theory to the classroom himself and most of the following recommendations are what other researchers have proposed based on Piagetian principles. Overall Piaget's theory has applications for *when* and *how* to teach.

WHEN TO TEACH
- Because of Piaget's ideas on stages of development, the notion of '**readiness**' is important - children show qualitatively different kinds of thinking at different ages and should only be taught concepts suitable for their underlying level of cognitive development.

CURRICULUM IMPLICATIONS
- Some researchers have suggested that because of the notion of readiness certain concepts should be taught before others or even in a specific *order*, for example conservation of number, followed by conservation of weight, followed by conservation of volume.
- New knowledge should be *built on pre-existing schemas*, which should be expanded through accommodation. Concrete operational children should therefore start with concrete examples before progressing onto more abstract tasks.
- However there should be a *balance* between accommodation (learning new concepts) and assimilation (practising and utilising those concepts).

LIMITATIONS ON PROGRESS
- Piaget proposed that cognitive development should *not* be speeded up because of its dependence on biological maturation. Teaching children a concept before they are biologically ready prevents them from discovering it for themselves – resulting in incomplete understanding.
- Piaget disagreed with Bruner over the ability of *language training* to advance cognitive reasoning.

HOW TO TEACH
Because of Piaget's emphasis on the individual child's self construction of its cognitive development, education should be *student centred* and accomplished through **active discovery learning**.

THE ROLE OF THE TEACHER
The role of the teacher in the Piagetian classroom is as a *facilitator*. Teachers should be involved in the indirect imparting of knowledge, not direct tuition and should therefore:

1 Focus on the *process* of learning rather than the end product of it.
2 Assess the *level* of the child's development so suitable tasks can be set.
3 Choose tasks that are *self-motivating* for the child, to engage its interest and further its own development.
4 Set tasks that are challenging enough to put the child into *disequilibrium* so it can accommodate and create new schemas.
5 Introduce abstract or formal operational tasks through *concrete* examples.
6 Encourage *active interaction* not just with task materials but with other children. In small group work children can learn from each other.

THE THEORIES OF BRUNER AND VYGOTSKY APPLIED TO EDUCATION
- Bruner and Vygotsky both disagreed with Piaget's strict notion of readiness and argued that the teacher should *actively intervene* to help the child develop its understanding - instruction *is* an important part of the learning process. The teacher, or more knowledgeable other, provides the 'tools' or 'loan of consciousness' required for the child to develop cognitively by providing structure, direction, guidance and support, not just facts. The following concepts are therefore important in education according to the theories of both Bruner and Vygotsky:

THE SPIRAL CURRICULUM
The '*spiral curriculum*' involves material being structured so that complex ideas can be presented at simplified levels first and then *re-visited* at more complex levels later on. This opposes Piaget's idea of readiness.
Children should be made aware of the structure and direction of the subjects they study, and progression should proceed via an *active problem solving* process.

SCAFFOLDING
'*Scaffolding*' is a kind of hypothetical support structure around the child's attempt to understand new ideas and complete new tasks. The scaffolding allows the child to climb to the higher levels of development in manageable amounts by
1 Reducing degrees of freedom (simplifying the tasks)
2 Direction maintenance (motivating and encouraging the child)
3 Marking critical features (highlighting relevant parts or errors)
4 Demonstration (providing model examples for imitation)

THE ZONE OF PROXIMAL DEVELOPMENT AND EDUCATION
- Tharp and Gallimore (1988) propose the following definition of teaching according to Vygotsky's ideas - "*Teaching consists in assisting performance through the ZPD. Teaching can be said to occur when assistance is offered at points in the ZPD at which performance requires assistance*" and go on to quote Vygotsky (1956) who said that teaching was only good when it "*awakens and rouses to life those functions which are in a stage of maturing, which lie in the zone of proximal development*".
- Teachers should assist performance by working sensitively and *contingently* within the ZPD. Bruner developed this idea of contingency (responding appropriately and flexibly to the child's individual needs only when required) in his own work, and Wood and Middleton (1975) have investigated contingency by watching mothers help their children build a puzzle. The mothers showed contingency by offering different levels of help depending on how much difficulty the child was having.

Contemporary issue - Do cognitive changes persist into old age?

The issue of whether cognitive changes, such as those relating to intelligence and memory, persist into old age is one that has important implications for the way that the elderly:

1 are treated by society, in terms of ageist discrimination for example
2 view themselves, and the effects such views may have on their behaviour and cognitive abilities

Cognitive developmental psychologists are interested in the issue since they investigate:

1 changes in cognitive abilities over time
2 whether such changes are qualitative in kind or quantitative in degree
3 whether such changes are more a result of biological maturation or social environment.

---

1. DO CHANGES IN COGNITIVE ABILITIES OCCUR IN OLDER PEOPLE?

The overall answer to this question is *yes, some genuine changes* in cognitive abilities do occur with old age, however:

- The degree of change is likely to be *exaggerated* by *negative stereotypes* in some cultures, such as older people becoming senile.
- There are *large individual differences* between older people in *how much change* occurs and *how late* in the life span it occurs.
- Some of the changes reflect the influence of *variables other than just age* on cognitive abilities, such as those resulting from the *cohort effect*. This is when different age groups in a society at any one time will differ in other characteristics, such as the level of education or nutrition they have experienced, which may influence cognitive abilities but be unrelated to the duration of their lives. This is supported by the finding that *longitudinal studies* of the same individuals over time *reveal less change* in cognitive abilities than *cross-sectional studies* that compare different people of different ages.

---

2. ARE COGNITIVE CHANGES IN OLD AGE QUALITATIVE OR QUANTITATIVE IN KIND?

- Both changes in degree and kind of memory and intellectual ability have been suggested.
- Intelligence - while research has shown that older people show decreases in the speed of their mental processing, a steady accumulation of life experience may provide the greater expert knowledge and insight into life associated with wisdom in old age. This may link with the finding that *crystallised intelligence* (which involves the use of knowledge that has already been acquired) appears to increase with age, while *fluid intelligence* (which concerns the ability to solve problems that have not been encountered before) seems to decrease with age. Some cognitive developmental researchers have even suggested a *fifth, post-formal stage* of intellectual ability in late adulthood, involving an acceptance of contradiction, ambiguity and complexity.
- Memory – Salthouse (1990) found evidence for a decline in the efficiency of *working memory* in elderly participants. Performance on tests of recall is worse in older than younger people, but there seems little or no difference in tests of recognition.

---

3. ARE COGNITIVE CHANGES IN OLD AGE A RESULT OF BIOLOGICAL OR SOCIAL FACTORS?

As with childhood cognitive development, changes in cognitive abilities in old age may be a result of both biological and social factors.

- Biological deterioration of mental abilities can be caused by the degeneration of neurones resulting from either natural cell death with age or diseases such as Alzheimer's. Studies have shown that *dramatic* cell loss, particularly in parts of the temporal lobe and hippocampus of the brain can occur in people with Alzheimer's disease, but is not an inevitable consequence of ageing.
- A number of social environmental changes that occur in old age can affect mental abilities. The elderly may experience decreasing activity levels and *less stimulating environments* which could adversely affect their cognitive abilities - especially in cultures where older people have less family and social contact or are put in care homes with poor facilities, repetitive routines and limited social variability. Such environments may not present sufficient opportunity to practice and apply fluid intelligence. Baltes and Willis (1982) found that training older adults on the aspects of IQ that usually decline over time significantly improved their performance, even in long term follow-up studies of those adults in their early 80s.
In addition, negative cultural stereotypes about the forgetfulness of old age or positive stereotypes about the wisdom old age bestows, may affect memory abilities by becoming *self-fulfilling prophecies*. This was supported by Levy and Langer (1994) who found that older American participants exposed to negative stereotypes about the effect of age on memory performed worse on memory tests than younger Americans (for whom the negative stereotype did not yet apply), older deaf Americans (who would have been less exposed to the stereotype) and older Chinese participants (who are exposed to positive stereotypes about age bringing wisdom).
- There are a number of cognitive psychological explanations for mental deficits in old age that cannot always be clearly distinguished as either biological or social. Slower mental processing speed could result from either neuronal deterioration or older people having more ways of solving problems available to them. Retrieval of memory may decline with age because of trace decay, interference from a greater number of memories, or a lack of cues in their present life to prompt the access to memories of the past.

'Does the autistic child have a 'theory of mind'?' Baron-Cohen, Leslie and Frith (1985)

INTRODUCTION
- Baron-Cohen et al describe childhood autism as a severe developmental disorder affecting around 4 in 10,000 children and see the key symptom as being a **profound problem in understanding and coping with the social environment** - finding it unpredictable and confusing. This causes impaired verbal and non-verbal communication and a failure to develop normal social relationships – autistic children seem to treat people and objects in the same way and tend to be withdrawn or disruptive in their interactions with others.
- Autistic social problems could be partly caused by other symptoms that such children show – many for example are mentally retarded. However autistic children with normal IQs also lack social competence, while non-autistic retarded children such as those with Down's Syndrome are relatively socially competent. Baron-Cohen et al therefore suggest that autistic children **lack a specific cognitive mechanism** that is distinct from general IQ, namely a '**theory of mind**'.
- A theory of mind enables one to realise that '**other people know, want, feel, or believe things**' and as such is vital for social skills. It is a form of '**second –order' representation**' or metarepresentation (a representation of another person's representation of the world, or a belief about another's belief), which also gives the ability to pretend in play – something autistic children are very poor at.

AIM
If a theory of mind that enables one to attribute mental states to others:
1 is specifically lacking in autistic children and is not related to general intelligence
2 allows people to work out what others *believe* about certain situations and thus predict what they will do next
then it can be hypothesised that autistic children whose IQs are in the average range will perform significantly worse on a task that requires such belief based prediction than non-autistic but severely retarded children with Down's Syndrome.

METHOD
Design A natural or quasi experiment was used, employing an independent measures design.
The independent variable was the type of child, naturally manipulated in 3 conditions; autistic, Down's Syndrome, clinically 'normal'.
The dependent variable was the ability to correctly answer the belief question of the Sally-Anne test.
Subjects 20 autistic children aged around 6-16 years old (average approx. 12) of higher average intelligence than the other groups.
14 Down's Syndrome children aged around 6-17 (average approx. 11).
27 clinically 'normal' pre-school children aged around 3-5 (average approx. 4 and a half).
Procedure The experimenter sits at a table opposite the child with two dolls, Sally and Anne. Sally puts a marble into her basket, then leaves the scene. Anne transfers the marble and hides it in her box. Sally returns and the experimenter asks the critical **Belief Question** – "Where will Sally look for her marble?". If the children point to the previous location of Sally's basket they pass the belief question since they can represent the doll's false belief. If they point to the current location of Anne's box then they fail the question since they cannot take into account Sally's false belief. The scenario was repeated, but this time the marble was transferred to the experimenter's pocket.
Controls –To ensure the validity of the belief question, 3 control questions were asked – the Naming Question asking which doll was which (to ensure knowledge of the dolls' identities), the Reality Question "Where is the marble really?" and the Memory Question "Where was the marble in the beginning?" (to ensure knowledge of the marble's location at each point in the scenario).

Sally places her marble in the basket

Exit Sally

Anne transfers Sally's marble to box

Re-enter Sally — Where will Sally look for her marble?

RESULTS

% failure on Questions	Autistic group	Down's Syndrome group	'Normal' pre-schoolers
Naming, Reality, Memory	0%	0%	0%
Belief Question	80% on both trials	14% on both trials	15% on both trials

Belief Question differences were significant at P<0.001. All 16 autistic children who failed pointed to the current marble location.

DISCUSSION
The controls rule out explanations of position preference, negativism, random pointing, misunderstanding/forgetting the task or general intellectual ability. The experimenters therefore conclude that the autistic children specifically lacked a theory of mind to enable them to attribute belief to the doll and thus distinguish their own belief from the doll's. The four autistic children who did not fail the Belief Question may have possessed a theory of mind and were predicted by Baron-Cohen et al to show differences from the other autistic children in their type of social impairment and pretend play deficiency (testing of this was not reported). The *conceptual* perspective-taking tested here is distinguished from the *perceptual* perspective-taking tested by Piaget and Inhelder's 'three mountain' test.

EVALUATION
Methodological The scenario and use of dolls is rather artificial (dolls do not believe!). Realistic tests using people have confirmed the results.
Theoretical The study initiated a large amount of research into theory of mind and links with certain aspects of Piaget's egocentrism.
Links Child cognitive development. Natural or quasi experimentation.

The physiological approach to psychology

ORIGINS AND HISTORY

- Sometimes known as the biological, biopsychological, neurophysiological, nativist (considering nature rather than nurture) or innate approach.
- The biological approach to psychological matters has integrated with and run parallel to the rest of psychological thought since early Greek times - the Greek physician Galen suggested that personality and temperament may be linked to the levels of body fluids such as blood and bile in the body.
- As knowledge of human anatomy, physiology, biochemistry, and medicine developed, important insights for human behaviour and experience were gained. Penfield for example mapped the role of various areas of the cerebral cortex through microelectrode stimulation with conscious patients. Sperry investigated the effects of splitting the cerebral hemispheres on consciousness and psychological function.
- The field will progress still further as the technology to isolate the effects of genes and scan the living brain develops.

Roger Sperry
'All that is psychological is first physiological' Anon.

ASSUMPTIONS

Biologically orientated psychologists assume that
- all that is psychological is first physiological - that is since the mind appears to reside in the brain, all thoughts, feelings and behaviours ultimately have a physical/biological cause
- human genes have evolved over millions of years to adapt physiology and behaviour to the environment. Therefore, much behaviour will have a genetic basis
- psychology should, therefore, investigate the brain, nervous system, endocrine system, neurochemistry, and genes
- it is also useful to study why human behaviour has evolved in the way it has, the subject of evolutionary/sociobiological theory

METHODS OF INVESTIGATION

Common techniques include
- laboratory experimentation - e.g. stimulating, giving drugs to, or removing parts of the brain to see what effect it has on behaviour
- laboratory observations - controlled observations of physical processes, e.g. sleep or the scanning of the structure and activity of the brain.
- correlations - e.g. between twins and adopted family members to discover the genetic influence on intelligence or mental disorders.

CONTRIBUTION TO PSYCHOLOGY

Physiological researchers have contributed to an understanding of
- **gender development** - e.g. the influence of genetic and hormonal predispositions on gender behaviour and identity
- **aggression** - e.g. investigating the role of the limbic system
- **abnormality** - e.g. the dopamine hypothesis and enlarged ventricle theory of schizophrenia
- **memory** - e.g. brain scans of areas involved during memory tests or the effect of brain damage on memory
- **motivation** - e.g. the role of the hypothalamus in homeostasis
- **awareness** - e.g. biological theories of sleep, dreams and body rhythms
- **localisation of function** - e.g. the effect on behaviour of brain damage to certain areas

CONTRIBUTION TO SOCIETY

Physiology's main applications have been to
- **therapy** - e.g. drug treatment, psychosurgery, or electroconvulsive therapy for mental disorders such as schizophrenia or depression
- **health** - e.g. research on the causes, effects and management of stress
- **industry** - e.g. research on jet lag and shift work
- **sport** - e.g. the effect of arousal on performance
- **education** - e.g. the genetic basis of ability

STRENGTHS

Physiology has contributed to psychology in many ways:
- The approach is very scientific, grounded in the hard science of biology with its objective, materialistic subject matter and experimental methodology.
- It provides strong counter-arguments to the nurture side of the nature-nurture debate.
- Physiology's practical applications are usually extremely effective, e.g. the treatment of mental disorder.
- The physiological approach has contributed to psychologists' understanding of a very wide range of phenomena.

WEAKNESSES

- Reductionism - the biopsychological approach explains thoughts and behaviour in terms of the action of neurones or biochemicals. This may ignore other more suitable levels of explanation and the interaction of causal factors.
- The approach has not adequately explained how mind and body interact - consciousness and emotion are difficult to study objectively.
- Over simplistic - biopsychological theories often over-simplify the huge complexity of physical systems and their interaction with environmental factors.

Methods of investigating brain function - measurement

MEASURING/OBSERVATIONAL TECHNIQUES

DIRECT RECORDING OF NEURONAL ACTIVITY

Microelectrodes are inserted into single neuronal cells and record their electrochemical activity, e.g.

Hubel and Wiesel measured the activity of single neuronal cells in the visual cortex of monkeys. By keeping the head still, various visual stimuli could be presented to different areas of the retina to discover both the area the cell represented and the stimuli it most responded to.

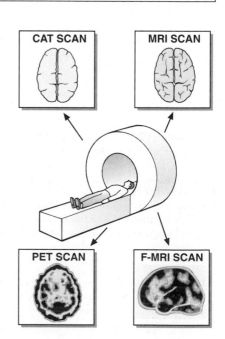

EVALUATION
Advantages
*   Extremely precise - a very accurate way of studying the living function of neurones.

Disadvantages
*   Very time-consuming - thousands of neurones occupy even a tiny area of brain.
*   Too focused - it neglects the interactions between nerve cells that are responsible for brain functions.
*   Invasive method - it, thus, has ethical problems, especially if applied to humans.

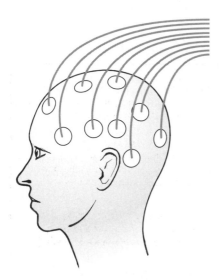

EXTERNAL RECORDING OF BRAIN ACTIVITY

Aims to detect brain activity from measurements made at the surface of the skull, e.g.
*   electroencephalograms (EEG) - electrodes are attached to areas of the scalp, and the electrical activity of the brain beneath that they detect is amplified to reveal the frequency of the 'brain wave'. The frequency is the number of oscillations the wave makes in a second and ranges from 1-3 hertz (delta waves) to 13 hertz or over (beta waves).
*   evoked potentials - record the change in the electrical activity of an area of brain when an environmental stimuli is presented or a psychological task is undertaken.
Electrooculargrams (EOG) measure electrical activity of eye movements, whereas Electromyograms (EMG) record activity from muscles to measure tension or relaxation.

EVALUATION
Advantages
*   Non-invasive techniques - no alteration or intervention makes these methods of measuring brain activity more natural and ecologically valid.
*   Practically useful - these methods can distinguish between levels of sleep and different types of subject, e.g. brain damaged, epileptic, those with Alzheimer's disease, etc.

Disadvantages
*   Crude measure - the activity of millions of neurones is measured and averaged. EEGs indicate the activity level but not the precise function of the neurones involved.

SCANNING TECHNIQUES
1   **STILL PICTURES** - detailed three dimensional or cross-sectional images of the brain can be gained by the following non-invasive techniques:
    a   **Computerised Axial Tomography** (CAT scan) - is produced by X-ray rotation.
    b   **Magnetic Resonance Imaging** (MRI scan) - where magnetic fields are rotated around the head to produce an extremely detailed picture.

2   **DYNAMIC PICTURES** - moving coloured images of brain activity levels in different parts of the brain over time can be gained by techniques such as:
    a   **Positron Emission Tomography** (PET scan) - which detects the metabolism level of injected substances (e.g. glucose) made mildly radioactive to show which parts of the brain are most active (using up energy) over a period of minutes.
    b   **Functional Magnetic Resonance Imaging** (F-MRI scan) - shows metabolic activity second by second without injected tracers.
    c   **Magnetoencephalography** (MEG scan) - detects actual nerve cell firing over thousandths of a second.

EVALUATION
Advantages
*   Detailed knowledge - scans can gain information about the brain structure and function of conscious patients, some while they are performing psychological tasks.

Disadvantages
*   Scanning techniques - are expensive and scans can be difficult to interpret and are sensitive to disruption, e.g. by small movements.

Methods of investigating brain function - alteration

ALTERATION/EXPERIMENTAL TECHNIQUES

ACCIDENTAL DAMAGE

Researchers use these natural experiments to compare the alteration in psychological functioning with the location of damage (by scan, surgery or autopsy). Damage may be caused by

- **strokes/tumours** - e.g. blood clot damage has revealed much about the location of motor, sensory, and linguistic functioning in the brain.
- **head trauma** - e.g. a railroad construction accident blew a 3 foot long metal rod through Phineas Gage's left frontal lobe in 1848, changing his personality to make him impulsive and irritable.
- **virus** - e.g. the virus herpes simplex damaged the temporal lobe and hippocampus of Clive Wearing causing anterograde amnesia.

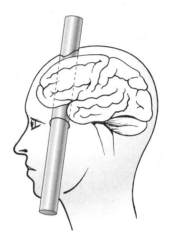

EVALUATION
Advantages
- The altering damage occurs 'naturally' so there are less ethical problems compared to other methods.

Disadvantages
- Lack of precision - the exact extent of damage is not controllable and may be difficult to assess.
- Comparison problems - comparison of the functioning in the individual before and after the damage is less objective, since it is often based on retrospective accounts of previous behaviour and abilities.
- Confounding variables - other non-physical effects of the damage may be responsible for behavioural differences. Social reactions to Phineas Gage's physical deformity may have affected his personality.

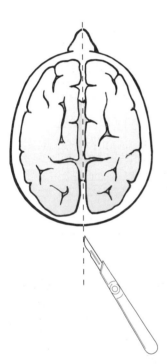

DELIBERATE DAMAGE

ABLATION/LESION STUDIES - aim to investigate function by removing areas of the brain or destroying links between areas. Some of the psychological functions investigated have included
- **Motivation** - ablation studies on the hypothalamus of rats have caused disrupted eating behaviour.
- **Aggression** - removing the amygdala of some animals has reduced their aggression.
- **Memory** - Lashley removed large portions of rat brains to find the location of memory.
- **Consciousness** - Sperry cut the corpus callosum of epileptic patients, producing a 'split mind'.
- **Psychopathology** - prefrontal lobotomy was performed on mental inmates to control behaviour.

EXPERIMENTAL EXPOSURE EFFECTS - aim to influence brain physiology by using environmental distortion or deprivation. Common examples are found in perceptual studies, e.g. Blakemore and Cooper's study of the visual cortex of cats exposed to an environment of vertical lines.

EVALUATION
Advantages
- Greater control - greater precision in the location of damage and the ability to compare behaviour before and after alteration leads to higher certainty over the effects of the damage.

Disadvantages
- Ethical problems of intervention - the deliberate change of behaviour is radical and irreversible.
- Non-human findings - may not be legitimately generalised to humans due to qualitative differences.
- Plasticity - the brain is a very flexible system which can compensate for damage. Removing one part of it will only show the performance of the rest of the system, not necessarily the missing part.

STIMULATION OF THE BRAIN

ELECTRICAL STIMULATION - aims to stimulate brain areas with microelectrodes to reveal their function through behavioural change. Examples include
- animal studies - Delgado stimulated areas of the limbic system to provoke aggression in monkeys and inhibit aggression in a charging bull (while standing in front of it!) by remote control.
- human studies - Penfield stimulated areas of the cortex in patients undergoing brain surgery and found locations that would produce body movement (primary motor cortex), body sensations (primary sensory cortex), memories of sound (temporal lobe) and visual sensations (visual cortex).

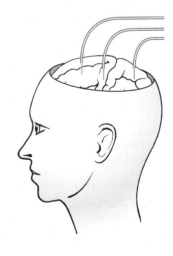

EVALUATION
Advantages
- Less harmful - the aim is to stimulate the brain rather than damage it (therefore more ethical).
- More valid - stimulation seems a better way of investigating the 'living' function of brain areas.

Disadvantages
- Invasive technique - the techniques still involve surgical operation, which can be risky.
- Interconnectedness - it is not easy to know exactly how far the stimulation has spread to other areas and the behaviour produced may not be natural, indeed it is often more stereotyped.

'Brain abnormalities in murderers indicated by positron emission tomography' Raine et al (1997)

INTRODUCTION

Previous research using a variety of techniques (e.g. brain damage effects and EEG measurements) on both humans and other animals has indicated that dysfunction in certain localised brain areas may predispose individuals to violent behaviour. Such brain structures include the prefrontal cortex, corpus callosum, left angular gyrus, amygdala, hippocampus and thalamus.

AIM

By using recent brain imaging techniques on a large group of violent offenders who have committed murder and a control group of non-murderers, this study hypothesises that dysfunction in the above brain structures should be found more often in the murderers than
1　dysfunction of the same areas in non-murderers
2　dysfunction in other areas of the murderers' brains that have been implicated in non-violent psychiatric disorders (e.g. the caudate, putamen, globus pallidus, midbrain and cerebellum)

METHOD

Subjects –The 'murderers' were 41 prisoners (39 male, 2 female) with a mean age of 34.3 years (standard deviation of 10.1), charged with murder or manslaughter in California. They were referred for brain imaging scans to obtain evidence or information relating to a defence of not guilty by reason of insanity, incompetence to stand trial or diminished capacity to reduce sentencing having been found guilty. The reasons for scanning referral were very diverse, ranging from schizophrenia (6 cases) to head injury or organic brain damage (23 cases). No murderer had psychoactive medication for 2 weeks before scanning (each was urine screened).

Controls – Each murderer was matched with a 'normal' subject for age, sex and schizophrenia where necessary. Each was screened to exclude physical and mental illness, drug taking and, of course, a history of murder.

Procedure - After practice trials, all participants were injected with a tracer substance (fluorodeoxyglucose) that was taken up by the brain to show the location of brain metabolism (activity) while they conducted a continuous performance task (CPT) requiring them to detect target signals for 32 minutes. A positron emission tomography (PET) scan was then immediately given to show the relative brain activity (glucose metabolised) for 6 main cortical areas (the outside of the brain) and 8 subcortical areas (inside the brain).

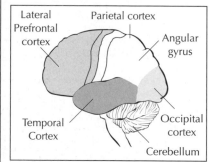
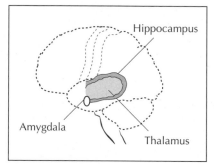
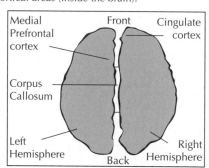

RESULTS

	Brain structure	Murderers' metabolic activity level	Interpretation
Cortex	Prefrontal cortex	Lower activity than controls	Linked to loss of self control and altered emotion.
	Parietal cortex	Lower activity than controls especially in the left angular and bilateral superior gyrus	Lower left angular gyrus activity linked to lower verbal ability, educational failure and thus crime.
	Temporal cortex	No difference compared to controls	No difference was expected.
	Occipital cortex	Higher activity than controls (unexpected)	May compensate on CPT for lower frontal activity.
Subcortex	Corpus callosum	Lower activity than controls	May stop left brain inhibiting the right's violence.
	Amygdala	Lower activity in left than right side of the brain in murderers than controls	These structures form part of the limbic system (thought to control emotional expression). Problems with these structures may cause a lack of inhibition for violent behaviour, fearlessness and a failure to learn the negative effects of violence.
	Medial (inner) temporal including hippocampus	Lower activity in left than right side of the brain in murderers than controls	
	Thalamus	Higher activity on right side in murderers	
	Cingulate, caudate, putamen Globus pallidus, midbrain and cerebellum	No significant differences were found in these structures between murderers and controls.	No differences were expected in these structures (which are involved in other disorders), supporting the specificity of brain areas involved in violence.

No significant differences were found for performance on the CPT, handedness (except left-handed murderers had significantly less abnormal amygdala asymmetry than right handed murderers), head injury or ethnicity.

DISCUSSION

Strengths – a large sample was used with many controls to rule out alternative effects on brain activity.

Limitations – the PET scan method can lack precision, the findings apply only to a subgroup of violent offenders (not to other types of violence or crime) and caution in the interpretation of the findings is needed, which need to be replicated.

The findings do not mean violence is caused by biology alone (other social, psychological and situational factors are involved), do not demonstrate that the murderers are not responsible for their actions, do not mean PET scans can diagnose murderers and do not say whether the brain abnormalities are a cause or effect of behaviour.

EVALUATION

Methodological　No control over the level of violence used in the murder. Brain scans can be difficult to interpret.
Theoretical　Previous findings on brain structures involved in violence are supported and new findings revealed.
Links　Brain scanning. Cortical functions. Freewill. Ethical implications of socially sensitive research.

'Hemisphere deconnection and unity in conscious awareness' Sperry (1968)

AIM
To present studies investigating the behavioural, neurological and psychological consequences of surgery in which the two cerebral hemispheres are deconnected from each other by severing the corpus callosum. Sperry uses these studies to argue that the 'split brain' shows characteristics during testing that suggest each hemisphere
- has slightly different functions
- possesses an independent stream of conscious awareness and
- has its own set of memories which are inaccessible to the other

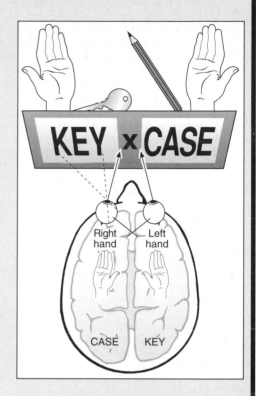

METHOD
Subjects: A handful of patients who underwent hemispheric deconnection to reduce crippling epilepsy.

Design: A natural experiment. Severing the corpus callosum prevents communication between the left and right hemispheres.

Procedure: Since each hemisphere receives information from, and controls the functioning of, the opposite side of the body, the capabilities of each can be tested by
- presenting visual information to either the left or right visual field when the subject is focusing straight ahead. If this is done at fast speeds (about 1 tenth of a second) the eye does not have time to move and re-focus. Thus information presented to the left visual field, will be received by the right hemisphere of the brain
- presenting tactile information to either the left or right hand behind a screen (to remove visual identification). Thus tactile information from objects felt by the right hand will be received by the left hemisphere.

RESULTS
Visual stimuli presented in one visual field at a time
- Objects shown once to a visual field are only recognised if presented again in the same visual field, not the other - implying different visual perception and memory storage for each hemisphere.
- Objects presented in the right visual field, and therefore received in the left hemisphere, can be named verbally and in writing, indicating the presence of speech comprehension and production as well as writing ability.
- Objects presented in the left visual field, and therefore received in the right hemisphere, can <u>not</u> be named verbally or in writing, but can be identified through pointing, indicating that the right hemisphere has language comprehension but not speech or writing.
These tests imply that the two hemispheres of the brain have different abilities and functions.

Different visual stimuli presented simultaneously to different visual fields
- If different visual stimuli are presented simultaneously to different visual fields, e.g. a dollar sign to the left, a question mark to the right, and the subject is asked to draw with the left hand (out of sight) what was seen, the subject draws the stimuli from the left visual field (the dollar sign). If asked what the *left hand has just drawn*, the subject's verbal, left hemisphere replies with what was seen in the right visual field (the question mark).

- If two related words are simultaneously presented to the different visual fields, e.g. 'key' to the left and 'case' to the right, the left hand will select a key from amongst a variety of objects, whereas the right hand will write what it saw in the right visual field (a case) without being influenced by the meaning of the word in the left visual field.

Tactile stimuli presented to different hands
- If an object has been felt by the left hand only, it can be recognised by the left hand again but cannot be named by the subject or recognised by the right hand from amongst other objects.
These tests imply that one side of the brain does not know what the other side has seen or felt.

Tests of the non-dominant right hemisphere
- The left hand can pick out semantically similar objects in a search for an object presented to the left visual field but not present in the search array of objects, e.g. a watch will be selected in response to a picture of a wall clock. The left hand can sort objects into meaningful categories.
- The right brain can solve simple arithmetical problems (pointing out the correct answer) and is superior in drawing spatial relationships.
- The right brain appears to experience its own emotional reactions (giggling and blushing in embarrassment at a nude pin up presented to the left visual field) and can show frustration at the actions of the left hemisphere.

EVALUATION
Methodological: *Validity* - Being a natural experiment there is a lack of control over variables - in particular the subjects' mental abilities may have been atypical before the operation.

Theoretical: There do seem to be functional asymmetries between the hemispheres. However, research has revealed many individual differences - the above findings appear most typical of right-handed men. It should not be forgotten that the left and right hemispheres share many functions and are highly integrated.

Applications: The research has implications for helping patients with brain damage.

Links: Cortical functions, consciousness, psychosurgery.

Body rhythms

CIRCADIAN RHYTHMS

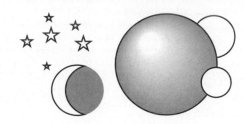

- Circadian rhythms cycle over 24 hours ('circa' = approximately, 'diem' = day). Humans show physiological changes over a 24 hour cycle in hormone levels, body temperature and heart, respiration and metabolic rate. Of most interest to psychologists however, has been the circadian sleep-waking cycle because of the dramatic changes in behaviour it produces.

THE SLEEP-WAKING CYCLE
The circadian sleep-waking rhythm determines our alertness and activity levels during the day and night. In humans it is regulated by:
- **The endogenous pacemakers or internal body clock** of the *suprachiasmatic nucleus* (SCN) and the *pineal gland*. The SCN is part of the hypothalamus that regulates sleep-waking patterns by sending messages to the pineal gland to release melatonin - which is thought to stimulate the production of serotonin in the raphe nucleus to initiate sleep. Removal of the SCN in hamsters randomises their sleep - waking patterns. The sleep-waking body clock seems to be the product of evolution and is largely inherited, SCN cells will fire in a rhythmic way even if removed and placed in culture. In humans it seems to naturally run on a slightly longer cycle than a day (around 25 hours) but there seem to be inherited individual differences between people. If the SCN of mutant hamsters which causes different sleep-waking patterns is transplanted into normal hamsters who have had their SCN removed, they adopt the mutant's circadian patterns. The sleep-waking circadian rhythm can be adjusted to a certain degree by zeigebers, but seems mostly regulated by the internal body clock.
- The major **external re-setter (zeitgeber)** of the circadian body clock in humans is light, which is detected at the retina and can influence (via interconnecting nerve fibres) the SCN to synchronise our rhythms to the 24 hour cycle of the day. This has been demonstrated by studies that have removed the zeitgeber of light such as *Siffre's cave study*. However while the cycle/rhythm can slowly adjust to new starting points (as happens when zetigebers change due to human activities such as shift work or travel over time zones) and can be resisted with a struggle (e.g. in sleep deprivation studies) the basic pattern or ratio of sleep-waking activity is remarkably consistent due to its biological basis. Similar sleep-waking patterns are found cross-culturally, despite cultural zeitgebers such as siestas and environmental zeitgebers in countries who experience whole summers or winters of lightness and darkness (such as those in the arctic circle). The inflexibility of the rhythm has also been demonstrated under controlled laboratory conditions, where exposure to different ratios of light and dark hours do not affect the sleeping patterns of subjects beyond certain limits.

PSYCHOLOGICAL AND PHYSIOLOGICAL CHANGES OF THE CIRCADIAN RHYTHM

	PSYCHOLOGICAL EXPERIENCE	PHYSIOLOGICAL CORRELATES		
		EEG	EOG	EMG
WAKING STATES (Approx. 16 hours)	**Alertness** - involves open-eyed active consciousness with the full ability to concentrate on a task.	Beta waves (13 hertz or above)	Eye movements reflect task	Muscle activity reflects task
	Relaxation - involves a passive but awake conscious experience although the eyes may be shut.	Alpha waves (8 to 12 hertz)	Eye movements reflect cognition	Muscle activity reflects relaxation
SLEEP STATES (Approx. 8 hours - around 80% NREM 20% REM in adults)	**NON-REM SLEEP** - involves a series of stages.			
	Stage 1: Lightest stage of sleep. Easily awakened.	Theta waves (4-7 hertz)	Slow rolling eye movements	Muscles relaxed but active
	Stage 2: Light sleep. Fairly easily awakened. Some responsiveness to external and internal stimuli - name calling produces K-complex activity.	Theta waves sleep spindles, K-complexes	Minimal eye movement	Little muscle movement
	Stage 3: Deep sleep. Difficult to awaken. Very unresponsive to external stimuli.	Delta waves (1-3 Hz) 20-50% of the time	Virtually no eye movement	Virtually no muscle movement
	Stage 4: Very deep sleep. Very difficult to awaken. Very unresponsive to external stimuli.	Delta waves over 50% of the time	Virtually no eye movement	Virtually no muscle movement
	REM SLEEP It is difficult to awaken people from rapid eye-movement (REM) sleep. If woken, individuals report vivid dreaming far more often than if woken from non-REM sleep (Dement and Kleitman, 1957).	High levels of mixed wave brain activity	Eye movement - may reflect dream content	Muscles in a state of virtual paralysis

Key application - of physiological concepts to shift work and jet lag

WHAT PHYSIOLOGICAL CONCEPTS ARE RELEVANT?

- Physiological research into body rhythms such as the human sleep-waking circadian rhythm has revealed that both inner biological factors (**endogenous pacemakers** or body clocks) and external environmental factors (**zeitgebers**) can influence our pattern of sleeping and waking activity.
- However, research has also shown that the sleep-waking body clock is fairly consistent and slow to adjust, while zeitgebers such as work patterns and travel across time zones can change very quickly. Such a **mismatch between our natural body rhythms and activity patterns** can produce negative effects, which have been investigated by physiologically orientated psychologists.
- The **pattern of adjustment** is also important. Siffre, a French cave explorer, spent 6 months in a cave underground which effectively removed the external zeitgebers of the world above such as light levels and human activity patterns. No time cues were given via his telephone contact with the outside world and artificial lights were switched on when he woke up and off when he fell asleep. Under these conditions his natural body rhythms lengthened to around 25 hours so by the time he left the cave he had experienced fewer 'days' than everyone else. This means that adjustment to new zeitgebers is easier if they involve a **lengthening** of the day, since the **circadian cycle** itself seems to have a natural tendency to lengthen.

SHIFT WORK

Much shift work has involved three 8-hour working periods rotating anti-clockwise, e.g. from night shift to evening shift to day shift (a 'phase advance' rather than 'phase delay' schedule), frequently on a weekly basis or less. Physiological research on body rhythms informs us this can produce long-term disorientation, stress, insomnia, exhaustion and negative effects on reaction speed, co-ordination skill, attention and problem solving, since such work schedules:

1. Create a mismatch or desynchronisation between the body rhythms of arousal and the zeitgebers of activity levels.
2. Do not allow enough adjustment time for body rhythms to catch up with (become 'entrained' by) new activity levels.
3. Delay the catching up (entrainment) of body rhythms by shortening rather than lengthening the day.

This increases the chances of accidents occurring due to human error, even when other factors such as reduced hours of sleep, night-time supervision levels etc. are taken into account.

Czeisler et al (1982) studied a group of industrial workers who were following such a shift pattern and their suggestion that they moved clockwise in shifts (a phase delay schedule) on a three week rather than one week basis led to better worker health and morale, as well as higher productivity levels.

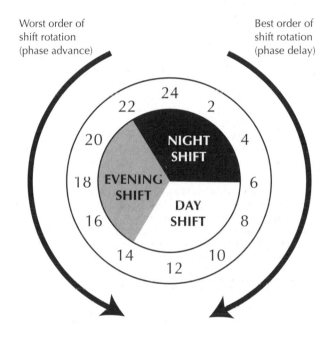

Worst order of shift rotation (phase advance)

Best order of shift rotation (phase delay)

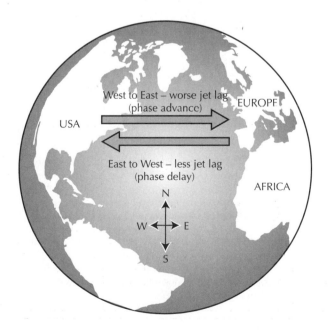

West to East – worse jet lag (phase advance)

East to West – less jet lag (phase delay)

USA | EUROPE | AFRICA

JET LAG

Rapid air travel across time zones can produce jet lag - general disorientation and symptoms similar to those described for shift work, though not always as severe. This also:

1. Results from a mismatch or desynchronisation between the body rhythms of the old time zone, stored in the body clock you take with you, and the zeitgebers of the new time zone, such as human activity levels (e.g. mealtimes) and light levels.
2. Is harder to adjust to if the zeitgebers shorten the day and the circadian cycle – causing a phase advance. This explains why rapid travel from the west to the east across many time zones tends to produce worse jet lag than travelling from east to west (which lengthens the day and causes phase delay).

The influence of zeitgebers and endogenous pacemakers on jet lag are harder to identify since many other variables involved in travelling could cause the symptoms, such as stress, excitement, unfamiliarity and restricted posture.

Slower travel over fewer time zones as well as taking drugs that affect melatonin activity at appropriate times may reduce the severity of jet lag symptoms.

Theories of the function of sleep

SLEEP DEPRIVATION - IS SLEEP NEEDED?

ANIMAL STUDIES:
- Jouvet (1967) deprived cats of sleep by putting them on a floating island in a pool of water so that when they fell asleep they fell in and woke up. The cats developed abnormal behaviours and eventually died.
- Rechtschaffen et al deprived rats of sleep. They had all died after 33 days.

HUMAN STUDIES:
- Psychological effects - increased desire to sleep, difficulty sustaining attention (however, problem solving is less impaired), delusions, and depersonalisation.
- Physiological effects - minor changes, such as problems with eye focusing, but no significant major adverse effects. Sleep after deprivation is not cumulative (not much longer than usual), although more time is spent in REM sleep (a REM rebound effect). However, sleep deprivation studies are not indefinite.

THEORIES OF SLEEP FUNCTION

RESTORATION THEORY
Oswald (1966) suggests that the function of sleep, especially REM sleep, is simply to restore bodily energy reserves, repair the condition of muscles and cells and to allow growth to occur. Sleep could also allow brain neurotransmitters to replenish and aid psychological recovery.

Evaluation
For:
- Longer sleep (particularly stage 4) occurs after large amounts of physical exercise, and in growing children (REM occupies 50% of sleep in babies, 20% in adults).
- Growth hormones are released during stage 4 sleep, deprivation of which causes physical problems such as fibrositis.
- Sleep is greater after periods of stress and improves mood.

Against:
- Sleep duration is not reduced with lack of exercise.
- Deprivation of REM sleep does not produce significantly adverse effects.
- REM sleep involves an increase in energy expenditure and blood flow which *inhibits* protein synthesis.

MEMORY CONSOLIDATION THEORY
Empson and Clarke (1970) propose that sleep, especially REM sleep, facilitates the reinforcement of information in memory.

Evaluation
For:
- Subjects exposed to information before sleep remember less in the morning if deprived of REM sleep rather than non REM sleep.
- Perhaps more REM sleep occurs in younger humans because they have more to learn.

Against:
- There is little evidence against the theory, but memory consolidation can occur without sleep.

SLEEPING TO DREAM
Sleep may occur because the dreams that take place in it have important functions (see dream theories).

EVOLUTIONARY THEORY
All mammals sleep (the porpoise even shuts down one side of its brain at a time to do so), although the length of time varies according to the species. Given its universal nature and the fact that this unconscious and defenceless state seems a dangerous behaviour to show, sleep probably has an important evolutionary survival function, possibly to
- conserve energy when food gathering has been completed or is more difficult (e.g. at night), and/or
- avoid damage from nocturnal predators or accidents by remaining motionless.

Meddis (1975) suggests the duration of sleep a species shows depends upon its food requirements and predator avoidance needs.

Evaluation
For:
- Lions (which have few predators and meet their food needs in short bursts) and squirrels (who have safe burrows) sleep longer.
- Cattle (which have many natural predators) and shrews (which have high metabolic rates) sleep very little.

Against:
- Some evolutionary arguments suggest that animals who are highly preyed upon need to sleep little to keep constant vigilance for predators, however others suggest the opposite - that they need to sleep longer to keep them away from harm by remaining motionless.

Theories of the function of dreaming

THEORIES OF DREAM FUNCTION

CRICK AND MITCHISON'S REVERSE LEARNING THEORY

Crick and Mitchison (1983) argue that dreaming can be regarded as the **random** and **meaningless by-product** of the bombardment of the cortex with random stimulation from the brain stem during REM sleep, to serve the biological function of **clearing the brain** of useless or maladaptive information.

Evaluation
For:
- The two mammals that do not show REM sleep (the dolphin and spiny anteater) have abnormally large cortexes, perhaps to contain the useless memories they are not able to unlearn.

Against:
- The theory lacks detail over exactly how 'useless' information is identified and 'unlearned', and also neglects the apparent meaningfulness of many dreams.

REPROGRAMMING THEORY

Evans (1984) suggests that REM sleep is required by the brain to update itself in the light of new information received **during the day**, and that dreams are the interpretation of this assimilation.
Foulkes (1985), however, proposes that dreams reflect the way our cognitive systems organise and reprogram the stimuli received from random brain activity **during REM sleep**.

Evaluation
For:
- Subjects given unusual tasks before sleep, spend longer in REM sleep.

Against:
- If dreams interpreted the processed information so logically, why would dreams be so strange and incoherent?

WISH FULFILMENT

Freud suggested that dreams were the disguised expressions of unconscious desires and impulses. The recalled manifest content of the dream has been disguised by the dream censor through methods like symbolism to protect our conscious self from the anxiety provoking latent (hidden) meaning of the dream.

Evaluation
For:
- Many researchers have agreed that dreams are meaningful.

Against:
- There is little empirical evidence for Freud's theory in general and little reason for dream meanings to always be disguised.

HOBSON AND McCARLEY'S ACTIVATION SYNTHESIS THEORY

Hobson and McCarley (1977) propose a biological theory which regards dreams as the **meaningless** result of **random brain activity**. The activation part of the theory involves the random firing of giant cells in the reticular activating system (triggered by the presence of acetylcholine) which activates the sensory and motor areas of the brain during REM sleep. The synthesis part of the theory involves the attempt of higher parts of the brain to organise and make sense of the random activity - producing the semi-coherent dreams we experience.

Evaluation
For:
- The theory has biological support and explains how the content of dreams could be influenced by particular areas of brain activation (balance areas may produce dreams of flying) or external stimulation while asleep (water splashed on a sleeper's face can be incorporated into their dreams).

Against:
- Foulkes (1985) proposes that dreams are **meaningful** interpretations of REM random brain activity in the light of our cognitive systems' organisational abilities. Dreams reflect the way we interpret information, relate it to past experience and help us prepare for situations not yet encountered. Hobson and McCarley have come to agree with this view that dreams can be meaningful.

PROBLEM SOLVING

Cartwright proposes that dreams are a meaningful way of considering worries or problems from conscious everyday life. Dreams may use metaphors (but are not deliberately disguised as Freud thought) and may provide solutions for problems.

Evaluation
For:
- Subjects given problems before sleep are more likely to solve them realistically if REM sleep is uninterrupted.

Against:
- There is little other evidence for the theory and most problems can be more quickly solved while awake.

'The relation of eye movements during sleep to dream activity: an objective method for the study of dreams' Dement and Kleitman (1957)

AIM

Aserinsky and Kleitman found a relationship between rapid eye movement (REM) during sleep and reports of dreaming. Dement and Kleitman aimed to provide a **more detailed** investigation of how objective, physiological aspects of rapid eye movement relate to the subjective, psychological experience of dreaming reported by subjects, by testing whether

- significantly **more dreaming** occurs **during REM sleep** than non-REM sleep under controlled conditions.
- there is a **significant positive correlation** between the objective length of **time** spent **in REM** and the subjective **duration of dreaming** reported upon waking.
- there is a significant **relationship** between the **pattern of rapid eye movements** observed during sleep and the **content of the dream** reported upon waking.

METHOD

Subjects: 7 adult males and 2 adult females - 5 of which were intensively studied, 4 of which were used to confirm results.

Design: Laboratory experimentation and observation.

Procedure: Subjects slept individually in a quiet dark laboratory room after a normal day's activity (except that alcohol and caffeine were avoided during the days before testing). Electrodes were connected near the eyes to register eye movement and on the scalp to measure brain waves during sleep - these were the objective measures of REM sleep. Subjects were awoken at various times during the night (fairly evenly distributed across the average sleeping time of the subjects) by a loud doorbell noise, and immediately reported into a recording device whether they had been dreaming and the content of the dream <u>before</u> any contact with the experimenter (to avoid bias). Subjects were never usually told whether their eyes had been moving before being awoken. Dreaming was only counted if a fairly detailed and coherent dream was reported - vague impressions or assertions of dreaming without recall of content were not counted.

STUDY ONE

Subjects were awoken in one of four different ways during either REM or non-REM sleep, and were compared to see if they had been dreaming.
- 2 subjects were awoken randomly
- 1 subject was awoken during 3 REM sleep periods followed by 3 non-REM periods, and so on.
- 1 subject was awoken randomly, but was told he would only be awoken during periods of REM sleep
- 1 subject was awoken at the whim of the experimenter

STUDY TWO

Subjects were awoken either 5 or 15 minutes after REM sleep began and were asked to decide whether the duration of their dream was closer to 5 or 15 minutes.
The length of the dream (measured in terms of the number of words in their dream narratives) was also correlated to the duration of REM sleep before awakening.

STUDY THREE

Subjects were awoken as soon as one of four patterns of eye movement had occurred for 1 minute, and were asked exactly what they had just dreamt.
- Mainly vertical eye movements
- Mainly horizontal eye movements
- Both vertical and horizontal eye movements.
- Very little or no eye movement

RESULTS

Generally, REM periods were clearly observed in all subjects and distinguished from non-REM sleep periods. REM sleep periods occurred at regular intervals specific to each subject (although on average occurring every 92 minutes) and tended to last longer later in the night.

STUDY ONE

Regardless of how subjects were awoken, significantly more dreams were reported in REM than non-REM sleep.
When subjects failed to recall dreams from REM sleep, this was usually early in the night.
When subjects recalled dreams from non-REM sleep it was most often within 8 minutes after the end of a REM period.

STUDY TWO

Subjects were significantly correct in matching the duration of their dream to length of time they had shown REM sleep for both the 5 minute periods (45 out of 51 estimates correct) and 15 minute periods (47 out of 60 estimates correct).
All subjects showed a significant positive correlation at the $P< 0.05$ level or better between the length of their dream narratives and duration of REM sleep before awakening.

STUDY THREE

There was a very strong association between the pattern of REMs and the content of dream reports.
- The 3 vertical REM periods were associated with dreams of looking up and down at cliff faces, ladders, and basketball nets.
- A dream of two people throwing tomatoes at each other occurred in the only mainly horizontal REM period.
- 21 periods of vertical and horizontal REMs were associated with dreams of looking at close objects.
- 10 periods of very little or no REMs were associated with dreams of looking at fixed or distant objects.

EVALUATION

Methodological: Dreams may be recalled easier in REM than non-REM sleep because the latter is a deeper stage of sleep - perhaps dreams occur in deeper sleep, but are more difficult to recall from it.

The study used a limited sample, mostly men, therefore showed a lack of generalisability.

Theoretical: The research provides support for the idea that dreams can be studied in an objective way. This then opens up areas of research for the effect of environmental stimuli on dreaming.

Links: Sleep and dream research. Laboratory studies.

Sources of stress

THE CONCEPT OF STRESS

The concept of stress has been viewed in different ways. Stress has been regarded as:

1 An *internal bodily response* - an essentially automatic biological *reaction* to external stimuli. This neglects the type of stimuli that causes the reaction.
2 An *external stimuli* that exerts a destructive force upon the organism. This neglects the fact that the same external stimuli will not always produce the same reaction.
3 An *interaction or transaction* between stimulus and response that depends upon *cognitive appraisal* of the situation – the stress reaction will only result if individuals *perceive* a mismatch between the demands of the situation and their ability to cope with it (regardless of actual demands and coping ability). This is currently the most common view and thus a widely used definition of stress is: "A pattern of negative physiological states and psychological responses occurring in situations where people perceive threats to their well being which they may be unable to meet" Lazarus and Folkman (1984).

Stress can result from:
- changeable or continuous causes (e.g. life-events or steady occupational demands)
- predictable or unpredictable causes (e.g. depending on the experience of control)
- biological sources (e.g. disruption of bodily rhythms, illness, fatigue), social sources (e.g. interpersonal and work related) or psychological causes (e.g. locus of control and personality type).

LIFE CHANGES AS A CAUSE OF STRESS

STRESSFUL LIFE EVENTS: Holmes and Rahe (1967) suggested that stress is caused by *change* and may lead to greater susceptibility to physical and mental health disorders. They compiled the 'Social Readjustment Rating Scale' (SRRS) a list of 47 life events involving stressful change and rated them for their severity out of one hundred (e.g. death of a spouse = 100, marriage = 50, change in school = 20 etc.). Scores of over 300 life change units in a year would represent a high risk for stress-related health problems.
Evaluation - The SRRS has been criticised for its over-generalised approach. There are many individual differences in what events people find most stressful and how they react to them. Positive and predictable changes may be less stressful than negative and unpredictable ones. The evidence for the scale relating to health is mostly correlational, illness may have contributed towards the development of stressful life events such as losing employment, rather than vice versa.

HASSLES & UPLIFTS: Researcher such as Lazarus and Kanner have proposed that more *everyday problems* or pleasant occurrences were more likely to affect stress levels and health. They designed the 'Hassles and Uplifts Scale' to measure these incidents and their effects.
Evaluation - The 'Hassles and Uplifts Scale' has been found to be a better predictor of health. Continuous diary monitoring of everyday stresses has enabled a causal link to be made with later illness (Stone et al, 1987).

CATASTROPHIC STRESS: *Single traumatic events* such as natural disasters, warfare or violent assault can provoke long lasting stress and health problems. Mental disorder classification systems term this Post Traumatic Stress Disorder. (**Evaluation** - see PTSD research).

BIOLOGICAL CAUSES: SRRS items relating to changing work and sleep patterns could cause stress through biological changes like the desynchronisation of body rhythms with new zeitgebers e.g. activity and light levels. (**Evaluation** - see shift work and jet lag research).

THE WORKPLACE AS A SOURCE OF STRESS

WORKPLACE STRESSORS: Occupational stress can result from factors relating to the nature of the job (e.g. its security, clarity of purpose, workload and intensity of skill use) and the social and environmental conditions in which it takes place (e.g. the co-worker relationships, organisational management, control of workload, career progression, physical workspace and noise). Workplace stressors therefore tend to result from stable characteristics rather than change (although changes in job and working conditions can also causes stress).
A common example is *work overload/underload* which involves stress resulting from a perceived mismatch between the time and skills the job requires and the time and skills available to complete it. Such a mismatch may cause feelings of unfairness, resentment and lack of control – especially in overload circumstances where the deadlines are important, there is external pressure to meet them and they are set by external sources. Relief from work overload stress is reduced by the lack of time left for other activities and the fatigue felt during such time.
Occupational burnout results from continual levels of stress due to highly demanding work requiring consistently high levels of concentration, responsibility, frustration or exposure to suffering, e.g. air traffic controllers or nurses.

CONTROL AND STRESS

The inability to control life event changes, everyday hassles, work schedules/deadlines and unexpected traumatic events etc. is a major cause of stress and consequent ill health. Weiss (1972) found rats that could **control** electric shocks were less likely to develop gastric ulceration than those who could do not, despite receiving an identical number of shocks. Workers with little control at the bottom of organisational hierarchies are often found to suffer the most ill health from stress. Rotter (1966) suggested that an 'external locus of control' leads people to think they have a lack of control over their lives and can result in less active coping strategies and greater stress-related illness. Even the illusion or possibility of control in humans can reduce the effects of stress. Feelings of control are thus important in increasing the perception that one has an ability to cope that is sufficient to match the demands of the situation (see definition of stress above). Very high levels of control however can also be stressful, especially when one is responsible for decisions and many choices are available – which may account for the executive stress of some managers.

Stress as a bodily response

Selye (1976) identified the **General Adaptation Syndrome** (GAS) - a **non-specific** physiological response that occurs to a **variety** of stressful stimuli. Much research has investigated the 3 phases of the GAS.

PHASE 1
ALARM REACTION
The physiological response triggered by stressful stimuli.

Perception of stressful stimuli

HYPOTHALAMUS

Activates pituitary gland to release adrenocorticotrophic hormone (ACTH)

Activates the sympathetic branch of the autonomic nervous system

ADRENAL GLAND

Activates adrenal cortex to release corticosteroids

Activates adrenal medulla to release adrenaline and noradrenaline

Inhibits immune system response, inhibits tissue inflammation, releases energy from the liver, etc.

Activates fight or flight reactions of increased heart and breathing rate, blood pressure, muscle tension, etc.

PHASE 2
STAGE OF RESISTANCE
If the stressor persists or is not dealt with, the body seeks to maintain arousal at a constant if lower level.

Individual differences may modify stress effects.
Factors that could mediate in the resolving or continuation of stress arousal or even modify its effects, include:

1 Behavioural coping style
Stress arousal will often not persist if fight or flight behaviours *deal with* the stressful stimuli. Optimal arousal theory states that up to a certain level stress can provide a beneficial motivating effect on behaviour (Selye called this 'eustress') that helps deal with the source of stress. However, although not all modern-day problems can be solved through physical means, different people use different **coping strategies** – some adopt **problem-focused strategies** and deal with the source of stress, others adopt **emotion-focused strategies** and try to deal with its effects.

2 Personality factors and cognitive style
Friedman and Rosenman (1974) argued that some people have **'Type A' personalities** that create and maintain high levels of stress in their life styles. These people are often aggressive, competitive and highly driven perfectionists who will not delegate and are impatient towards others. Kobasa (1979) suggests people with **'Hardy personalities'** are less vulnerable to the effects of stress because they have a greater sense of control over, and a more positive attitude towards, stressful events and a stronger sense of purpose. Rotter agrees that cognitive style, like a sense of control over stressful events (i.e. an *internal* rather than *external* locus of control) will moderate the effects of stress.

3 Gender and cultural factors
Genders and cultures may differ in the amount and type of stress experienced (e.g. discrimination in society and the workplace) or even physiological susceptibility. Men and those from capitalist / individualistic cultures may be more socialised into aggressive and competitive Type A behaviour towards stressful situations, and have different coping styles and levels of social support.

PHASE 3
STAGE OF EXHAUSTION
Eventually continued high arousal levels exhaust bodily resources producing negative physiological & psychological effects.

1 Physiological effects:

a Reduced resistance to infection
Studies on both animals and humans have shown that stress, especially in the long-term, can adversely affect the immune system as corticosteroids suppress its activity and thus increase vulnerability to infection. Stress has been associated with many illnesses, ranging from headaches (Gannon et al, 1987) and asthma (Miller and Strunk, 1979), to colds (Stone et al, 1987), stomach ulcers (Brady, 1958) and cancer (Jacobs and Charles, 1980).

b Heart and circulatory disorders
Stress-triggered increases in heart rate and blood pressure, as well as levels of glucose/fatty acids released into the blood stream, may result in the deterioration and blocking of blood vessels and thus increased cardiovascular disorder. Rosenman et al (1975) found in a 9 year study involving over 3 thousand men that type A personalities were more prone to suffer heart disease. However there is debate over whether the personality traits are a cause or result of stress, and which traits are the most important since some studies have not replicated Rosenman et al's results.

Stress may also indirectly cause physiological effects since it leads to unhealthy behaviour, e.g. lack of exercise, drinking and smoking.

2 Psychological effects:

a Anger and frustration - Can cause a vicious circle of stress production as they contribute to a more stressful environment. Hostility may be a key stress-provoking factor in type A behaviour.

b Depression and helplessness - Seligman (1975) found continual and unavoidable stress caused learned helplessness and depression which would be inappropriately generalised to different situations.

c Anxiety - Different types of stressful situation can produce different types of anxiety disorder, e.g. persistent, unresolvable stress could lead to generalised anxiety disorder, whereas 'one-off' traumatic events could cause post-traumatic stress disorder.

Managing and reducing stress

HOW CAN STRESS BE REDUCED?
There are really only two ways that stress can be reduced:

1 DEAL WITH THE CAUSES OF STRESS
Those strategies that focus on removing or coping with stressful *stimuli* or *situations* before they produce a stress reaction are known as 'problem-focused strategies'. This is obviously the best way to deal with potential stress, but may not be possible since:
- there are a huge variety of sources for stress, it may therefore be impossible to deal with them all
- the individual may be unaware of the source of stress or may only realise after the stress reaction has occurred
- not all sources of stress can be avoided, some may be an inevitable part of living and working life, others may be mental worries that physical action cannot deal with. Problem-focused strategies become counter-productive under such conditions.

2 DEAL WITH THE EFFECTS OF STRESS
Those strategies that focus on removing or coping with stress *reactions* once they have occurred are known as 'emotion-focused strategies'. This is the approach that most methods employ.

People use a variety of coping strategies in everyday life, however specific physiological and psychological techniques have also been developed to help manage stress that individuals feel unable to deal with sufficiently on their own. Most of these techniques are emotion-focused strategies but some aim to incorporate elements of problem-focused strategy as well.

NATURAL COPING STRATEGIES FOR STRESS
Appropriate behaviour - These range from dealing with the source of stress, e.g. time management planning and avoiding stressful situations, to natural behavioural reactions that combat its effects, e.g. rest and relaxation (holidays), laughter, arguments, exercise and sport.

Defence mechanisms – Freud would argue that many of the above natural stress reduction methods are in fact the products of ego defence mechanisms. Stress-related psychic energy can be given cathartic expression through displacement and sublimation, e.g. aggression towards scapegoats, laughter and physical exercise, or alternatively repressed into the unconscious and/or dissociated from consciousness through denial (which could lead to anxiety or even dissociative disorders if long-term stress was experienced).

Social support – individuals who perceive they have social support (e.g. reassurance, advice and practical aid) suffer less physiological stress effects than those without such support, e.g. those with no intimate friends (Brown and Harris, 1978) or partners (Tache et al, 1979).

EVALUATION
Natural coping strategies are not always sufficient on their own and some, e.g. arguments and aggression, may actually contribute towards further stress. Freudian defence mechanisms have not always been supported by empirical evidence and may be counter productive - only providing short-term solutions while creating long-term problems. Social support is significantly correlated with lower mortality rates, but causation is difficult to determine.

BIOLOGICAL TECHNIQUES FOR STRESS MANAGEMENT
Anti-stress drugs
Beta-blockers - act on the autonomic nervous system to reduce physiological stress arousal.
Anxiolytic drugs - minor tranquillisers, e.g. Valium, combat anxiety without causing sleepiness.
Anti-depressant drugs - less often used, but can be appropriate for severe anxiety.

Other drugs
Alcohol is an often sought remedy for stress, its sedative effects slow down neural and bodily functions and its effect on loosening inhibitions can lead to cathartic behaviour.

Biofeedback
Feedback signals on body processes can help control the adverse physiological effects of stress such as increased heart rate and blood pressure.

EVALUATION
Anti-anxiety drugs can cause psychological and physical dependence and other unpleasant side effects. Drugs are only short-term stress remedies that temporarily reduce its effects but may make dealing with its causes more difficult or even create further sources (especially alcohol). Although there is debate over how it works, biofeedback can lower heart rate and blood pressure, but again it only treats the symptoms not causes of stress.

PSYCHOLOGICAL TECHNIQUES FOR STRESS MANAGEMENT
Therapy - *Stress inoculation training* (Meichenbaum, 1977) and *Hardiness training* (Kobasa, 1986) are both cognitive behavioural techniques designed to increase stress resistance or 'hardiness' by:
1 Analysing - Getting clients to learn to analyse sources and physical signs of stress.
2 Teaching coping strategies and techniques to combat stressful situations - e.g. relaxation, positive self-instructional statements and specific skills with stress inoculation therapy, or the re-living and reconstruction of stressful situations in hardiness training.
3 Changing behaviour – e.g. practising skills in simulated and real situations so a successful change is produced (with stress inoculation) or reinforcing a sense of control through performing manageable tasks (with hardiness training).

Mental state relaxation – Meditation and hypnosis (including self-hypnosis) reduce stress effects through mentally inducing relaxation.

EVALUATION
Cognitive behavioural therapies are effective although it is unsure whether the behavioural aspects (successfully dealing with a stressful situation) are more important than the cognitive ones (stress reducing statements and a sense of control). The techniques aim to deal with the source as well as the effects of stress and so are potentially more effective in the long term. Meditation and hypnosis do not have the side effects and equipment needs of physiological methods but also focus on the effects and ignore causes.

Schachter and Singer's cognitive labelling theory

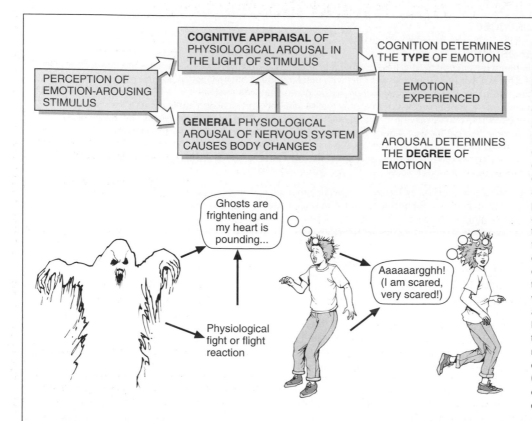

COGNITIVE APPRAISAL OF PHYSIOLOGICAL AROUSAL IN THE LIGHT OF STIMULUS

PERCEPTION OF EMOTION-AROUSING STIMULUS

GENERAL PHYSIOLOGICAL AROUSAL OF NERVOUS SYSTEM CAUSES BODY CHANGES

COGNITION DETERMINES THE **TYPE** OF EMOTION

EMOTION EXPERIENCED

AROUSAL DETERMINES THE **DEGREE** OF EMOTION

Ghosts are frightening and my heart is pounding...

Physiological fight or flight reaction

Aaaaaargghh! (I am scared, very scared!)

The cognitive labelling theory of emotion states that emotion-arousing external stimuli will cause a **general** physiological arousal response that will be **interpreted** by a cognitive appraisal of the stimuli as a **particular** emotional feeling. Thus, the external stimuli of a dangerous object will cause a general 'fight or flight' physiological response **and** a cognitive evaluation of this arousal in the light of, for example, past experiences involving this object (i.e. having learnt that ghosts are frightening) which leads to the appropriate emotion of fear. Physiological **arousal** is, therefore, **necessary** for most genuine emotions to occur but **not sufficient** (since cognitive appraisal can label it as a variety of emotions).

SUPPORT

Schachter and Singer (1962) told subjects that they were going to test the effects of a vitamin injection on their vision, but instead injected them with adrenaline. Subjects were then either:

A informed of the real effects (e.g. increased heart/respiration rate)

B misinformed of the effects - told false symptoms, e.g. itching

C given no information on the effects

A fourth group (**D**) were injected with a placebo of saline solution in place of adrenaline to provide a control group.

All subjects were then left in a waiting room with another subject (really a confederate of the experimenter) who began to act either

1 angrily, e.g. complaining about and then ripping up a questionnaire, or

2 Euphorically, e.g. laughing and throwing paper around.

The subjects were then rated by external observers who found groups **B** and **C** were more likely to follow the confederate's behaviour.

The results showed some support for cognitive labelling theory in that

- those who did not have an accurate explanation for their physiological arousal (groups **B** and **C**) used the cues of the confederate's behaviour to identify and label their own emotion.
- those who already had an accurate explanation (group **A**) for the effects did not need other cues, so did not follow the confederate.
- those who changed their behaviour (groups **B** and **C**) did so according to cognitive appraisal of their emotions, rather than specific physiological arousal, indicating that only general arousal is required.

Dutton and Aron (1974) found further evidence for cognitive labelling of emotions. Male subjects approached by an attractive female experimenter on a high suspension bridge were shown to mislabel their fear as sexual attraction.

Hohmann's (1966) study appears to support the necessity of physiological arousal for genuine emotional feelings. He studied 25 males with spinal cord injury, and found the greater the damage to their nervous system feedback, the less intense were their emotional experiences. Subjects still reported emotions but when angry, for example, would describe it as 'a mental kind of anger'.

CRITICISMS

Schachter and Singer's (1962) experiment has been criticised in a number of ways:

- There was no assessment of the subjects' emotional state before the experiment began, or the emotional effect of receiving an injection.
- The emotional states produced by artificial injections under laboratory conditions are probably not typical of normal emotional reactions.
- Significant results were only found for the behavioural changes rated by the observers - no significant differences were found in the subjects' self report of their emotions.
- The results were not highly significant and other researchers such as Marshall and Zimbardo (1979) have not replicated Schachter and Singer's findings.

While the misattribution of emotions (the most typical experimental support for cognitive labelling theory) is perhaps an unusual occurrence in everyday life, it does indicate an important role for cognitive appraisal. Researchers such as Lazarus (1991) argue that cognitive processes can initiate both physiological arousal and emotion feelings, and that a cognitive appraisal of environmental stimuli at some level (conscious or unconscious) is a basic requirement for the elicitation of any emotion.

Although the majority of current theories on emotion involve cognitive appraisal, there is still some debate over its importance. Psychologists such as Zajonc (1984) still argue that cognition and emotion involve relatively separate systems, and that emotion can occur without any cognitive appraisal. Recent research indicates that emotional centres in the brain can receive information directly from the sensory areas.

'Cognitive, social, and physiological determinants of emotional state' Schachter and Singer (1962)

AIM

To describe an experiment that provides support for Schachter's (1959) theory of the interaction between physiology, cognition, and behaviour in emotional experience. Schachter believes that cognitive factors (thought processes) are very important in determining which emotion is felt. He argues that emotion-provoking stimuli, such as a gun being pointed at you, will automatically cause a general physiological level of arousal (the activation of the sympathetic nervous system), which is interpreted (cognitively) as fear (the emotion) in the light of our knowledge about the dangerous nature of guns. Schachter and Singer, therefore, propose the 3 following predictions from this theory:

A Given an **unexplained** state of general **physiological arousal**, the individual experiencing it will attempt to describe or **label it as a particular emotion** in terms of his **cognitive explanations** of its causes. Thus, the same state of arousal could be described or labelled as joy or fury, depending upon the situation he is in.

B Given a state of general **physiological arousal** for which an individual already has an **appropriate explanation** (e.g. I feel this way because I have been injected with adrenaline) there will be **no need** to use external situational cues **to label** his arousal as an emotion.

C Given **no** state of general **physiological arousal, despite situational cues** to label emotions with, an individual will experience **no** emotion.

METHOD

Subjects: 184 male college students, 90% of whom volunteered to get extra points on their exams.

Design: Laboratory experiment. Based on the above predictions, three independent variables were manipulated in an independent measures design to affect the dependent variable of experienced emotional state (measured by behavioural observation and self-report).

Independent variable	Conditions manipulated
1 Physiological arousal	**a** *Injection of epinephrine* (adrenaline) **b** *Injection of a placebo* (saline solution)
2 Explanation of arousal	**a** *Informed* (told correct symptoms) **b** *Misinformed* (told wrong symptoms) **c** *Ignorant* (told no symptoms)
3 Situational emotion cues	**a** *Euphoric stooge* **b** *Angry stooge*

Procedure: Subjects were told the experiment was a study of the effect of Suproxin - supposedly a vitamin supplement - upon vision. Subjects were tested individually and asked whether they would mind receiving a Suproxin injection (in fact either epinephrine or a placebo) and were assigned to one of the following conditions:

1 **Epinephrine informed** - given a Suproxin injection that was *really epinephrine* and told of its *real side effects* (general physiological arousal of the sympathetic nervous system causing accelerated heartbeat/breathing, palpitations etc.).
2 **Epinephrine misinformed** - given a Suproxin injection that was *really epinephrine* and told *false side effects* (e.g. itching, numbness, etc.)
3 **Epinephrine ignorant** - given a Suproxin injection that was *really epinephrine* and told there would be *no side effects* at all
4 **Control ignorant** - given a Suproxin injection that was *really a placebo* (a saline solution which has no direct effect on arousal of the sympathetic nervous system) and told there would be *no side effects* at all.

All subjects (with the exception of the epinephrine misinformed group, who were not exposed to the angry stooge) were then left alone with either
- **the euphoric stooge** (subjects saw a confederate behaving happily - throwing paper and playing with a hula hoop) or
- **the angry stooge** (subjects saw a confederate complain and behave in a outraged way, ripping up a questionnaire)
and then observed through a one-way mirror to rate their behaviour for how similar it was to the stooge's behaviour (implying that they were in the same emotional state). Self-report scales were also used to assess how good or angry they felt.

RESULTS

For subjects observing euphoric stooges:
- Self-reports of emotions and behaviour were mostly significantly happier in epinephrine ignorant and misinformed subjects (who did not have a relevant explanation for their arousal) than the epinephrine informed group (who did not need to use the external cues to explain their arousal). This supports predictions **A** and **B** above.
- There was no significant difference in mood between the epinephrine ignorant or misinformed subjects, and the placebo control subjects.
  This indicates that prediction **C** above is not supported.

For subjects observing angry stooges:
Only behavioural observations were used, since subjects feared self-reports of anger at the experimenter would endanger their extra exam points.
- Epinephrine ignorant subjects behaved significantly more angrily than epinephrine informed or placebo subjects.
This supports predictions **A**, **B**, and **C**. However, placebo subjects still followed the angry behaviour more than the epinephrine informed subjects. The results support the predictions more strongly if adrenaline misinformed and ignorant subjects who attributed arousal to their injection and the placebo subjects who showed physiological arousal in response to just having an injection, are removed from the data.

EVALUATION

Methodological: *Artificiality* - Injection is an artificial way of generating physiological arousal and can cause (fear) arousal in itself. The laboratory lacks ecological validity and the situation of experiencing unexplained physiological arousal is rare.
Validity - Only male subjects and two-tailed tests were used and the results have not always been replicated.
Ethics - Deception over purpose of study and content of injection. Injection (although by permission) hurt.

Theoretical: Supports the importance of cognitive factors in emotional experience. Provides some support for Schachter's theory that physiological arousal and cognitive interpretation are **both necessary** but **not sufficient on their own** to cause emotions.

Links: Emotion.

Contemporary issue - genetic research and behaviour

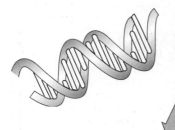

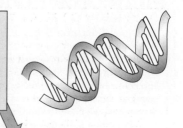

The inherited basis of human behaviour has long interested philosophers, genetic biologists, psychologists, politicians and the general public, and has caused a good deal of debate and controversy. An understanding of the assumptions and methods of the physiological approach in this area can help explain the implications of research into the genetic basis of behaviour and the controversy it has generated.

ASSUMPTIONS OF GENETIC RESEARCH

Some genetic researchers have attempted to discover the influence of inherited factors on behaviour and mental abilities, assuming that genetic factors must influence such characteristics to some extent, since they are produced by bodies which are constructed based on the instructions contained in our DNA. Unfortunately, however, researchers have differed in their assumptions over exactly how strong genetic influences are and have often leapt to conclusions based on a faulty understanding of how genes express their influence. These conclusions have important implications and have caused strong disagreements between psychologists who favour the importance of nature and those who champion nurture. A more variable influence of inherited factors in combination with environmental ones has gradually become accepted as research revealed that:

- genes can only build bodies based on the environmental resources available, and environmental factors can influence the genes themselves
- human characteristics may be influenced by many genes (pleiotropy) , not all of which will necessarily be inherited
- some genes, e.g. those involved in Huntingdon's disease, have more direct and inevitable effects than others, e.g. those involved in Alzheimer's disease
- genes express their effects in many different and often subtle ways

Genetic research now implicitly investigates how genes interact with environmental factors to create behaviour and tries to determine the balance of influences for specific characteristics.

GENETIC RESEARCH METHODS

Two techniques used to investigate genetic influences include:

- Family resemblance correlations – these measure the degree of similarity in characteristics between genetically related (e.g. parents and offspring, siblings, cousins, etc.) and unrelated individuals on the assumption that the closer the genetic relationship the greater the similarity. Genetically identical (monozygotic) twins in particular have been compared with non-identical (dizygotic) twins, while adoption studies have helped control for the similar environments related individuals are more likely to share.
- Molecular genetics – modern technology now allows researchers to extract genetic material from individuals with a certain characteristic and see how it differs from that of people without the characteristic. This can reveal the coding of the genes correlated with the characteristics and their location amongst the 23 pairs of human chromosomes.

There are many problems with these methods however, so results gained from them have to be carefully interpreted. For example since adoption studies are natural experiments, they can never completely control for environmental effects. Molecular genetic research has found that individuals can possess the genes associated with a characteristic, without necessarily developing it themselves. At the moment, the possession of most human behaviour and abilities cannot be predicted with 100% certainty by either of the above methods.

IMPLICATIONS OF GENETIC RESEARCH

Given the variable effects of genes upon behaviour and the methodological problems involved in assessing them, particular care needs to be taken in how knowledge of genetic influences is used and interpreted.

In the past genetic research has been used for selection purposes based on faulty assumptions and methodology, for example research into the genetic basis of intelligence. The application of genetic research by society to control the selection of 'desirable' characteristics is known as eugenics and has led to horrific social injustice and genocide.

With improving technology, such as genetic screening and gene therapy, further ethical implications regarding the use of genetic knowledge for selection and control purposes will have to be considered. Employers may want to select their employees, insurance companies their customers, and parents their children (through abortion or gene therapy) based on the results of genetic screening. Some argue that just because the choice to genetically screen and control is placed in the hands of individuals rather than society does not make it any less 'eugenic'.

However, resistance to the idea that genes affect behaviour is often based on the mistaken assumption that genetic inheritance dictates our fate. For the reasons expressed above it is very unlikely that psychological characteristics are determined by genes in such an inevitable way, in most cases genes seem just as 'deterministic' as environmental influences. The positive effects of genetic screening and gene therapy should also not be ignored.

Genetic research on intelligence

Much early research on the inheritance of intelligence was:

- politically motivated by eugenic beliefs, often carried out by researchers biased towards discovering innate causes
- conducted using poorly controlled family resemblance studies and culturally biased IQ tests on different 'races'

Unsurprisingly it revealed that IQ was largely (around 80%) inherited, and was used to justify the selection of naturally bright individuals for jobs, special education at an early age and right of immigration into the USA. In some countries those thought genetically doomed to mental deficiency were sterilised to prevent them spreading their low intelligence in society.

Later research indicates that around 50% of IQ is individually inherited, the rest is influenced by conditions in the womb and the social and family environment. The way genes influence intelligence is still a mystery however. Genes associated with intelligence may directly affect aspects of cognitive ability such as processing speed or indirectly evoke environmental influences on IQ by creating characteristics such as ability to concentrate, motivation to learn etc. Alternatively perhaps the genes promote resistance to disease and the healthy development of the brain - lacking such genes might prevent the genius a fully healthy brain would give us all!

Understanding how genes influence intelligence may help us to adjust the environment to produce the most improvement in those who require it, without resorting to genetic manipulation.

The learning theory approach to psychology

ORIGINS AND HISTORY

- The learning theory approach in psychology was initiated mainly by the behaviourists, who were influenced by the philosophy of **empiricism** (which argues that knowledge comes from the environment via the senses, since humans are like a 'tabula rasa', or blank slate, at birth) and the physical sciences (which emphasise scientific and objective methods of investigation).
- **Watson** started the behaviourist movement in 1913 when he wrote an article entitled 'Psychology as the behaviourist views it', which set out its main principles and assumptions. Drawing on earlier work by Pavlov, behaviourists such as Watson, Thorndike and Skinner proceeded to develop theories of **learning** (such as classical and operant conditioning) that they attempted to use to explain virtually **all** behaviour.
- The behaviourist approach dominated experimental psychology until the late 1950s, when its assumptions and methods became increasingly criticised by ethologists and cognitive psychologists. The behaviourist theories have been modified to provide more realistic explanations of how learning can occur, for example by psychologists such as Bandura with his social learning theory.

John Watson

'Give me a dozen healthy infants... and my own specified world to bring them up in and I'll guarantee to take any one at random and train him to become any type of specialist I might select - doctor, lawyer... and yes, even beggarman and thief.'

ASSUMPTIONS

The behaviourists believed:

1 the majority of all behaviour is **learned** from the **environment** after birth (behaviourism takes the nurture side of the nature-nurture debate), and so
  a psychology should investigate the **laws** and **products** of learning
  b behaviour is **determined** by the environment, since we are merely the total of all our past learning experiences, freewill is an illusion.
2 only **observable** behaviour not minds should be studied if psychology is to be an objective science, since we cannot see into other people's minds, and if we ask them about their thoughts they may lie, not know, or just be mistaken. Most learning theorists still adopt this scientific approach.

METHODS OF INVESTIGATION

The behaviourists adopted a very scientific approach, using strict laboratory experimentation, usually conducted on animals such as rats or pigeons. Animals were tested because the behaviourists believed:

- the laws of learning were universal
- there was only a quantitative difference between animals and humans
- animals are practically and ethically more convenient to test

CONTRIBUTION TO PSYCHOLOGY

The behaviourists' discoveries concerning the laws of learning were vigorously applied to explain many aspects of behaviour, such as:

- **Language acquisition,** e.g. Skinner's theory.
- **Moral development,** e.g. conditioned emotional responses of guilt and conscience.
- **Attraction,** e.g. Byrne & Clore's reinforcement affect model.
- **Abnormality,** e.g. the classical conditioning of phobias and their treatment.

+ aggression, prejudice, gender role identity, etc.

CONTRIBUTION TO SOCIETY

- The behaviourist learning theory approach has produced may practical applications for education (such as programmed learning) and the treatment of those suffering behavioural disturbances (such as systematic desensitisation for phobias, behaviour shaping for autism, and token economies for institutionalised patients).
- Operant conditioning principles have been used in training animals to perform tasks, from circus animals to guide dogs.
- Watson applied behaviourist theory to both child rearing and advertising, while Skinner offered many suggestions regarding the large scale manipulation of behaviour in society in his books such as *Beyond Freedom and Dignity* and *Walden Two.*

STRENGTHS

Behaviourism contributed to psychology in many ways:

- Behaviourism was very scientific and its experimental methodology left a lasting impression on the subject.
- It provided strong counter-arguments to the nature side of the nature-nurture debate.
- The approach is very parsimonious, explaining a great variety of phenomena using only a few simple (classical and operant) principles.
- Behaviourism has produced many practical applications, some of which have been very effective.
- Social learning theory has overcome some of the weaknesses of the behaviourists' theories.

WEAKNESSES

Behaviourist views have been criticised by other approaches for a number of reasons.

- Ethologists argued that the behaviourists ignored innate, built-in biases in learning due to evolution, but also disagreed with the behaviourists' use of animals and laboratory experimentation, saying that there is a biologically qualitative difference between humans and other animals and that experiments only demonstrate artificial, not natural learning.
- Cognitive psychologists think that behaviourism ignores important mental processes involved in learning; while the humanistic approach disliked their rejection of conscious mental experience.

Classical conditioning

Classical conditioning is concerned with **learning by association**, and refers to the **conditioning of reflexes** - how animals learn to **associate new stimuli with innate bodily reflexes**. The principles of classical conditioning were first outlined by **Pavlov**, and were then adopted by behaviourists, such as Watson, who attempted to use them to explain how virtually all of human behaviour is acquired. Pavlov was a physiologist who, while studying the salivation reflex, found that the dogs he was using in his experiments would sometimes start salivating before the food had reached their mouths, often at the sight of the food bucket. Clearly the dogs had learnt to **associate new external stimuli** (such as sights and sounds), with the **original stimulus** (food) that caused the salivation reflex. In a series of thorough and well controlled experiments, Pavlov found many new stimuli could be associated with reflexes and went on to introduce special terms for, and investigated many aspects of, the conditioning process.

Pavlov's apparatus

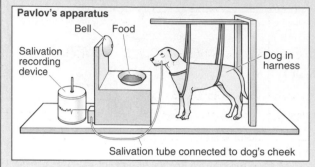

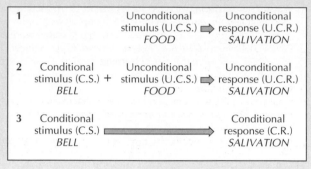

1. Unconditional stimulus (U.C.S.) ➡ Unconditional response (U.C.R.)
   FOOD — *SALIVATION*

2. Conditional stimulus (C.S.) + Unconditional stimulus (U.C.S.) ➡ Unconditional response (U.C.R.)
   BELL — *FOOD* — *SALIVATION*

3. Conditional stimulus (C.S.) ➡ Conditional response (C.R.)
   BELL — *SALIVATION*

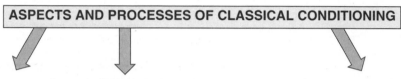

ASPECTS AND PROCESSES OF CLASSICAL CONDITIONING

TIMING

The law of temporal contiguity
Pavlov found that for associations to be made, the two stimuli had to be presented close together in time. If the time between the presentation of the C.S. (bell) and the presentation of the U.C.S. (food) is too great, then learning will not occur.

Variations in contiguity
There are different ways to present the C.S. and U.C.S. together.
- **Forward conditioning** - involves presenting the C.S. (bell) just before and during presentation of the U.C.S. (food), producing the strongest learning.
- **Backward conditioning** - is where the C.S. (bell) is presented after the U.C.S. (food), but produces very little learning.
- **Simultaneous conditioning** - is where the C.S. (bell) and U.C.S. (food) are presented at the same time.
- **Trace conditioning** - involves presenting and removing the C.S. (bell) before the U.C.S. (food).

DURATION

Reinforcement
The learning link will last as long as the U.C.S. (food) is occasionally re-presented with the C.S. (bell).
It is the reflex-based U.C.S. which acts as the reinforcer and strengthens the learning link.

Extinction
If the C.S. (bell) is continually presented without the U.C.S. (food), then the C.R. (salivation) will gradually die out or extinguish.

Spontaneous recovery
If a period of time is left after the C.R. has extinguished, then the C.R. will be exhibited again if the C.S. is presented.

Inhibition
The fact that the C.R. can show spontaneous recovery at a later date after extinction shows that the C.R. does not fade away, but has been actively inhibited by the non-presentation of the U.C.S.

FLEXIBILITY

Generalisation

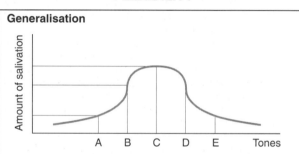

Pavlov found that the C.R. could be triggered by stimuli which resembled the original C.S. - the closer the resemblance the greater the C.R., e.g. if the original C.S. bell had a tone of C, then the dogs would salivate to a lesser degree to tones of B and A.

Discrimination

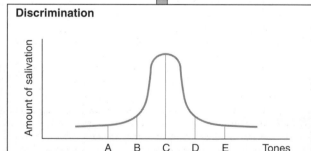

By only presenting the U.C.S. with the original C.S., discrimination from the similar C.S.s occurs.

Higher order conditioning
Once the C.S. is reliably producing the C.R., the C.S. acquires some reinforcing properties itself - a new C.S. can be associated with the original C.S., until the new C.S. will also produce the C.R.

Classical conditioning and phobias

PHOBIAS AS CONDITIONED EMOTIONAL RESPONSES

Behaviourist learning theorists such as Watson suggested that phobias were conditioned emotional responses. Certain stimuli, such as sudden loud noises, naturally cause fear reactions, and stimuli that become associated with them will acquire the same emotional response. In classical conditioning terms, if a rat does not originally produce fear, it can be made to do so by being associated with a loud noise, as follows.

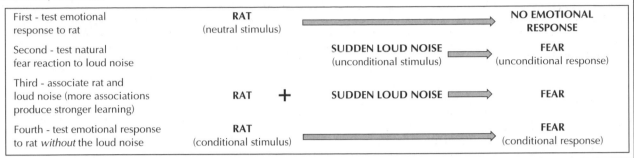

First - test emotional response to rat	**RAT** (neutral stimulus)	⟶	**NO EMOTIONAL RESPONSE**
Second - test natural fear reaction to loud noise		**SUDDEN LOUD NOISE** (unconditional stimulus) ⟶	**FEAR** (unconditional response)
Third - associate rat and loud noise (more associations produce stronger learning)	**RAT** **+**	**SUDDEN LOUD NOISE** ⟹	**FEAR**
Fourth - test emotional response to rat *without* the loud noise	**RAT** (conditional stimulus)	⟶	**FEAR** (conditional response)

THE CASE OF LITTLE ALBERT – WATSON & RAYNER (1920)

Watson and Rayner aimed to provide experimental support for the conditioning of emotional responses such as phobias using a 'stolid and unemotional' young infant, Albert B, to test four questions:

1   ***Can a fear of an animal e.g. a white rat be conditioned by visually presenting it and simultaneously striking a steel bar to create fear?***
   - At approx. 9 months Albert, who had been reared almost from birth in a hospital environment, was suddenly presented with stimuli such as a white rat, a rabbit, a dog, a monkey, masks (with and without hair), cotton wool and burning newspapers. Albert showed no fear reaction at any time – a typical response since he practically never cried and had never been seen to show either fear or rage before.
   - Two stimuli were used to try and produce a fear response in Albert – the sudden removal of support (dropping and jerking the blanket he was lying on) and sharply striking a suspended steel bar with a hammer behind his head. The first stimuli was tried exhaustively but was not effective in producing a fear response, while the second stimuli caused Albert to start violently, catch his breath and raise his arms on the first blow, do the same but pucker and tremble his lips on the second blow, and burst into tears on the third blow.
   - At 11 months and 3 days of age the bar was struck behind Albert's head as he began touching the white rat that had been suddenly presented to him. He jumped violently and fell forward, burying his face in the mattress. When he touched the rat with his other hand, the steel bar was struck a second time – having the same effect and causing him to whimper.
   - At 11 months and 10 days of age, Albert was presented with the rat and appeared apprehensive about touching it. After five further joint presentations of the rat and the noise, the rat was again presented alone. The instant he saw it he began to cry, fell over, and then crawled away so fast that he was caught with difficulty before reaching the edge of the table.

2   ***Is there transfer (stimulus generalisation) of the conditioned emotional response to other objects?***
   - At 11 months and 15 days of age, Albert was presented with a variety of stimuli. He reacted with most fear to the rat and rabbit, slightly less fear to the dog and a seal fur coat and showed avoidance towards cotton wool, Watson's hair and a Santa Claus mask. He played happily with his blocks (smiling and gurgling) and with the hair of other people however.
   - At 11 months and 20 days the reactions to the rat and rabbit were not as violent so the bar was struck again with the rat, rabbit and dog to strengthen the response before Albert was moved to a different room. The fear did transfer to this new location, but with less intensity.

3   ***What is the effect of time upon conditioned emotional responses?***
   Since Albert was due to leave the hospital, only a one-month delay could be left before further testing. At 1 year and 21 days of age Albert showed avoidance of the Santa Claus mask, fur coat, rat, rabbit and dog. He cried on contact with the coat, rabbit and dog, but not the rat (he just covered his eyes with both his hands).

4   ***Can conditioned emotional responses be removed?***
   Albert was removed from the hospital on the day the above tests were made and so the authors stated 'the opportunity to build up an experimental technique by means of which we could remove the conditioned emotional responses was denied us'. They suggested they might have tried continually presenting the fearful stimuli to encourage fatigue of the fear response, associating the fearful stimuli with pleasant stimuli, e.g. stimulation of the erogenous zones or food, and encouraging imitation of non-fearful responses.

EVALUATION

Methodological The study has serious ethical problems. Watson and Rayner reported that they hesitated about proceeding with the experiment but comforted themselves that Albert would encounter such traumatic associations when he left the sheltered environment of the nursery anyway. This is not a very good ethical defence, especially since they believed such associations might persist indefinitely and did not leave sufficient time to remove them afterwards, despite knowing Albert was due to leave.

Theoretical The authors claim the study supports the conditioning of emotional responses and point out that their ideas contradict Freudian theories on the primacy of the emotion of love/sex and the origin of phobias. Nevertheless Albert did show a good deal of resistance to the conditioning process and did not show a fear reaction if he was allowed to suck his thumb.

Operant conditioning

THE BASIC THEORY

Operant conditioning involves learning through the consequences of behavioural responses. The principles of operant conditioning were first investigated by **Thorndike**, and were then thoroughly developed by the famous behaviourist Skinner, who applied them to explain how many aspects of human behaviour are acquired.

Thorndike studied the way cats would learn to escape from his puzzle box by **trial and error**. Cats did not immediately acquire the desirable escape behaviour, but gradually increased in their ability to show it over time. Nevertheless, Thorndike found that any response that led to desirable consequences was more likely to occur again, whereas any response that led to undesirable consequences was less likely to be repeated - a principle which became known as the **Law of Effect**.

However, as with classical conditioning, the law of contiguity applies - associations between responses and consequences have to be made close together in time for learning to occur.

Thorndike's puzzle box

Cats had to emit the response of pulling the string inside the box to release the catch on the door to provide escape (a pleasant consequence). Time to escape decreased with each trial (the number of times the cat was put back in the box).

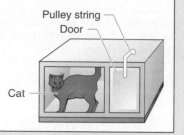

Skinner box

Rats had to press a lever to receive a food pellet, which would increase the likelihood of the lever pressing response reoccurring.

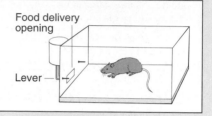

ASPECTS OF REINFORCEMENT

CONSEQUENCES

Positive reinforcement
This increases the likelihood of a response by providing pleasant consequences for it, e.g. food.

Negative reinforcement
This increases the likelihood of a response that removes or provides escape from unpleasant consequences, e.g. stopping an electric shock.

Punishment
This decreases the likelihood of a response being repeated if it is followed by inescapable negative/unpleasant consequences, e.g. an electric shock.

Secondary reinforcement
Secondary reinforcers are those that are associated with naturally occurring primary reinforcers (e.g. food, water, warmth, etc.), for example money, tokens, or parents.

FREQUENCY

Schedules of reinforcement
Continuous schedules - involve reinforcing every response made.

Partial schedules - involve reinforcing responses in varying frequencies to affect response and extinction rates, for example:
- *Fixed ratio schedule* - reinforcing a fixed number of responses (e.g. a food pellet for every ten lever presses in a Skinner box).
- *Variable ratio schedule* - reinforcing an average number of responses (e.g. a food pellet on average every ten lever presses, sometimes after 8 sometimes after 12 presses).
- *Fixed interval schedule* - reinforcing after a fixed amount of time (e.g. a food pellet for a lever press each minute in a Skinner box).
- *Variable interval schedule* - reinforcing after an average amount of time (e.g. a food pellet on average each minute, sometimes after 50 seconds sometimes after 70.

Extinction
If the response is not reinforced, it will gradually die out or extinguish.

FLEXIBILITY

Generalisation

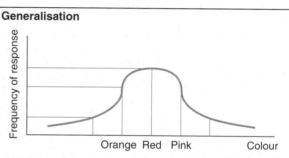

Skinner found animals would make responses that resembled the originally reinforced response - a pigeon reinforced for pecking a red key, would also peck (although less frequently) at an orange or pink key.

Discrimination

Occurs by only reinforcing the original response.

Behaviour shaping
By reinforcing responses that increasingly resemble a desired end behaviour in a step by step manner, very complex behaviour can be built up from simple units.

The first responses are reinforced until perfected and then reinforcement is withheld until the behaviour is refined to the next desired behaviour.

Language acquisition - Skinner's learning theory approach

The Behaviourist learning theorist Skinner, in his book 'Verbal Behaviour' (1957), argued that language was acquired through the principles of **operant conditioning** - trial-and-error learning, selective reinforcement and behaviour shaping.
It is important to remember that words, according to Skinner, are merely behavioural responses emitted because they have been reinforced by the environment. In the case of language, reinforcement is provided by the parents whose smiles, attention and approval are pleasant to the child (parents are secondary reinforcers because they are associated with the primary rewards of food, warmth etc.).
Any verbal response that leads to pleasant consequences is more likely to be repeated again (the Law of Effect)

The acquisition of language behaviour

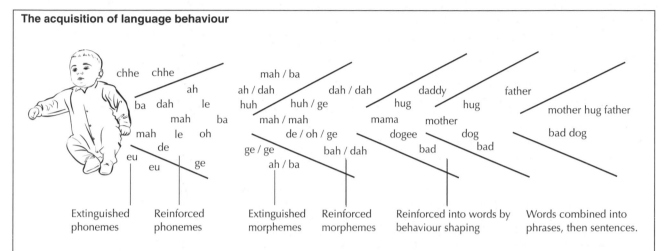

| Extinguished phonemes | Reinforced phonemes | Extinguished morphemes | Reinforced morphemes | Reinforced into words by behaviour shaping | Words combined into phrases, then sentences. |

The acquisition of phonemes
Babies utter many different phonemes (basic units of sound, e.g. 'mah', 'le', 'ge', 'eu', 'chhe') while babbling and as echoic responses (imitations). Parents respond by *reinforcing familiar* phonemes from their own language by smiling or paying increased attention, thereby making them more likely to be *repeated*, and *ignore unfamiliar* sounds (such as the 'eu' phoneme if the parents are English rather than French) thereby *extinguishing* them as responses.
By *selective reinforcement* the child therefore produces more and more suitable phonemes for the language.

Acquisition of morphemes
During babbling, different phonemes will, by trial and error, combine to form morphemes (basic units of meaning, e.g. 'mah / mah' or 'dah /dah'). Since these sound even more like a language that the parents recognise they will draw even more attention and reinforcement for the baby and are therefore more likely to be repeated. Those *trial* and *error* combinations that are not recognised (e.g. 'ah / ba' or 'ge / ge') are not paid attention to, are not reinforced and are therefore more likely to be extinguished as responses.

Acquisition of words
Morphemes become refined into words by behaviour shaping. Parents will want their children to produce more accurate words for communication and will gradually reinforce morpheme combinations that sound more and more like proper words. Step by step, correct words will be spoken more frequently while 'baby' pronunciation will be extinguished.

Phrases and sentences.
Through the processes of trial and error, selective reinforcement and behaviour shaping words will be shaped into telegraphic two-word utterances, then into phrases and then into sentences until the full language has been acquired.

The acquisition of the 'meaning' of words.
Producing words in the right context is also reinforced , as words gain their 'meaning' (not a word favoured by the behaviourists) through their associations, either classical or operant, with objects, events or activities. The word 'more' for example will be produced to gain additional food, cuddles etc. because it has previously been associated with increases in these pleasurable stimuli. Skinner distinguished between two different types of verbal behaviour that parents will reinforce in different ways:

1 A 'mand' is verbal behaviour that is reinforced by the child receiving something it wants. For example the word 'chocolate' is reinforced by receiving some.

| Child sees chocolate | Appropriate verbal behaviour (mand) | Receives chocolate and reinforcement |

2 A 'tact' is verbal behaviour caused by imitating others, e.g. parents in the correct context, and is reinforced by approval. For example the word 'tree' is caused by imitating the parent's speech and is reinforced by a smile and / or approval.

| Parent uses word in a context = the stimulus | Child imitates word = verbal response (tact) | Parent approves = reinforcement |

'Teaching sign language to a chimpanzee'
Gardner and Gardner (1969)

BACKGROUND
- One way to investigate whether another species might be able to learn human language is to try and teach it. Chimpanzees, being regarded as intelligent and sociable animals (although strong and occasionally difficult to handle), are regarded as good subjects for this kind of study.
- Past attempts at teaching chimps vocal language, e.g. Hayes and Hayes (1951) with the chimpanzee Vicky, failed because of the chimpanzee's inappropriate vocal apparatus. Since chimpanzees employ a variety of gestures in their natural environment, the aim of the study was to see if a chimpanzee could be taught American Sign Language.

METHOD
Design: a longitudinal case study of one chimpanzee.

Subject: Washoe (named after the county where the University of Nevada was situated) was a wild caught female chimpanzee aged between 8 and 14 months in June 1966 when the study began. Although Washoe was at first very young and dependent, it was decided to work with a chimpanzee so young in case there was a critical time period for language acquisition.

Equipment: trainers able to communicate in American Sign Language (ASL), a gestural language used by the deaf, were required. Although some ASL gestures are symbolically arbitrary, others are quite representational or iconic (they resemble what they stand for). Finger spelling was avoided as far as possible. Since ASL is currently used by humans, comparisons of young chimpanzee and human performance could be made. Washoe was always in the company of the researchers during her waking hours, all of whom used ASL in their games and activities with her.

Procedure: training methods made use of
imitation - past researchers noted that chimpanzees naturally imitated visual behaviour, so the researchers repeatedly signed in Washoe's presence. Washoe would readily imitate gestures but not always on command or in appropriate situations at first, so correct and exaggerated gestures were repeatedly made as prompts until Washoe emitted the correct sign. Routine activities, such as bathing, feeding, and tooth-brushing also helped produce (delayed) imitation.
babbling - Washoe's spontaneously emitted gestures were encouraged and shaped into signs by indulging in appropriate behaviour.
instrumental conditioning - tickling was used as a reinforcer to shape more accurate signs by withholding it until a clearer version of the sign was shown.

RESULTS
- **Measurement:** detailed records of daily signing behaviour were kept until 16 months, when their increasing frequency made such record keeping difficult. From 16 months, new signs were recorded on a checklist when three different observers noted a sign occurring in the correct situation without specific prompting. A sign was said to have been acquired when it was correctly used without prompting at least once a day for 15 consecutive days.

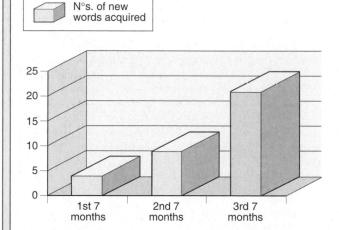

- **Vocabulary:** thirty signs met the above criteria by the end of the twenty-second month, plus four more which occurred on more than half the days of a 30 consecutive day period. Four new signs were shown in the first 7 months, nine signs during the next seven months and 21 during the following seven months.

- **Differentiation:** Washoe's signing became more context and object specific over time, even showing the ability to distinguish between the use of 'flower' (originally used for all smells) and 'smell'

- **Transfer:** Washoe spontaneously generalised signs acquired in one context to other contexts, e.g. 'picture' to all pictures, 'dog' to unknown dogs, etc.

- **Combinations:** Washoe used signs in combination once she had 8 to 10 signs at her disposal. Some combinations were shown spontaneously, before they had been used by the researchers, e.g. 'gimme tickle' or 'listen dog'.

EVALUATION
Methodological: The training and testing conditions were not ideal (although controlled tests were being developed) and there are many practical problems with trying to teach chimpanzees language (they get distracted and frustrated).

Theoretical: There are many problems involved in deciding whether Washoe was acquiring language. She seemed to be showing semanticity, displacement, and productivity (creativity) but did not show structure dependence (no grammatical word order - although this was not reinforced by the researchers).

Ethics: The research has implications for the rights of apes, if they can talk should they not be given human rights?

Links: The debate over animal language. The use of animals as subjects. The ethics of testing animals.

Evaluation of classical and operant conditioning

EVALUATION OF METHODOLOGY

STRENGTHS - The theories of classical and operant conditioning were the product of behaviourist psychology with its emphasis on observable behaviour and laboratory experimentation. With such objective and standardised methodology the principles of classical and operant conditioning could be reliably replicated while reducing the effect of possible confounding variables. Animals such as dogs, cats, pigeons and rats were frequently used as experimental subjects since the behaviourists believed the laws of learning were universal and they have the advantage of being practically and ethically easier to test (they can be tested under more controlled conditions, do not try to work out the nature of the test and are given less ethical rights etc.).

WEAKNESSES – Unfortunately the methods employed also had disadvantages. The experimental subjects often demonstrated learning of only a small range of unnatural responses, e.g. animals pressing levers or pushing buttons, under artificially controlled conditions, e.g. Albert B was not allowed to suck his thumb (he failed to show the same fear response when he did so). This may have led the behaviourists to ignore behaviour their subjects might have found difficult to learn and neglect other influences upon the learning process. This criticism was especially relevant to the study of non-human animal learning which may be qualitatively different to human learning in important ways. There were also serious ethical problems with some of the procedures used in classical and operant conditioning studies.

EVALUATION OF CLASSICAL AND OPERANT CONDITIONING THEORIES

STRENGTHS - The behaviourists used the theories of classical and operant conditioning to explain a wide variety of psychological phenomena, from the processes of learning to the products of it such as phobia and language acquisition. In addition many practical applications of the theory were developed, from animal training to human education and the treatment of disordered behaviour. In many cases such applications have been shown to be efficient in producing behavioural change.

WEAKNESSES – Unfortunately classical and operant conditioning did not take into account the role of inherited and cognitive factors in learning, and are thus incomplete explanations of the learning process in humans and other animals. By focusing on just a few species such as rats or pigeons and generalising the results to all animals, the behaviourists not only ignored the differing cognitive influences on learning that different species show (e.g. the ability of humans to learn by observation and imitation), but importantly neglected the innate abilities in learning that every species will have evolved to better adapt themselves to their environmental niche.

INNATE BIASES IN LEARNING ABILITY

Ethologists would argue that animals have `built-in` biases in natural learning ability that they have evolved to better adapt them to their environment. The laws of learning are therefore not the same for all species, for example:

- **Selectivity of associations and phobias** - Garcia and Koelling (1966) found that rats given a novel tasting solution and made to feel sick up to 3 *hours* afterwards would still learn to associate the two events and avoid that solution on future occasions, even after *only one* such trial in some cases. It therefore seems likely that rats have evolved a highly sensitive learning capability between taste and sickness, especially since this sensitivity makes `evolutionary sense` - it aids survival. Seligman (1970) proposed the concept of **biological preparedness** and argued that humans have also evolved selective associations for survival reasons, in the form of **phobias** for example. The most frequently occurring phobias, e.g. of heights, snakes, spiders etc., all share the evolutionary characteristic of being dangerous to us, and these sort of stimuli have been experimentally shown to be more easily classically conditioned with fear than non-dangerous stimuli such as flowers and grass, which are far more rarely found as phobias. Also of interest is the finding that modern day dangerous objects such as guns and cars are also rare phobias since evolution has not had time to *prepare* us for these stimuli.

- **Imprinting and language acquisition** - Lorenz (1935) showed an increased learning sensitivity to particular stimuli could occur at *certain times* in an animal's life when it is most important to acquire this learning. In his studies of imprinting he found that goslings would form strong attachments to moving, conspicuous objects in their environment during the first hours after hatching, and will follow and stay close to this object.
  In a similar way some researchers have argued that human *language acquisition* takes place during a sensitive time period early in life. A species-specific, evolved human potential for language (a Language Acquisition Device according to Chomsky) would account for the ease with which young children learn to speak and understand complex grammar as well as the failure to teach human language to apes to the same standard.

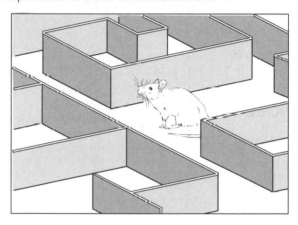

COGNITIVE FACTORS IN LEARNING

Classical and operant conditioning also ignore the cognitive factors between the stimulus and response that influence learning. In operant conditioning for example, a number of researchers have demonstrated that learning does not always happen by trial and error, reinforcement is not always necessary for learning to occur and learning can produce changes in mental representations rather than just behaviour.

- **Insight learning** – Kohler found primates often seem to solve problems in a flash of insight (involving a cognitive rearrangement of the elements of the problem) rather than by laborious trial and error.
- **Latent learning** – Tolman found rats will learn mazes without reinforcement and that they acquire mental maps of the mazes rather than a series of left and right turning behaviours.
- **Social Learning theory** – suggests:
1 Humans can learn *automatically* through *observation* rather than requiring reinforcement through personal experience.
2 Observed behaviour may be *imitated* if desirable consequences are expected (whole 'chunks' of behaviour can be copied without the need for gradual trial-and-error practice).

Social learning theory and aggression

SUPPORTING EVIDENCE

Bandura et al (1963) allowed one group of children to watch an adult model perform certain aggressive acts with an inflatable 'Bobo doll' which were unlikely to occur normally, such as throwing the doll up in the air, hitting it with a hammer and punching it while saying things like 'pow' and 'boom'. When these children were left in a playroom with the inflatable doll, they frequently imitated the same acts of aggression, compared to a control group who had not seen the model and showed none of the behaviours.

Bandura (1965) used a similar experimental set-up, but showed different consequences for the model's aggression to three groups of children. One group saw the model's aggression being rewarded, one group saw the model being punished for the aggression, and another group saw no specific consequences.
When allowed to enter the playroom, the children who had seen the model punished showed less imitative aggression than the other two groups. However, if all the children were offered rewards for doing what the model had done, all groups showed high levels of imitation.
The children in the model punished group had clearly learnt the aggression by observation, but had not shown their potential to imitate it because they expected negative consequences.

SOCIAL LEARNING THEORY AND AGGRESSION

Social learning theory was developed mainly by Bandura and Walters, and suggests that much behaviour, including aggression, is **learnt** from the environment (rather than being instinctual) through reinforcement and the process of **modelling**. Modelling involves learning through the **observation** of other people (models), which may lead to **imitation** if the behaviour to be imitated **leads to desirable consequences**.

Bandura distinguished between the learning of behaviour and the performance of it. Behaviour may be learnt from models through observation, but the likelihood of it being imitated depends on the perceived consequences of the model's actions - if a child sees a model's behaviour being rewarded, this acts as vicarious (indirect) reinforcement for the child who will proceed to imitate it. If the child sees others punished for their actions then, although the behaviour is learnt, it is less likely to be imitated. The social learning theory can easily be applied to explain the learning and performance of aggressive behaviour. Models can be parents, peers or media characters (thus this theory has implications for the portrayal of behaviour like violence on television).

EVALUATION
Methodological
Bandura's social learning theory laboratory experiments have been accused of being overly **artificial** (hitting a Bobo doll is not the same as inflicting aggression on a real person) and of inducing **demand characteristics** (the children may have believed that they were meant to behave aggressively).
However, other experimental studies have demonstrated that children are more likely to hurt other children after viewing violent behaviour (Liebert and Baron, 1972).

Theoretical
The theory neglects the role of innate factors in behaviour like aggression. However, social learning theory does provide a more credible explanation of the transmission of behaviour like violence than the traditional behaviourist view of learning, and has investigated the types of models and behaviours that are most likely to be imitated. Social learning theory provides a more complete approach to explaining learning and has attempted to integrate cognitive and even psychoanalytic concepts with traditional behaviourist learning theory.

IMPLICATIONS FOR REDUCING/CONTROLLING AGGRESSION
The implication of social learning theory is that if aggressive behaviour is not observed or reinforced in a society, then it will not naturally occur.

However many examples of aggression already frequently occur in the great majority of societies, and so the theory would be more realistically applied to reducing aggression.

This could be achieved by ensuring that aggression is not reinforced, or that negative consequences are seen to follow it. The direct punishment of aggression raises problems though, since it may itself be perceived as an aggressive act that is socially approved of - indeed research consistently demonstrates that 'aggression breeds aggression'. Munroe and Munroe (1975) found cross-culturally that childhood aggression is highest in societies whose families highly punish their children for showing aggression.

Social learning theory would suggest that media violence should be dramatically reduced.

'Transmission of aggression through imitation of aggressive models' Bandura, Ross, and Ross (1961)

AIM
To demonstrate that learning can occur through mere observation of a model and that imitation can occur in the absence of that model. More specifically:
- Children shown aggressive models will show significantly more imitative aggressive behaviour than those shown non-aggressive or no models.
- Children shown non-aggressive, subdued models will show significantly less aggressive behaviour than those shown aggressive or no models.
- Boys should show significantly more imitative aggression than girls, especially with the male rather than female aggressive model.

METHOD
Subjects: 72 children, 36 boys and 36 girls, aged 37-69 months (with a mean age of 52 months) were used.

Design: Laboratory experiment, in which the independent variable (type of model) was manipulated in three conditions:
- Aggressive model shown
- Non-aggressive model shown
- Control condition, no model shown

The dependent variable was the amount of imitative behaviour and aggression shown by the children.

A matched pairs design was used with 24 children (12 boys and 12 girls) assigned to each condition, with an effort made to match subjects according to pre-existing levels of aggression. In addition to the above manipulations, in the experimental conditions:
- Half the subjects observed a same sex model.
- The other half observed opposite sex models.

Procedure: In the experimental conditions children were individually shown into a room containing toys and played with some potato prints and pictures in a corner for 10 minutes while either:
- The non-aggressive adult model (either male or female) played in a quiet and subdued manner for 10 minutes, or
- The aggressive model distinctively aggressed against a 5 foot inflated Bobo doll by **a** sitting on it and repeatedly punching it on the nose, **b** striking it on the head with a mallet, and **c** throwing it up in the air and kicking it around the room. The aggressive model also uttered verbally aggressive statements such as 'sock him in the nose', 'throw him in the air' and 'pow', as well as two non-aggressive statements - 'he keeps coming back for more' and 'he sure is a tough fella'.

All children (including the control group) were then individually taken to a different experimental location and subjected to mild aggression arousal by being stopped from playing with some very attractive toys. This arousal took place in order to give all groups an equal chance of showing aggression and also to allow the group shown the non-aggressive model to demonstrate an inhibition of aggressive behaviour.

All children were then shown into another room which contained both aggressive toys (e.g. a 3 foot high Bobo doll, a mallet, dartguns, and a tether ball) and non-aggressive toys (e.g. a tea set, dolls, and colouring paper), and were observed through a one-way mirror for 20 minutes.

Observers recorded (with inter-scorer reliabilities of .90 correlation coefficient) behaviour in the following categories:

- **Imitation behaviour of aggressive model:**
  a physical aggression, e.g. sitting on the doll and repeatedly punching it on the nose.
  b Verbal aggression, e.g. 'sock him' or 'pow'.
  c Non-aggressive speech, e.g. 'he sure is a tough fella'.
- **Partial imitation behaviour of aggressive model**, e.g. mallet aggression against other objects or sitting on the Bobo doll without punching it.
- **Non-imitative physical and verbal aggression**, e.g. just punching the Bobo doll, physical aggression with other objects and verbal non-imitative remarks 'shoot the Bobo' or 'horses fighting, biting'.
- **Non-aggressive behaviour**, e.g. non aggressive play or sitting quietly.

RESULTS
1 Children in the aggressive model condition showed significantly more imitation of the model's physical and verbal aggression and non-aggressive verbal responses than children who saw the non-aggressive model or no model at all in the control condition.
2 Children in the aggressive model condition usually showed more partial imitation and non-imitative physical and verbal aggression than those who saw the non-aggressive model or no model at all, but not always to a significant degree.
3 Children in the non-aggressive model condition showed very little aggression, although not always significantly less than the no model group.
4 Children who saw the same sex model were only likely to imitate the behaviour significantly more in some of the categories. For example, boys would imitate male models significantly more than girls for physical and verbal imitative aggression, non-imitative aggression and gun play; girls would imitate female models more than boys for verbal imitative aggression and non-imitative aggression only, but not significantly.

EVALUATION
Methodological:

Procedure -	Not completely standardised presentation of model's behaviour (later experiments used videotape presentation)
Artificiality -	Bizarre acts of aggression were shown and imitated against a Bobo doll, not a real person.
Ethical problems -	Aggression was induced in, and taught to, children. Exposure to an adult stranger's aggression may have been frightening for the children.

Theoretical: The research provides reasonable support for the social learning theory idea that behaviour can be acquired through observation rather than direct personal experience, and that reinforcement is not required for learning to occur. This study has important implications for the effects of media violence on children.

Links: Social learning theory, aggression, socialisation, gender differences.

Contemporary issue - How does the media affect behaviour?

LABORATORY EXPERIMENTS ON MEDIA VIOLENCE

Bandura's experiments showed that aggression could be learnt and imitated from live, filmed or cartoon models. Liebert and Baron (1972) found that children who had watched a violent programme were more likely to hurt another child. However laboratory studies may produce artificial results.

CORRELATIONS ON MEDIA VIOLENCE

Eron (1987) found a significant positive correlation between the amount of aggression viewed at age 8 and later aggression at age 30.
Phillips (1986) has found correlations between highly publicised incidents of aggression, such as murder cases or boxing matches, and the number of corresponding incidents in society at large. Correlation is not causation however.

NATURAL EXPERIMENTS ON MEDIA VIOLENCE

Joy et al (1986) measured children's levels of aggression in a Canadian town one year before and after television was introduced, and found a significant increase compared to the non significant increases in towns that already had television.

FIELD EXPERIMENTS ON MEDIA VIOLENCE

Parke et al (1977) showed juvenile delinquents in the USA and Belgium either violent or non-violent television for a week in their homes. Aggression was greater for the violent TV group especially in those who had previously shown higher levels. Field studies are hard to control and replicate however.

OBSERVATIONAL LEARNING

Violent behaviour could be learnt by observation and imitated if rewarding.

DISINHIBITION

Watching aggression could reduce inhibitions about behaving aggressively as it is seen as socially legitimate.

AROUSAL

Aggressive emotional arousal or excitement from watching aggression may lead to real violence.

DESENSITISATION

Watching aggression may lead to an increased acceptance or tolerance of it in society.

NEGATIVE EFFECTS (OF MEDIA VIOLENCE)

MEDIATING FACTORS

- The personality of the viewer. The effects of TV violence often depend on what the child brings to the screen.
- The amount of exposure to media violence.

HOW MIGHT THE MEDIA INFLUENCE BEHAVIOUR ?

NO EFFECT

Howitt and Cumberbatch (1974) analysed 300 studies concluding that TV violence has no direct effect on children's behaviour. Freedman (1984, 1986) argues that although there is a small correlation between levels of viewing and behaving aggressively, the causal connection is very weak.

POSITIVE EFFECTS OF MEDIA VIOLENCE

INOCULATION

Watching antisocial violence could provide the opportunity to discuss its immorality or to see it come to no good (the 'baddie' loses).

CATHARSIS

According to Freud's ideas, watching violence could provide a relief from pent up aggression, as it is released through emotional sympathy.

STUDIES ON THE CATHARTIC EFFECT OF TV VIOLENCE

Feshbach and Singer (1971) claimed that children shown aggressive programs over a 6 week period showed *less* aggressive behaviour than those who saw non-violent TV. However, this study has been accused of methodological flaws, and more recent studies have not replicated or have found the opposite findings.

POSITIVE EFFECTS OF PRO-SOCIAL MEDIA

POSITIVE ROLE MODELS

Just as aggression could be learnt from aggressive media models, so pro-social role models could also provide a basis for observational learning and imitation - especially if their behaviour produces rewards such as public praise, social respect etc. (the 'goodie' always wins in the end).

STUDIES ON THE EFFECTS OF PRO-SOCIAL TV

Sprafkin et al (1975) found over 90% of children chose to help a puppy instead of personal gain after watching a program that involved helping ('Lassie'), while Baron et al (1979) found children were more co-operative after watching the 'The Waltons'.
Hearold (1986) analysed approximately 200 studies and concluded that pro-social television has around twice the effect on children's behaviour than anti-social television.

Behavioural treatments - behaviour therapy (treatments using classical conditioning techniques)

SYSTEMATIC DESENSITISATION

TECHNIQUE

Aims to **extinguish** the fear response of a phobia, and **substitute** a relaxation response to the conditional stimulus **gradually**, step by step. This is done by

- forming a hierarchy of fear, a list of fearful situations, real or imagined, involving the CS that are ranked by the subject from least fearful to most fearful.
- giving training in deep muscle relaxation techniques.
- getting the subject to relax at each stage of the hierarchy, starting with the least fearful situation, and only progressing to the next stage when the subject feels sufficiently relaxed to do so.

APPLICATION

This therapy was developed mainly by Wolpe (1958). Mary Cover Jones applied systematic desensitisation to infants with phobias, such as the case of 'Little Peter'. Little Peter was a three year old child who had a strong phobia of rats and rabbits, and initially 'fell flat on his back in a paroxysm of fear when a white rat was dropped into his playpen', 'Walker (1984). Peter's treatment began by being presented with a rabbit in a cage at the same time as he ate his lunch, and ended 40 sessions later with him stroking the rabbit on his lap with one hand and eating his lunch with the other!

EFFECTIVENESS

This method of treatment has a very high success rate with specific phobias, e.g. of **particular** animals rather than agoraphobia (a **general** fear of being in open spaces), and is thought to work because it seems impossible for two opposite emotions (like fear and relaxation) to exist together at the same time.

APPROPRIATENESS

This conclusion is questioned by studies that claim to have found that neither relaxation or hierarchies are actually **necessary**, and that the essential factor is just **exposure** to the feared object or situation. Systematic desensitisation is considered more ethical and less directive because the patient has more control over the treatment - progression only occurs when they feel suitably relaxed.

IMPLOSION/FLOODING

TECHNIQUE

Both methods of forced reality testing aim to produce the **extinction** of a phobic's fear by the **continual** and **dramatic** presentation of the phobic object or situation.
In implosion therapy, the phobic individual is, therefore, asked to continually **imagine** the worst possible situation involving their phobia, whereas in flooding therapy the worst possible situation is actually **physically** and continuously presented.

APPLICATION

Wolpe (1960) forced a girl with a fear of cars into the back of a car and drove her around for 4 hours until her hysterical fear completely disappeared, while Marks et al (1981) used flooding on agoraphobics. Prolonged exposure and compulsive response prevention is used for obsessive compulsives.

EFFECTIVENESS

Marks et al (1981) found continued improvement for up to nine years after the treatment. The key to the therapy is that the dramatic presentation is continuous and **cannot be escaped from or avoided**. Therefore, the patient's anxiety is maintained at such a high level that eventually some process of stimulus 'exhaustion' takes place (you can not scream forever!) and the conditioned fear response extinguishes.

APPROPRIATENESS

These methods are considered to be
- the most successful at treating phobias, especially flooding, which Marks et al, 1971, found to be consistently more successful than systematic desensitisation, suggesting that **in vivo exposure** is crucial.
- quick and cheap but involve ethical problems of suffering and withdrawal from therapy (which could worsen the phobia).

AVERSION THERAPY

TECHNIQUE

Aims to **remove undesirable responses** to certain stimuli **by associating** them with other **aversive** stimuli, in the hope that the undesirable responses will be avoided in the future. In essence, this therapy actually tries to condition some kind of 'phobia' of the undesirable behaviour, although it is important to note that fear is not always the conditioned response.

APPLICATION

Aversion therapy has been used to treat alcoholism.

Alcohol	+	Emetic drug	⟶	Nausea
Alcohol		Emetic drug	⟶	Nausea
Alcohol			⟶	Nausea

More controversially, aversion therapy has been used to prevent a number of sexual behaviours, ranging from homosexuality to fetishism. Shocks have been paired with self damaging behaviours to stop them.

EFFECTIVENESS

Some studies have claimed limited success using aversion therapy to treat alcoholism - Meyer and Chesser (1970) found that about half their alcoholic patients abstained for at least one year following their treatment, although O'Leary and Wilson (1987) have reported mixed results. Marks et al (1970) claimed aversion therapy was effective on sexual behaviours for up to 2 years, although Marshall et al (1991) found no effectiveness.

APPROPRIATENESS

However, relapse rates are very high - the success of the therapy depends upon whether the patient can avoid the stimuli they have been conditioned against, to maintain the aversion. If the alcoholic continues to go to bars then the nausea response to alcohol may extinguish under repeated exposure. There are ethical problems involved in deliberately conditioning aversions.

The psychodynamic approach to psychology

ORIGINS AND HISTORY

- The psychodynamic approach was mainly initiated by *Sigmund Freud*, a Viennese doctor who specialised in neurology. Freud became interested in hysteria - the manifestation of physical symptoms without physical causes - and became convinced that **unconscious mental causes** were responsible not just for this disorder but for many disorders and even 'normal' personality. Freud developed psychoanalysis – a set of techniques for **treating** the unconscious causes of mental disorders and built up an underlying explanatory **psychoanalytic theory** of how human personality and abnormality develop from childhood.
- Freud's theory and approach were influenced by the ideas and society of his time, particularly by his early work with Charcot, the Parisian hypnotist, and Breuer the pioneer of the cathartic method. Freud's psychoanalytic approach had a great impact on psychology and psychiatry, and was developed in different ways by other **psychodynamic** theorists (those influenced by psychoanalytic assumptions) such as Jung, Adler, Klein, Anna Freud (his daughter) and Erikson.

Sigmund Freud (1856 - 1939)

"...I set myself the task of bringing to light what human beings keep hidden within them.....the task of making conscious the most hidden recesses of the mind is one which it is quite possible to accomplish".

ASSUMPTIONS

Psychoanalysis, as developed by Freud, had a very fixed set of assumptions that later psychodynamic theorists agreed with to differing extents. The most common shared assumptions of the approach are:

- **Unconscious processes** - many important influences on behaviour come from a part of the mind we have no direct awareness of, the unconscious.
- **Psychodynamic conflict** - different parts of the mind are in constant dynamic struggle with each other (often unconsciously) and the consequences of this struggle are important in understanding behaviour.
- **Emotional drives** – Freud believed behaviour is motivated by sexual and aggressive drives. The drives create psychic energy that will build up (like steam in a steam engine) and create tension and anxiety if it cannot be released in some form. While not all psychodynamic theorists agree with Freud's view, they do see emotional motivation as important.
- **Development** - personality is shaped by relationships, experience and conflict over time, particularly during childhood.

METHODS OF INVESTIGATION

- Freud used the **case study** method when treating his clients (seeing them individually and investigating them in detail), often using the clinical interview method to probe their past and question their behaviour. He **deeply** analysed and **interpreted** the **symbolism** of all they said and did. These methods remain the norm for most psychodynamic theorists.
- Two particular techniques Freud used were: **Free association** - the uninhibited expression of thought associations, no matter how bizarre or embarrassing, from the client to the analyst. **Dream analysis** - the 'royal road' to the unconscious, the analyst attempts to decode the symbols and unravel the hidden meaning of a dream from the dreamer's report.

CONTRIBUTION TO PSYCHOLOGY

Freud used his theory to explain a vast number of topics, such as:

- **Personality development** - due to fixation / defence mechanisms.
- **Moral / gender development** - the result of the Oedipus complex.
- **Aggression** - caused by hydraulic drives and displacement.
- **Abnormality** - the consequence of early trauma and repression.
- **Memory** - Forgetting caused by repression.

+ Slips of the tongue, the shaping of civilisation and customs, etc.

CONTRIBUTION TO SOCIETY

- The purpose of psychoanalysis was as a therapy to treat mental disorder. Once the unconscious cause of disorder was identified through dream interpretation etc., then a cure could be effected by getting it 'out in the open' to be discussed, resolved and controlled.
- Psychoanalysis can be applied to art and literature.

STRENGTHS

- Freud's ideas made a large impact on psychology and psychiatry and are still discussed and used today, around a 100 years after he started developing them.
- Freud thought case studies like 'Little Hans' and 'Anna O', his belief in determinism and his detailed collection of data provided scientific support for his theory.
- Psychodynamic therapies drew attention to the psychological causes of mental disorder.
- Psychoanalysis has enormous explanatory power and has something to say on a huge variety of important topics.
- Later psychodynamic theory tried to deal with the weaknesses of psychoanalysis and develop the strengths.

WEAKNESSES

Psychodynamic psychology has been accused of:

- Having vague concepts that can be used to explain anything but which can predict very little.
- Having concepts that are difficult to test and verify scientifically. Experimental research that has been conducted often fails to support psychodynamic ideas, and that which does seem to support them can often be attributed to alternative causes.
- Using unrepresentative samples and techniques that were not fully objective and therefore open to bias.
- Being linked with unsuccessful psychodynamic therapies.
- Having many concepts that can be explained by more scientific approaches such as cognitive psychology.

Freud's psychoanalytic theory of personality

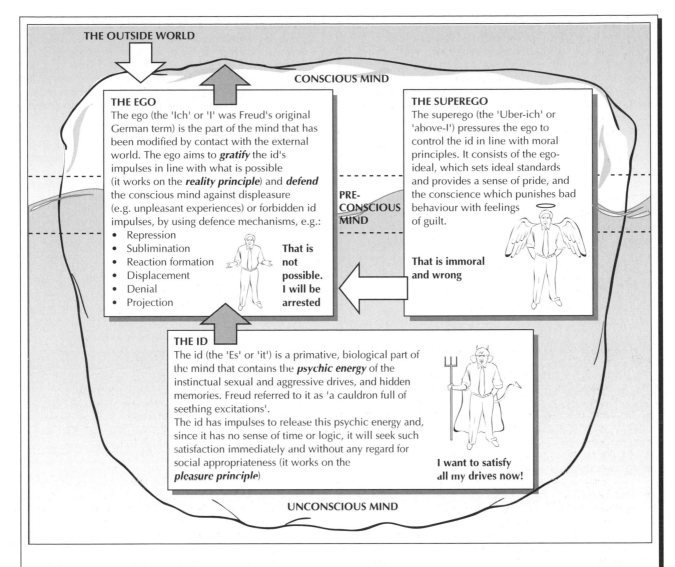

THE OUTSIDE WORLD

CONSCIOUS MIND

THE EGO
The ego (the 'Ich' or 'I' was Freud's original German term) is the part of the mind that has been modified by contact with the external world. The ego aims to *gratify* the id's impulses in line with what is possible (it works on the *reality principle*) and *defend* the conscious mind against displeasure (e.g. unpleasant experiences) or forbidden id impulses, by using defence mechanisms, e.g.:
- Repression
- Sublimation
- Reaction formation
- Displacement
- Denial
- Projection

That is not possible. I will be arrested

PRE-CONSCIOUS MIND

THE SUPEREGO
The superego (the 'Uber-ich' or 'above-I') pressures the ego to control the id in line with moral principles. It consists of the ego-ideal, which sets ideal standards and provides a sense of pride, and the conscience which punishes bad behaviour with feelings of guilt.

That is immoral and wrong

THE ID
The id (the 'Es' or 'it') is a primative, biological part of the mind that contains the *psychic energy* of the instinctual sexual and aggressive drives, and hidden memories. Freud referred to it as 'a cauldron full of seething excitations'.
The id has impulses to release this psychic energy and, since it has no sense of time or logic, it will seek such satisfaction immediately and without any regard for social appropriateness (it works on the *pleasure principle*).

I want to satisfy all my drives now!

UNCONSCIOUS MIND

FREUD'S TOPOGRAPHICAL MODEL
This divided the mind into three levels or layers of consciousness (these can be illustrated with the iceberg analogy above):
1. **The Conscious** - This contains all we are directly aware of, but only represents 'the tip of the iceberg' since although we may think we know why we do things, we often do not. According to Freud, unconscious causes are of great importance.
2. **The Pre-conscious** – This contains material that can become conscious.
3. **The Unconscious** – The part of the mind that is not accessible and contains our inner drives and repressed experiences. It is also where the unconscious struggles that affect our behaviour take place. The unconscious mind resembles a hydraulic closed energy system (like a steam engine) in that psychic energy from the drives builds up and, if not released, causes inner pressure or anxiety.

FREUD'S STRUCTURAL MODEL
Freud also suggested a model that involved dynamic struggle between three aspects of the mind – the **id**, **ego** and **superego** (illustrated above). The ego has the task of satisfying the demands of the id, superego and society, as well as attempting to keep unpleasant experiences out of consciousness. These *conflicting influences* have many important *consequences* for human behaviour, including *dreams*, *the development of personality traits* and *disordered behaviour*.

FREUD'S DREAM THEORY
- Freud suggested that dreams represent *unfulfilled wishes* from the id, which try to break into consciousness and seek satisfaction while we are 'off guard'. Dreams are the way these id wishes are *disguised* by the dream censor using defensive measures such as *symbolism* (using a dream image or event to stand for an id wish), condensation (the merging of many unconscious meanings into one dream image) and *displacement* (where emotions are separated from their true source and attached to trivial sources in the dream). Dreams still demonstrate many aspects of id 'thinking', being so disjointed, illogical, and generally showing little appreciation for time and reality, but can still act as the 'guardians of sleep' to protect us from our own unconscious while asleep.
- Dreams are thus a very important source of unconscious information since, by undoing the 'dreamwork' of the *manifest content* of the dream (what is consciously remembered) the *latent content* (the hidden id impulses or meaning) can be discovered. This is achieved by free associating to each element of the manifest content to trace it back to the latent content, decoding the symbolism of the manifest content (some symbols are personal but many have universal meanings, e.g. phallic symbols such as guns and knives) and identifying the event (within the previous 24 hours according to Freud) that acted as the trigger for the dream.

Freud's stage theory and personality development

PSYCHOSEXUAL STAGES OF DEVELOPMENT

Drives and development - Freud proposed that we are driven or motivated by our *instinctual drives*, which come from two basic instincts. Thanatos, the death instinct, is responsible for aggressive drives, whereas Eros, the life instinct, is responsible for the sex drive or libido. Freud saw the life instinct and sex drive as exerting the most influence in the early years of life and thus childhood is a time of key importance in personality development.

Freud proposed a stage theory of infantile psychosexual development that suggested that children are polymorphously perverse - able to derive sexual pleasure from any part of their bodies, but as they grow older the sexual drive becomes focused upon (and seeks expression and satisfaction from) different parts of the body. The stages are governed by biological maturation.

The stages of psychosexual development

*   **Oral stage** - where pleasure is gained first from passively and dependently sucking and swallowing (the oral receptive sub-stage) and later, as the teeth emerge, from biting and chewing (the oral aggressive sub-stage).
*   **Anal stage** - gratification shifts to the anus where pleasure is gained first from expelling and playing with faeces (the expulsive sub-stage) and then, during toilet training, from holding on to and controlling bowel movements (the retentive sub-stage).
*   **Phallic stage** - from around 3 to 5 or 6 years of age the libido becomes focused upon the genitals, and pleasure involving them becomes directed towards the opposite sex parent. Both boys and girls at this age unconsciously desire the opposite sex parent, but differ slightly in the way they deal with this situation, which Freud termed the Oedipus Complex.
    The Oedipus complex for boys involves sexual attraction towards the mother and wishing his rival for the mother's affection, his father, out of the way (ideally dead). However, the boy fears that the more powerful father will discover his illicit desires and will punish by depriving the boy of what he currently holds most dear - his phallus. This 'castration complex' is resolved when, out of fear of castration, the boy identifies with the father figure, introjecting all his values, attitudes and behaviour, so that in becoming like his father the boy can indirectly have the mother through his fantasies and later grow up to have mother-like figures in the same way as his father.
    The Oedipus complex for girls (sometimes referred to as the Electra Complex) involves the girl's desire for the father. The girl believes that she has already been castrated, and out of penis envy she turns to her father to provide her with a symbolic penis substitute - a baby. However, out of fear of losing her mother's love plus the symbolic gains of imitating a person the father is attached to, the girl identifies with her mother and by becoming like her she too can indirectly satisfy her sexual desires.
*   **Latency stage** - after the turmoil of the phallic stage the child enters a stage where the child's desires diminish somewhat.
*   **Genital stage** - occurs with the onset of puberty and involves the reawakening of the libido and its attachment to external love objects outside the family.

Id, ego and superego development - Freud suggested that by the end of the phallic stage, the three main aspects of the mind would have developed - the id, ego and superego. Babies begin life dominated by the unsocialised id, seeking immediate gratification (crying for food, sleeping and defecating) with no regard for time and place (as parents will testify!). The ego gradually develops through contact with the external world with all its restraints on behaviour, thus toilet training during the anal stage is a particularly important time for its development. The ego is free from moral constraint until the superego develops, mainly as a result of the internalisation of parental values in the Oedipus complex.

STAGES AND PERSONALITY DEVELOPMENT

Fixation and trauma - Freud therefore believed that the early years of development are of utmost importance, since the experiences of childhood shape the structure of the unconscious mind and the majority of human personality. Freud suggested that too much or too little pleasure at a stage might lead to *fixation* at it, causing the individual in later life to still want to indulge in its pleasures (stage *regression*). For example fixation at the oral receptive stage due to over-indulgence (the slightest whimper brought food and oral gratification) may lead to an optimistic personality or one that gains pleasure from being dependent and passive. Any traumatic events, especially of a sexual nature, in earlier life might also become hidden in the unconscious and influence later behaviour.

Defence mechanisms and stage fixations

The ego cannot allow many of the id's sexual and aggressive impulses to reach respectable, adult, conscious life and so uses defence mechanisms to control, alter, deny or redirect the impulses whenever they may occur. Ego defence mechanisms used to cope with fixations may thus affect personality, e.g.:

*   **Sublimation** - usually the most successful defence, it allows the expression of id impulses through behaviour that is a socially acceptable symbolic alternative. For example fixation at the oral stage may later lead to seeking oral pleasure, not from sucking the mother's breast in public, but from sucking at one's thumb, pen or cigarette. Anal expulsive desires to handle faeces may lead to an enjoyment of pottery. A phallically fixated desire to expose one's penis may lead to a later sublimated career choice of a fireman, who can happily drive large hoses and extending ladders with much attention through the streets, after sliding down the fire station pole (Kline, 1984).
*   **Repression** - not a very successful defence in the long term since it just involves forcing disturbing wishes, ideas or memories into the unconscious where, although hidden, they will create psychic pressure or anxiety and constantly seek expression. Thus someone may repress homosexual feelings and become a latent (hidden) homosexual who may consciously report attraction to the opposite sex, but has to use other defence mechanisms, such as denial or reaction formation, to control their unconscious urges.
*   **Reaction formation** - if unconscious impulses become too powerful then the ego can only maintain control by forcing the individual to consciously feel and act in *exactly the opposite* way to that unconsciously desired. Thus latent homosexuals may feel and show an excessive hatred of overt homosexuals, while those with an 'anal character' (an exaggerated concern for orderliness, cleanliness, control and routine) may be reacting against their anal expulsive desire to mess. If while reading this you are getting a little *too* angry in your objection to some of Freud's ideas, then your ego is probably helping you react against your anxiety provoking unconscious recognition of their truth!

There are many other defence mechanisms, like *displacement* where feelings are expressed by redirecting them onto something or somebody powerless and convenient rather than the original cause (we do not slam a door because we hate it!). They make humans and their society the way they are. Without the restraints defence mechanisms impose, civilisation would not be possible.

Balance - Freud also argued that the overall balance between the id, ego and superego would affect personality. A strong superego, for example, might result in a very moral person while a very weak one may result in an emotional psychopath. An over influential id might lead to irresponsible and impulsive behaviour or even violence and crime.

Jung's analytical psychology

JUNG & ANALYTICAL PSYCHOLOGY ASSUMPTIONS

Carl Gustav Jung (1875-1961) was a Swiss psychiatrist who worked in a Zurich mental hospital before moving on to his own private practice. He was, at first, a favourite disciple of Freud's, and applied psychoanalytic concepts to his study of schizophrenics, but increasingly developed his own theories that differed from Freud's Psychoanalysis and the two men parted company on bad terms in 1913. Jung pursued his 'Analytical Psychology', and developed a range of theories on personality and mental disorder.

In contrast to Freud, Jung put greater emphasis on:

- Processes occurring *within* the individual rather than on the relationships between individuals and society. Jung regarded the goal or end point of development as *individuation* – the self-actualisation of the individual's potential and the achievement of psychic balance, the integration of opposites and self-realisation.

  Thoughts, emotions and behaviour result from a *self-regulating* psyche / mind that constantly tries to *seek balance* and integration between the conscious and unconscious, and between different aspects of personality. Imbalance will cause *compensations*. Compensations result in personality characteristics, dreams and symptoms of mental disorder.

- Spiritual and religious rather than physical aspects of human nature – people seek more than honour, power, wealth, fame, and the love of women as Freud put it. Jung believed everyone needs a myth or set of beliefs to live by to give their life some meaning and purpose. These myths do not necessarily have to been objectively 'true' to have this positive function. If people become alienated from their beliefs, as indeed Jung himself felt alienated from Orthodox Christianity, anxiety and a sense of incompleteness results.

METHODS

Jung employed similar methods to Freud, but often used and interpreted them in different ways.

- **Analysis and interpretation of symbolism** – Jung spent more time on the cross-cultural study of symbolism in mythology. He frequently found important similarities in the myths and symbols of cultures that did not seem to have any contact with each other, especially mystical 'mandala' symbols, such as circular shapes, crosses or other divisions of four, that represent psychic balance and harmony. He interpreted this as evidence for a collective unconscious.

- **Word association tests** - like free association, a person has to reply with the first word that comes to mind that is associated with other words. Jung carried this out in a more scientific way, not just recording the associated word but also measuring the exact time it took for an association to be made to each word in his list as well as the physiological response to it (recorded by skin conductance using a polygraph or 'lie-detector' apparatus). Collections of words that produced variations from normal responses would indicate a common emotional link or 'complex'.

- **Dream interpretation** – Jung disagreed with Freud that dreams are always disguised wish fulfilment resulting from past circumstances. Jung suggested that dreams reflect current preoccupations and may be compensations for conscious attitudes and behaviour that are causing imbalance. Dreams are a symbolic language, difficult to always understand in linguistic terms, but not deliberately disguised. Dreams come from everyday emotional problems in the personal unconscious (and may suggest ways of solving such problems in the future) or from images/symbols from the deeper collective unconscious.

THEORY OF THE UNCONSCIOUS

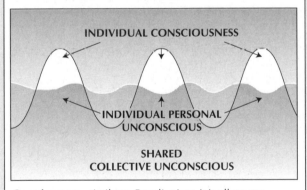

Consciousness - similar to Freud's view, it is all we are aware of.

Personal unconscious - the unconscious of each individual, it contains temporarily forgotten as well as truly repressed material and 'complexes' (clusters of linked emotions, memories and attitudes in the personal unconscious that can form mini sub-personalities in themselves) resulting from personal experience.

Collective unconscious - a level of consciousness shared with other members of our species that contains common archetypes. Archetypes are inherited predispositions to feel, act and experience the world in certain ways, thus people may behave in similar ways as their ancestors and people in other cultures they have never met. Important archetypes include The Persona (our social mask), The Shadow (our animal urges, similar to the id but more positive in its influence) and The Anima/Animus (our female or male sides).

THEORY OF PERSONALITY

Jung's analytical psychology suggests the psyche has many aspects and that personality can be influenced unconsciously by complexes and archetypes. In addition, however, Jung suggested that personality is also shaped by how we consciously react towards and experience the world.

Extraversion and introversion – These are two attitudes or ways of directing our libido (Jung saw this as more of a general life force rather than just sexual energy) towards the world. *Introverts* direct their libido inwards towards their mental world and so prefer to keeps themselves to themselves, avoid excessive social contact, and may be somewhat self-absorbed. *Extraverts* direct their libido outwards to the external world and so have an outgoing, confident and friendly nature that adapts easily to situations and seeks social stimulation.

The four functions – These are ways of experiencing the world:
Sensation (registering the existence of things)
Thinking (identifying and understanding things),
Feeling (judging the pleasantness or worth of things)
Intuition (anticipating or predicting things)
Jung suggested one function might predominate, and that sensation and intuition were opposed to each other, as were thinking and feeling. Thus those guided by emotion might not think logically through decisions, while those always anticipating the future might be blind to things happening under their very noses.

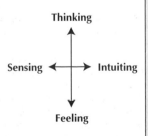

Evaluation of Freud's and Jung's theories

Freud's methods

- Freud used an unrepresentative sample and lacked objective data upon which to base his theory. He mostly studied himself, his disordered patients and only one child in detail. Freud thought this unimportant, believing in only a quantitative difference between people - we are all neurotic to some extent, including himself. Freud's case notes consisted of his memories of his clients' memories (often of early childhood), however since he regarded many childhood recollections as fantasies anyway he guessed at what had taken place in his patient's past.
- Freud may have shown researcher bias in his interpretations – since he originally wanted a general theory of sexual causation that would "open all secrets with a single key" he may have tended to interpret all symbols as sexual, only pay attention to or remember information that supported his theories and ignore information or other explanations that did not fit them. E.g. Little Hans' horse phobia may have resulted from his fright on seeing a horse collapse rather than an unconscious fear of castration from the father (Hans had actually been threatened with castration, but by his mother).

Psychoanalytic Theory

- Freud over-emphasised sexual causes - Breuer even said Freud was prone to "excessive generalisation".
- Freud's theory was biased by a cultural, sexist male viewpoint e.g. on female inferiority and penis envy.
- The unconscious is difficult to test objectively.
- The theory is very good at explaining but not predicting behaviour. Symbolism is so vague and subjective, and defence mechanisms are so flexible, that they can be used to support any theory of the unconscious, indeed they seem to make Freudian theory unrefutable (incapable of being shown wrong) and thus unscientific e.g. any research finding the exact opposite of what Freudian theory would predict could be explained through the defence of reaction formation. Kline (1972) argued that psychoanalytic theory can be broken down into testable hypotheses if they are made **two-tailed** to predict either outcome and refutable by finding no significant effect.

Freud's contribution

- Freud developed his theory throughout his life and proposed explanations for a huge variety of phenomena, from humour and forgetting to crowd behaviour, customs and warfare. Many psychologists and psychoanalysts, although often disagreeing with some of his ideas, have been inspired by his theories to develop their own. Psychoanalytic terms and concepts have become ingrained into western psychology and society, and Psychoanalysis is still practised today.
- Philosophers and writers had long considered the importance the unconscious, dream interpretation, defence mechanisms etc. whereas Freud's more original ideas concerning them have been criticised, leading psychologists e.g. Eysenck (1985) to agree with Ebbinghaus that "what is new in these theories is not true, and what is true is not new".
- More negatively, Freud's Oedipus complex may have led to genuine cases of child abuse being dismissed as childhood sexual fantasies.

EVALUATION OF FREUD'S PSYCHODYNAMIC THEORIES

Subsequent research

- Reviews of research attempting to scientifically validate Freudian concepts are largely negative in their conclusions because it is difficult to show that the unconscious mechanisms Freud proposed are responsible.
- Freud emphasised the importance of the Oedipus complex, calling it the `kernel of neurosis` yet while Social Learning Theory research has found imitation of same sex parents does occur, there has been no conclusive evidence that unconscious motives like castration fear are responsible.
- Freud regarded repression as `the cornerstone on which the whole of psychoanalysis rests`, yet although research has linked trauma to amnesia, the degree to which repressed events are truly unconscious has been questioned and other causes have been suggested as more likely.
- While *Kline and Storey* (1977) found evidence for oral and anal personality traits by using personality questionnaires, it has not been demonstrated that these traits have been caused by Freudian fixation at a stage.

- Freud suggested that a woman's desire for a baby was a symbolic substitute for their desire to gain the penis they envy in men and feel they have been deprived of. Harris and Campbell (1999) investigated whether unconscious motivations might be involved in pregnancy. They thought pregnancy might involve other symbolic gains. Harris gave semi-structured interviews to 128 North London women designed to measure the quality of their lives and sexual partnerships and their degree of **secondary gain** from becoming pregnant (e.g. an improvement in their circumstances or relationships). Women with unplanned pregnancies were found to be significantly more likely to have been in a situation of secondary gain, especially relating to their partnerships, than women with planned pregnancies or no pregnancy. This was particularly the case for those women with unplanned pregnancies who were shocked when they found out they were pregnant. Unfortunately the study cannot conclusively demonstrate that the motivations were truly unconscious – the women were not asked to rate the secondary gain themselves and there are problems relying on retrospective data (based on their memory of events before they were pregnant) gained from interview and self report methods (the secondary gain scale only had an inter-rater reliability of .69)

- **Developmental theory** – Jung focuses very much on the development of the *individual* and their inner life, and tends to ignore human relationships, the past and childhood experiences.
- **The collective unconscious and archetypes** – While evolutionary theory also argues for inherited species-specific characteristics and tendencies, the cross-cultural similarities in myth and symbolism Jung found could just have resulted from similar *experiences* shared by different cultures rather than a shared unconscious.

EVALUATION OF JUNG'S ANALYTICAL PSYCHOLOGY

- **Therapy** –Jung's therapy became increasingly focused on middle-aged clients with high levels of insight, time and money, and with relatively minor problems or just those seeking more meaning in their lives. Lacking objective therapeutic outcomes, it is unclear when full individuation is reached.
- **Contribution to psychology and society** – Jung's ideas have not been as popular as Freud's, perhaps because they were a little more mystical and obscure, and less clearly explained. However some of Jung's ideas influenced humanist psychology and Eysenck used introversion and extraversion as the basis for his personality dimensions.

Key application - of psychodynamic concepts to mental health

FREUD AND THE CAUSES OF MENTAL HEALTH PROBLEMS

A number of Freudian psychoanalytic concepts have been applied to explain the origin of mental disorders:

- **Repression of traumatic events** – traumatic experiences, especially in childhood, may be repressed and become a later source of unconscious anxiety. Freud concluded that neurotics suffer from reminiscences (memories).
  Evidence - research on traumatic events leading to dissociative states like fugue (where people forget their previous life and start a new one) or multiple personality disorder (where a person may have different personalities that are unaware of each other's existence due to amnesic barriers) supports the possibility of repression and its effects.
- **Sublimation into somatic symptoms** – underlying anxiety may be symbolically expressed in physical symptoms as in hysteria. Hysteria, as it was understood in Freud's time was a medical term applied to patients who seemed to be suffering symptoms of disorder to the nervous system (e.g. pain or temporary paralysis or blindness), for which no *physical* neurological cause could be found.
  Evidence - Freud presents numerous case study examples of his patients' hysterical disorders as evidence, e.g. Anna O.
- **Regression** – the disorganised and delusional thinking of schizophrenia may result from a regression to a self absorbed state of 'narcissism' in the early oral stage where the irrational id dominates and there is no well developed ego to make contact with reality. Depression may also result from regression to an early state of dependency due to a loss in later life triggering the emotional effects of a more serious childhood loss.
  Evidence - many studies have supported the idea that early parental loss and childhood trauma are correlated with later mental disorder, but are not able to tell whether repression and regression are the causes.
- **Displacement** – unconscious anxiety may be displaced onto external symbolic objects and situations, resulting in phobias.
  Evidence - Freud regarded the case of Little Hans as good supporting evidence for this.

FREUD AND THE TREATMENT OF MENTAL HEALTH PROBLEMS

Traditional psychoanalytic therapy involves first identifying the unconscious source of disorder (such as the blockage of id impulses or the repression of traumatic experiences) and then trying to relieve the blockage by making the unconscious causes conscious. This is not easy since the patient is not only unaware of what is causing their problems, but will show resistance to the therapist's attempts to interpret them as the ego tries to maintain its defences.

1 **Identifying the problem** - Freud used three methods for un-rooting the unconscious causes of disorder:
- **Free association** - thought associations expressed from the client to the analyst without inhibition could contain clues regarding the source of unconscious anxiety. Pauses in, or drying up of, associations meant unconscious resistance was being met.
- **Dream analysis** - which Freud regarded as the 'royal road' to the unconscious. By unravelling the disguised symbolism of the manifest content of the dream (what was remembered), the latent content (what the dream actually meant) could be revealed.
- **Behaviour interpretation** - Freud believed that both normal (e.g. slips of the tongue) and abnormal behaviour were due to unconscious causes which could be carefully deduced from what people said and did - "He that has eyes to see and ears to hear may convince himself that no mortal can keep a secret. If the lips are silent, he chatters with his finger-tips; betrayal oozes out of him at every pore" (Freud 1901).

2 **Producing improvement** - this is achieved by:
- **Catharsis** – Freud originally thought that discharging the emotion (psychic energy) associated with repressed impulses or traumatic memories brought about improvement, but what seemed more important was that the unconscious conflict was brought out into the open for discussion. This is where transference is important.
- **Transference** - the process whereby unconscious feelings of love and hate are projected onto the analyst. These feelings provide a basis for identifying, accepting and discussing the analyst's interpretation of the problem.
- **Insight** – Freud regarded this as the crucial therapeutic element since it increases ego control over revealed unconscious causes.

JUNG AND THE CAUSES OF MENTAL HEALTH PROBLEMS

Jung generally agreed with Freud's interpretations of hysterical neuroses, but thought his theory of schizophrenia too incomplete. A number of Jung's analytical psychological concepts have also been applied to explain the origin of mental disorders:

- **Individuation and growth** - If a person is not able to proceed in their growth then neurosis will develop. Unlike Freud, Jung believed neurosis was caused by *present rather than past problems*, which only trigger memories of similar troubles from childhood as a result. Neuroses were even sometimes a result of the spirit of the times.
- **Balance** – Mental and behavioural disorder, like dreams and personality traits, are the result of *imbalance* in the psyche. Jung believed excessive introversion might lead to complete withdrawal from reality and schizophrenia, while excessive extraversion may lead to hysteria.
- **Compensation** - Since symptoms are the result of compensation, they can often be regarded as serving a *positive function*, indicating deficiencies and ways in which a more healthy and balanced set of behaviour or attitudes could be achieved in the future. Jung believed that even schizophrenic delusions were attempts of the mind to create new explanations of, or ways of seeing, the world.
- **Archetypes and complexes** - Since the self is not one personality but many, Jung saw the fragmentation of schizophrenic and dissociative disorders such as multiple personality as differing only in extreme (quantitatively not qualitatively) from 'normality' (a term Jung disliked). Problems may result from the imposition of complexes and archetypes, e.g. infatuation with a member of the opposite sex usually involves the projection of the archetypical anima or animus upon them, leading to an exaggerated view of their perfection.

JUNG AND THE TREATMENT OF MENTAL HEALTH PROBLEMS

Jung's therapy was more of a face-to-face (Freud sat out of his client's view, Jung sat opposite them), co-operative and joint process between therapist and client, both seeking answers to the problems. Analysis was less frequent, partly to ensure patients did not lose touch with their everyday lives, and aimed to restore balance and meaning to the client's life. Balance could be restored by bridging the gap between the conscious and unconscious through creative and imaginative activities (such as painting and play) or imaginary dialogues with archetypal figures, and by engaging in activities *opposite* to a dominant attitude (introversion/extraversion) or function (thinking, feeling, intuiting etc.).

'Analysis of a phobia in a five-year-old boy' Freud (1909)

AIM
To present the case study of Little Hans, a young boy who was seen as suffering from anxiety that led to a number of phobias. Freud uses this case study as strong support for his psychoanalytic ideas concerning:
- **Unconscious determinism** - Freud argues that people are not consciously aware of the causes of their behaviour. Little Hans was not consciously aware of the motivations for his behaviour, fantasies, and phobias.
- **Psychosexual development** - Psychoanalytic theory proposes that the sex drive seeks gratification through different erogenous zones at different ages, e.g. oral stage (0-1 years), anal (1-3 years), phallic stage (3-5 or 6 years). Little Hans was currently experiencing the phallic stage, according to Freud, gaining pleasure through masturbation and showing an interest in his own and other people's genitals.
- **The Oedipus complex** - Central to Freud's theory of personality, this occurs during the phallic stage as young boys direct their genital pleasure towards the mother and wish the father dead. However, young boys fear that their illicit desires will be found out by the father who will punish in the worse way possible - castration. Out of castration anxiety, the boy identifies with the father. Little Hans was regarded as a 'little Oedipus' wanting his father out of the way so he could be alone with his mother.
- **The cause of phobias** - Freud believed that phobias were the product of unconscious anxiety displaced onto harmless external objects. Little Hans's unconscious fear of castration by the father was symbolically displaced as a fear of being bitten by white horses.
- **Psychoanalytic therapy** - Aims to treat disturbed thoughts, feelings and behaviour by firstly identifying the unconscious causes of the disturbance, and secondly bringing them 'out into the open' to consciously discuss and resolve them. Thus Little Hans' behaviour was analysed, and its unconscious causes inferred and confronted.

SUMMARY OF THE CASE
Little Hans started showing a particularly lively interest in his 'widdler' and the presence or absence of this organ in others, and his tendency to masturbate brought threats from the mother to cut it off. When he was three and a half, he gained a baby sister, whom he resented, and consequently developed a fear of the bath. Later Hans developed a stronger fear of being bitten by white horses which seemed to be linked to two incidents - overhearing a father say to a child 'don't put your finger to the white horse or it will bite you' and seeing a horse that was pulling a carriage fall down and kick about with its legs. His fear went on to generalise to carts and buses. Little Hans, both before and after the beginning of the phobias, expressed anxiety that his mother would go away and was prone to frequent fantasies including imagining: **a** being the mother of his own children, whom he made to widdle, **b** that his mother had shown him her widdler, **c** that he had taken a smaller crumpled giraffe away from a taller one, **d** that a plumber had placed a borer into his stomach while in the bath on one occasion and had replaced his behind and widdler with larger versions on another occasion, and **e** that he was the father of his own children with his mother as their mother and his father as their grandfather. Having received 'help' from his father and Freud, his disorder and analysis came to an end after this last fantasy.

METHODS OF ANALYSIS
Little Hans was analysed and treated through his father (a firm believer of Freud's ideas) based on the latter's reports of Hans's behaviour and statements. Treatment was achieved by
- inferring the unconscious causes of Hans' behaviour through rich interpretation and decoding of psychoanalytic symbols
- confronting Hans with the unconscious causes by revealing to him his hidden motivations and consciously discussing them

RESULTS OF ANALYSIS

Event	Freudian Interpretation	Conclusion
Anxiety of mother's desertion	Sexual arousal of being taken into mother's bed for comfort	
Fear of bath	Death wish against sister due to jealousy over mother's attention	
Asking why mother did not powder his penis	Seduction attempt	Oedipus complex love for the mother
Taking smaller giraffe from the bigger one	Taking mother away from father	
Fear of heavily loaded carts and buses	Fear of another birth due to jealousy over mother's attention	
Fear of being bitten by white horses	Father (with spectacles and moustache) symbolic of white bus horse (with black blinkers and muzzle), bitten finger symbolic of castration	Fear of castration by father
Fantasy of plumber providing larger widdler	Wanting to be like (identifying with) his father	
Fantasy of being father with his mother	Fulfilment of growing up to have mother while making his father a grandfather instead of killing him	Resolution of Oedipus complex

EVALUATION
Methodological:
Case study method - Advantageous for therapeutic use but also many disadvantages, e.g. generalising results.
Lack of objectivity - Analysis was conducted second hand via the father and all data interpreted in the light of psychoanalytic theory. Freud was aware of objectivity problems and putting words in Little Hans' mouth, but argued 'a psychoanalysis is not an impartial scientific investigation but a therapeutic measure. Its essence is not to prove anything, but to alter something'.

Theoretical: There are many other explanations of Little Hans' behaviour that are more credible, e.g. those of Fromm (castration anxiety from the mother), Bowlby (attachment theory) and learning theory (classical conditioning of phobias).

Links: Freud's theory of socialisation, personality development and abnormality (its causes and treatment).
Links to case study of Thigpen and Cleckley in methodology.

Contemporary issue - Should people undergo traditional psychoanalysis?

The debate over the effectiveness and appropriateness of psychodynamic therapies was first sparked off by criticisms of Freudian Psychoanalysis. Many attacks were made on Freud's underlying psychoanalytic theory and methodology, and this naturally led people to question whether a therapy based on such disputed foundations could be worthwhile. Since Freud developed his therapeutic techniques, many other psychodynamic therapists have developed their own variations of the therapy that often differ in important respects from traditional psychoanalysis, and all should not be tarred with the same brush. It is instructive, however, to look at some of the issues surrounding the debate over just how effective and appropriate Freud's therapy is, since the debate is more complicated than it appears.

WHAT ARE THE AIMS OF PSYCHOANALYSIS?

Aims - The notion of a cure, according to Freud, involves not merely eradicating symptoms but identifying the deeper, underlying unconscious mental causes of disorder and dealing with them as best as possible. However, since Freud regarded all humans as neurotic to some extent his notion of a cure was very modest, to "turn neurotic misery into common unhappiness" by providing the client with more self control - "where id was, there shall ego be" (Freud, 1933).
Freud discovered the unconscious causes of disorder by interpreting the symbolism of his clients' behaviour, dream reports and free associations. The process (cathartic and transference) of revealing the hidden causes of their behaviour and above all the insights Freud provided regarding them provided the relief of anxiety and ego control required to improve their condition.

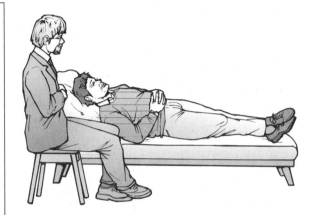

EFFECTIVENESS

Freud's own patients - It has been suggested (e.g. by Webster, 1995) that Breuer and Freud may have misdiagnosed their patients and that many who were supposedly cured through psychoanalysis, including Anna O, continued to show their symptoms after treatment by it. Some patients would have probably been classified as suffering from organic, physical disorders today, such as forms of epilepsy (Anna O), Tourette's Syndrome (Emmy von N, Freud's first hysterical patient treated by psychoanalysis) or even tumours (M-I, who died from a tumour of the stomach, had her stomach pains diagnosed as hysterical by Freud).

Criteria of success and the causes of psychoanalytic effectiveness

This is difficult to assess since psychoanalysis aims to change the unconscious processes that cause disturbed behaviour. However
1   unconscious progress may not always produce immediate observable changes (this affects the criteria and measurement of success)
2   unconscious changes can not be measured and may not be responsible for changes in behaviour.
Lacking an objective goal for therapeutic success, Freud's therapy essentially involved retrieving information about the patient until a cause could be found, but the only way the problem memories could be identified was when talking about them coincided with improvement in the patients symptoms. Freud stated "I accustomed myself to regarding as incomplete any story that brought about no therapeutic improvement". Since psychoanalysis took so long, the symptoms may have spontaneously recovered (disappeared on their own) and the 'story' being recalled at the time could just have been coincidental.

Effectiveness studies

Eysenck (1952) found that psychoanalytic therapy had lower success rates (44%) than alternative psychotherapies (64%) or spontaneous remission (72%). This finding has been hotly disputed, because of its very high spontaneous remission rate (some research suggests 30%) and criteria for success. When the criteria are changed, psychoanalytic success rates improve. A meta-analysis of general therapeutic success rates by Smith and Glass (1977) shows that psychoanalysis is more effective than no therapy at all for most people, but has slightly lower success rates than other therapies. Sloane et al (1975) found psychoanalysis was most effective for clients with less severe problems.

APPROPRIATENESS

Who can benefit? – Rather than asking 'should people undergo psychoanalysis?' a better question might be '*who* should undergo psychoanalysis?' Freud applied psychoanalysis to a range of disorders such as hysteria, phobias and obsessive compulsive disorder (e.g. the 'Rat Man'), yet it seems more appropriate for minor neuroses and anxiety disorders, with more intelligent and articulate clients. Freud himself argued psychotic disorders could not be treated because they lacked insight and the ability to form transference attachments to the therapist (although psychoanalysis with schizophrenics has been attempted in combination with drug therapy). In addition free-association may be inappropriate for obsessive-compulsive patients and transference may encourage further dependency in depressed patients.
What are the costs and benefits? – Psychoanalysis offers a therapy distinct from most other therapies and, using certain criteria, can produce progress and self-reports of improvement (although the latter, as with all therapies, may just reflect the patients' and therapists' justification of the time and effort they have committed). In terms of costs, the need for long-term analysis makes psychoanalysis very expensive and time consuming, although shorter versions have been developed, e.g. Malan's Brief Focal Therapy. Ethically speaking psychoanalytic therapy can be distressing for the patient (some say it can be counter-productive for schizophrenics because of its emotional stress) although it is not the only therapy with negative side effects. In terms of therapist-patient power and control the therapy involves complete trust in the interpretations of the analyst. Because of the concept of unconscious resistance, the therapist may directly or indirectly discourage the patient's right to withdraw from therapy since refusing or leaving therapy could indicate ego defence to progress in uncovering hidden truths.

Attachment in infancy 1

WHAT IS MEANT BY ATTACHMENT?

- An attachment is a strong, long lasting and close emotional bond between two people, which causes distress on separation from the attached individual.
- Psychologists have been particularly interested in the development of first attachments in infancy since they appear to have important consequences for later healthy development, especially concerning later relationships.

HOW DOES ATTACHMENT DEVELOP?

Attachment in infancy occurs gradually over a sequence of phases:

- Pre-attachment phase — 0 - 3 months — Infant preference for humans over other objects is shown by preferential looking and social smiling (before 6 weeks the infant is said to be asocial).
- Indiscriminate attachment phase — 3 - 7 months — Infant can distinguish between people and allows strangers to handle it.
- Discriminate attachment phase — 7 - 9 months — Infant develops specific attachments to certain people and shows distress on separation from them. Avoidance or fear of strangers may be shown.
- Multiple attachment phase — 9 months onward — Infant becomes increasingly independent and forms other bonds despite the stronger prior attachments.

THEORIES OF ATTACHMENT

PSYCHOANALYTIC

- Freud believed that infants become attached to people who satisfy their need for food at the oral stage. Oral gratification causes drive reduction, which is experienced as pleasant.
- While Freud was right that attachment is important for later development, his drive theory and idea that attachment is due to food has not been supported.

COGNITIVE

Schaffer (1971) points out that infants usually form attachments:

- Once they can reliably distinguish one caregiver from another.
- With the caregivers that stimulate and interact with them the most intensely.

LEARNING THEORY

- Learning theory suggests that attachment should occur as parents become associated with pleasant stimuli such as food and comfort via classical conditioning.
- Harlow and Harlow (1969), however, showed that rhesus monkeys had an innate preference to form attachments to surrogate mothers that provide contact comfort rather than food.

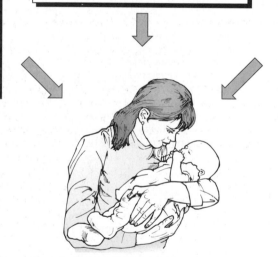

BOWLBY'S ATTACHMENT THEORY

- Bowlby (1951), influenced by ethological studies on imprinting, suggested infants were genetically programmed to form attachments to a single carer (the mother in most cases), within a critical time period (approximately 2 and a half years). Bowlby argued that attachment between infant and caregiver has evolved because it is an adaptive behaviour that aids survival. In particular, attachment provides food, security, a safe base from which to explore the world, exposure to important survival skills shown by the parent and an internal working model of relationships with others. For the parent it ensures a greater likelihood of their offspring surviving (and thus passing on their own genes for attachment formation). Various innate social releasers have also evolved to elicit care giving, such as crying and smiling. If attachments have not been formed by the end of the critical time period then Bowlby suggested that a number of negative effects would result (see deprivation and privation).
- While Bowlby's ideas on attachment were important, research indicates that multiple attachments can be formed, within a sensitive time period (Rutter, 1981). Many researchers have disputed the idea that an internal working model of relationships formed during attachment always influences later relationships and behaviour (see deprivation and privation research).

Attachment in infancy 2

HOW DO WE KNOW AN ATTACHMENT HAS FORMED?

Attachment can be tested via the 'Strange Situation' method developed by Ainsworth et al (1971), where the mother and child are taken to an unfamiliar room and subjected to a range of timed, increasingly stressful (for an attached child) set of scenarios, such as:

1 A stranger is introduced to the child in the presence of the mother.
2 The mother leaves the infant with the stranger.
3 After the mother returns and re-settles the infant, it is left alone.
4 A stranger enters and interacts with the lone infant.
5 Mother returns again and picks up infant.

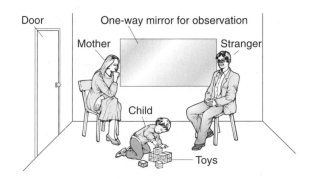

WHAT DIFFERENT KINDS OF ATTACHMENT ARE THERE?

Ainsworth et al (1978) discovered three main types of infant attachment using the Strange Situation, which occurred in various proportions:

Type A - Anxious-avoidant or **detached** (approx. 20% of sample)
The infant ignores the mother, is not affected by her parting or return and although distressed when alone is easily comforted by strangers.

Type B - Securely attached (approx. 70% of sample)
The infant plays contentedly while the mother is there, is distressed by her parting, is relieved on her return and although not adverse to stranger contact treats them differently from the mother.

Type C - Anxious-resistant or ambivalent (approx. 10% of sample)
The infant is discontented while with mother, playing less, is distressed by her parting, is not easily comforted on her return and may resist contact by mother and stranger.

Replicating studies have revealed slightly different proportions.

WHAT CAUSES DIFFERENCES IN ATTACHMENT?

Parental sensitivity - Ainsworth et al (1978) suggested that secure attachment is dependent upon emotionally close and responsive mothering, whereas insecure attachments result from insensitive mothers. Although other factors are involved the effects of maternal sensitivity have been supported.

Infant temperament - Researchers such as Kagan (1982) suggest innate differences in infant temperament and anxiety may cause certain kinds of parental reaction and attachment.

Family circumstances - Attachment type may vary over time and setting with social and cultural environmental conditions, e.g. if a family undergoes stress (Vaughn et al, 1979).

Reliability of classification - Strange Situation methodology has been criticised and other attachment types proposed, e.g. D, insecure-disorganised/disorientated.

CROSS-CULTURAL DIFFERENCES IN ATTACHMENT

Using the Strange Situation method (Ainsworth et al, 1978) cross-cultural studies of differences in attachment types have been conducted. Van Ijzendoorn and Kroonenberg (1988) compared the results of 32 cross-cultural studies and found that there was often more consistency across cultures than within them in terms of variation in attachment. However, while the majority of children in each culture seem to be securely attached, there do seem to be variations in the proportion of avoidant and resistant attachments in certain countries. German infants appear to have a slightly higher proportion of avoidant attachments which Grossman et al (1985) have suggested might result from a cultural tendency for German parents to maintain a large interpersonal distance and wean offspring early from close contact. Some studies of Israeli children raised on kibbutzim have revealed a higher proportion of resistant attachments, e.g. Sagi et al (1985), which may result from the fact that the children have contact with parents but are mainly raised communally in a large group. However, the Strange Situation may be based on American cultural assumptions and therefore be a flawed technique for making cross-cultural comparisons.

Country	Number of studies	Percentage of each type of attachment		
		Secure	Avoidant	Resistant
WEST GERMANY	3	57	35	8
GREAT BRITAIN	1	75	22	3
NETHERLANDS	4	67	26	7
SWEDEN	1	74	22	4
ISRAEL	2	64	7	29
JAPAN	2	68	5	27
CHINA	1	50	25	25
UNITED STATES	18	65	21	14
Overall average		65	21	14

Percentages to nearest whole number reported by Van Ijzendoorn and Kroonenberg (1988).

Deprivation of attachment in infancy

BOWLBY'S MATERNAL DEPRIVATION HYPOTHESIS

Bowlby (1951) proposed that if infants were deprived of their mother (whom he regarded as their major attachment figure), during the critical period of attachment of the first few years of life, then a range of serious and permanent consequences for later development would follow. These included mental subnormality, delinquency, depression, affectionless psychopathy and even dwarfism.

Evidence for:
- Goldfarb (1943) studied children raised in institutions for most of the first three years of their lives, and found they later showed reduced IQ compared to a fostered control group.
- Bowlby (1946) studied 44 juvenile thieves and argued that their affectionless psychopathy was the result of maternal deprivation.
- Spitz and Wolf (1946) investigated infants in South American orphanages and found evidence for severe anaclitic depression in them.
- Harlow and Harlow (1962) researched the effects of social deprivation on rhesus monkeys. Deprived of an attachment figure, they interacted abnormally with other monkeys when they were eventually allowed to mix with them and were unable to form attachments to their own offspring after being artificially inseminated.

Evidence against:
- All the above studies had their methodological flaws, from failing to take into account the amount of environmental stimulation available in institutions, to generalising from animal studies.
- Rutter (1981), in 'Maternal Deprivation Reassessed', a thorough review of research in the area, concluded that Bowlby:
  1 was not correct in his ideas about monotropy (attachment to one figure only) or strict critical periods for attachment.
  2 failed to distinguish between the effects of deprivation (losing an attachment figure) and privation (never having formed an attachment).

POSSIBLE EFFECTS OF DEPRIVATION

SHORT-TERM EFFECTS
- Symptoms of the 'Syndrome of Distress':
  1 Protest – the infant expresses their feelings of anger, fear, frustration, etc.
  2 Despair – the infant then shows apathy and signs of depression, avoiding others.
  3 Detachment – interaction with others resumes, but is superficial and shows no preferences between other people. Re-attachment is resisted.

- Temporary delay in intellectual development.

LONG-TERM EFFECTS
- Symptoms of 'Separation Anxiety':
  1 Increased aggression.
  2 Increased clinging behaviour, possibly developing to the point of refusal to go to school.
  3 Increased detachment.
  4 Psychosomatic disorders (e.g. skin and stomach reactions).

- Increased risk of depression as an adult (usually in reaction to death of an attachment figure).

Evidence

Robertson and Bowlby (1952) based their conclusions regarding the short-term effects of deprivation on observations of the behaviour of children aged between 1 and 4. These children were being hospitalised or placed in residential nurseries. However, the emotional and behavioural effects of the attachment separation may be difficult to distinguish from effects relating to their new environment and situation.

Cockett and Tripp (1994) found more long-term attachment deprivation effects in children from re-ordered families (where parents had divorced and the child now lived away from a parental attachment figure) than those children who lived in intact but discordant (arguing parent) families. However, factors relating, for example, to the disruption of moving house rather than attachment deprivation could also be responsible.

EVALUATION

According to Rutter (1981), there are many sources of individual differences in vulnerability to the short and long-term effects of deprivation, including:

- Characteristics of the child, e.g.
  1 Age – children are especially vulnerable between 7 months and 3 years (Maccoby, 1981).
  2 Gender – boys, on average, respond worse to separation than girls.
  3 Temperament – differences in temperament, like aggressiveness, may become exaggerated.

- Previous mother-child relationship – The infant's reaction to separation may depend upon the type of attachment, e.g. secure, anxious-resistant or anxious-avoidant (Ainsworth et al, 1978).

- Previous separation experience – Infants experienced in short-term stays with (for example) relatives are more resistant to the effects of deprivation (Stacey et al, 1970).

- Attachments to others – Since Schaffer and Emerson (1964) revealed that multiple attachments are possible (in opposition to Bowlby's (1951) ideas), infants who are not deprived of all attachment figures manage the effects better.

- Quality of care – Research has revealed that both the short- and long-term effects of deprivation can be dramatically reduced by high quality care in crèches and institutions respectively.

- Type of separation – Some research has indicated that long-term separation due to death or illness, if accompanied by harmonious social support, has less of a long-term effect than separation due to divorce.

Privation of attachment in infancy

- According to Rutter (1981), the most serious long-term consequences for healthy infant development appear to be due to privation - a lack of some kind - rather than to any type of deprivation/loss. However, in his review of the research, Rutter found that the many proposed adverse effects of privation were **not** always **directly** due to a lack of an emotional attachment bond, but often to a deficiency of other important things that an attachment figure may provide (e.g. food, stimulation or even family unity), but an orphanage or dysfunctional family may not. An extreme example of this is the case of Genie (Curtiss, 1977).

MAJOR CONSEQUENCES OF PRIVATION AND THEIR PRECISE LIKELY CAUSES
Rutter (1981)

Intellectual retardation
Due to a deficiency of stimulation and necessary life experiences.

Developmental dwarfism
Due mainly to nutritional deficiencies in early childhood.

Affectionless psychopathy
Due to failure to develop attachments in infancy.

Anti-social behaviour/delinquency
Due to distorted intra-familial relationships, hostility, discord or lack of affection.

Enuresis
Bed-wetting is mainly associated with stress during the first six years.

MEDIATING FACTORS

Factors likely to affect the severity of privation effects include:

- **Type of childcare available** - orphanages, for example, which provide a high standard of care may reduce the effects of lack of stimulation or stress, but may still have a high turnover of staff that prevents attachments forming with the orphans.
- **The duration of the privation** - the longer the time delay before making an attachment, the greater the chance of failure to form an attachment and thus developing affectionless

psychopathy. Although research unequivocally says that experiences at all ages have an impact it seems likely that the first few years do have a special importance for bond formation and social development.

- **Temperament and resilience of the child** - perhaps most importantly, there has been the repeated finding that many children are not excessively damaged by early privation, and that the effects of it can be reversed.

EVIDENCE FOR THE REVERSIBILITY OF PRIVATION EFFECTS

CASE STUDIES OF EXTREME PRIVATION

Freud and Dann (1951) studied six 3-year-old orphans from a concentration camp who had not been able to form attachment to their parents. These children did not develop affectionless psychopathy, probably because they formed close attachments with each other (rather like the two twins raised in extreme privation studied by Koluchova, 1972), and despite developing a number of emotional problems, their intellectual recovery was unimpaired.

Such extreme case studies clearly involve many sources of privation, not just of attachment figures, but also indicate the strong resilience that children's development can show.

ISOLATED RHESUS MONKEYS

Novak and Harlow (1975) found that rhesus monkeys kept in social isolation from birth could develop reasonably normally if they were given 'therapy' by later being allowed to occasionally play with monkeys of their own age.

However, despite indicating the possibility of recovery from total social isolation, generalising the results from rhesus deprivation studies to human deprivation ignores the large differences between the two species.

ADOPTION STUDIES

Hodges and Tizard (1989) found that institutionalised children (who had not formed a stable attachment), adopted between the ages of two and seven, could form close attachments to their adoptive parents.

However, the children returned to their own families had more problems forming attachments and all the institutionalised children had problems with relationships outside their family.

Kadushin (1976) studied over 90 cases of late adoption, where the children were over five years old, and found highly successful outcomes, indicating that early privation does not necessarily prevent later attachment.

'Social and family relationships of ex-institutional adolescents' Hodges and Tizard (1989)

AIM

To investigate (longitudinally and with a matched comparison group of control children) whether experiencing early institutionalisation with ever-changing care-givers until at least two years of age will lead to long term problems in adolescence for adopted and restored children. Early studies by Bowlby (1951) and Goldfarb (1943a) found that there were many short and long term effects of the early institutionalisation of children, which were attributed to maternal deprivation or privation and were regarded as largely irreversible. However, later studies by Tizard and others on a group of adopted, fostered and restored children with early institutional experience showed that there were markedly less dramatic effects on intellectual and emotional development (probably due to improved conditions) but still difficulties in interpersonal relationships. The children were studied at age 4 and again at age 8, by which time the majority had formed close attachments to their parents, but showed, according to their teachers, more problems of attention seeking behaviour, disobedience, poor peer relationships and over-friendliness. The present study was conducted as a follow up study to see:

- If these children would continue to 'normalise' and lose further effects of early institutionalisation at age 16 or worsen with the stresses of adolescence.
- If adopted children would continue to do better than restored children by age 16, as earlier studies had indicated.

METHOD

Subjects:

All 51 children studied at age 8 were located, of which 42 were available to study at age 16. From these, 39 were interviewed: 23 adopted (17 boys, 6 girls), 11 restored (6 boys, 5 girls) and 5 in institutional care (3 boys, 2 girls). A comparison group of children who had not experienced institutionalisation was gathered for the **family** relationship study, matched, for example, in terms of age, gender, parental occupation and position in the family. Another comparison group of children who had not experienced institutionalisation was formed for the **school** relationship study from the classmate nearest in age of the same sex.

Procedure:

- The adolescents were interviewed on tape and completed the 'Questionnaire of Social Difficulty' (Lindsay and Lindsay, 1982).
- Mothers or careworkers were interviewed on tape and completed the 'A' scale questionnaire (Rutter et al, 1970).
- Teachers were asked to complete the 'B' scale questionnaire (Rutter et al, 1970) on the adolescent's behaviour.

RESULTS

- Institutionalised children differed in their degree of attachment to their parents in that
  - a adopted children were **just as attached** to their parents as the comparison group
  - b restored children were **less attached** to their parents than the comparison group and adopted children.
- Institutionalised children had **more problems** with siblings than the comparison group, especially the restored children.
- Adopted children were **more affectionate** with parents than restored children (who were less affectionate than the comparison group).
- No difference was found in confiding in, and support from, parents between institutionalised children and comparisons, although the former were less likely to turn to peers.
- Institutionalised children showed significantly worse peer relationships, were less likely to have a particular special friend, and were noted by teachers to be more quarrelsome and less liked by, and show more bullying of, other children.

EVALUATION

Methodological:

Longitudinal methods -	Many advantages and disadvantages, e.g. loss of subjects using this method.
Design -	Lack of control over this natural experiment, since children were obviously not randomly assigned to adoptive, restored and control groups, there always remains some doubt over the effect of the children's personality characteristics on the results.
Procedure -	Problems of self-report questionnaires and interviews as far as socially desirable answers or deception is involved on the subject's part, and experimenter expectation on the interviewer's part.
Data analysis -	A thorough statistical analysis was conducted on the results.
Ethical problems -	Of asking children and their guardians questions that might disrupt their interpersonal relationships, e.g. asking mothers if they loved all their children equally.

Theoretical: Implies that while Bowlby was wrong about many of the more dramatic effects of early institutionalisation, some long lasting effects on interpersonal relations do persist into adolescence. Further follow up study needs to be conducted to see if adolescent behaviours and feelings persist into adulthood, however. There are some important practical implications for adoption practices from this study.

Links: Child attachment, longitudinal studies.

The effects of day care

Day care refers to the minding of children by people other than the family they live with, either in their home or outside it, when the family is away during the day. Day care became an issue of concern as increasing levels of external female employment and the reduction of the extended home family in industrialised societies, led to a greater need for outside carers. These factors, combined with Bowlby's research on maternal deprivation and various social / political agendas, have created concern that day care will have:

1 Negative effects on children – although it is now clear that children can form multiple attachments and to carers other than the mother, the concern was that, once the mother went to work, there would be no consistent carer left to provide for the child's attachment and stimulation needs, and that outside carers would not meet these needs in the same way.

2 Negative effects on parents – in particular the sexist pressure of society on women to either stay at home to provide the care and feel frustrated (and possibly resent, and thus negatively affect, their child care) or go to work and feel guilty about the effects it may have.

Overall, research has tended to reveal no significant negative effects of high quality day care. Early studies were a little too simplistic in their approach and the current opinion is that the effects of day care depend upon an interaction of influences.

PARENTAL INFLUENCES
Parents can affect:
- The security of their children's attachment bond through their sensitivity / responsiveness
- The level of stimulation they provide outside of day care
- The quality of day care through their economic status and concern over choices available
- The amount of time away

QUALITY OF DAY CARE
Good-quality day care involves:
- Consistency of care – in terms of prolonged contact with the same carers who are able to devote sufficient time
- Quality of stimulation – in terms of degree of verbal interaction, emotional responsiveness and activity resources.

CHILD INFLUENCES
There are individual differences in how children respond to day care based upon, for example:
- Their prior temperament and sociability, e.g. level of shyness
- Their prior security of attachment
- The age at which they experience day care

RESEARCH METHODOLOGY
Assessment of the emotional, social and cognitive effects of day care depends upon the validity of the tests used to measure them. The Strange Situation method may not be a valid test of emotional effects in some studies since the child could have other (or more important) attachment figures than the mother who are not involved in the test. Also, the reactions day care children show on their mother's return may reflect their increasing independence or enjoyment of day care rather than just their emotional reaction to her. Different studies may use different cognitive and IQ tests of varying reliability and validity.

SOCIAL-EMOTIONAL EFFECTS
- It has been suggested that day care could result in:
  1 The child being unable to form an attachment (causing privation effects) or disruption to the bond if attachment had been already made (causing deprivation effects).
  2 Increased sociability and social skills due to greater exposure to the outside world.
- Belsky and Rovine (1988) found infants were more likely to develop insecure attachments if they received day care for over 20 hours per week before they were a year old, while other research in America has linked greater child care with worse peer relationships and emotional health.
- However, these effects are not inevitable and may ignore the pre-existing attachments and quality of day care.
- Kagan et al (1980) set up their own nursery with consistent and high quality day care and compared 33 infants from a variety of backgrounds who attended it from 3.5 months of age with a matched home care control group. They found no significantly consistent differences between the two groups in attachment and sociability.
- Clarke-Stewart et al (1994) found peer relationships were more advanced in children who had experienced day care.
- Other research indicates that the length of time in day care in itself does not significantly affect attachment and that the individual differences children show to it is more related to the quality and consistency of the day care, maternal sensitivity and the child's pre-existing characteristics.

COGNITIVE EFFECTS
- It has also been suggested that day care could result in:
  1 Less verbal interaction, stimulation and exploration by the child due to a lack of a secure attachment figure as a base, if the day carers encourage quietness and passivity, do not want to form emotional attachments and are often changed.
  2 More stimulation, interaction and educational activities for children who would not otherwise receive them.
- Operation Headstart in the USA in the mid-1960s involved several hundred thousand socially disadvantaged pre-school children receiving intensive day care education. Initial short term gains in school and cognitive performance were found as well as longer term academic and social benefits.
- While the limited duration of the school performance gains in the Headstart programme and those studies that find worse cognitive development if day care takes place before one year of age should not be ignored, it should be noted that the cognitive effects depend upon the quality of day care relative to that the child would otherwise have received.
- Andersson (1992) conducted a longitudinal study on 100 Swedish children and found those who entered day care before the age of one had better school performance at age 8 and 13 than those who did not have any day care (who performed the worst). However, the former did have richer parents. Sweden has very high standards of day care and its greater parental leave allowance probably enables stronger attachments to be made before the child enters day care.

Defining abnormality

STATISTICAL INFREQUENCY

Abnormality can be defined as deviation from the average, where statistically common behaviour is defined as 'normal' while **statistically rare behaviour** is 'abnormal'. Thus autism is sufficiently statistically rare (it occurs in 2 - 4 children per 10,000) to be `abnormal`, as is multiple personality disorder. This does not necessarily mean the behaviour concerned is qualitatively different from 'normal' - many human characteristics are shown by everyone in the population to a certain degree, and if they can be measured every individual can be placed upon a dimensional scale or continuum that will reveal how common their score is in comparison to everybody else's. These comparisons can be standardised by the use of **normal distribution curves**. Many characteristics could be placed upon normal distribution curves as dimensions, such as intelligence. Most people fall somewhere in the middle of these continuums, but if an individual shows an extreme deviation from this average then they may be regarded as abnormal.

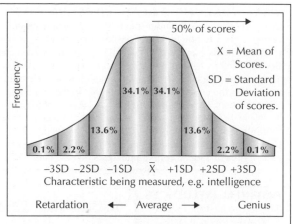

Evaluation

1 There are problems deciding how statistically rare (2 or 3 standard deviations?) behaviour has to be to be considered abnormal.
2 Some currently accepted mental disorders are probably not statistically rare enough to be defined as abnormal, e.g. phobias.
3 Statistical deviation from the average does not tell us about the desirability of the deviation - both mental retardation and genius are statistically rare (at + 3 standard deviations) but only the former is regarded as abnormal.
4 By this definition different subcultures may show behaviour that is statistically rare in the majority culture and be defined as abnormal.

DEVIATION FROM SOCIAL NORMS

Norms are expected ways of behaving in a society according to the majority and those members of a society who do not think and behave like everyone else break these norms and so are often defined as abnormal. The definition is based on the facts that:

1 Abnormal behaviour is seen as vivid and unpredictable, causes observer discomfort and violates moral or ideal standards (Rosenhan and Seligman, 1989) because it differs from most other people's behaviour and standards.
2 Abnormal thinking is delusional, irrational or incomprehensible because it differs from commonly accepted or usual beliefs and ways of thinking.

The deviation from social norm definition of abnormal behaviour is thus a **socially based definition** and is explained by social constructionism and social identity theories. Researchers such as Szasz (1960) have argued that 'abnormality', especially relating to certain mental disorders, is a socially constructed concept that allows people who show different, unusual or disturbing (to the rest of society) behaviour to be labelled and thus treated differently from others – often confined, controlled and persecuted. Social identity theory would argue that people who do not share similar behaviour and beliefs are not included in the 'in-group' (in this case the majority in a society) and are therefore categorised as 'other' (abnormal) and discriminated against.

Evaluation

Since deviation from social norms is a socially based definition, it implies that different societies with different norms will define different behaviours as abnormal and may even disagree over whether the same behaviour is abnormal. This means that an objective definition of abnormal behaviour that is fixed and stable across cultures and time is difficult if not impossible to achieve, and this may lead to unfair and discriminatory treatment of minorities by majorities. Indeed concepts of abnormal behaviour have been shown to differ cross-culturally (a belief in voodoo in one culture may be thought to be paranoia in another) and in the same culture over time (unmarried mothers in Britain and political dissidents in the Soviet Union have been confined to institutions for their 'abnormal' behaviour).

FAILURE TO FUNCTION ADEQUATELY

Maladaptive behaviour, which causes a failure to function adequately in the social and physical environment, seems a more objective way of defining abnormality. Everyone experiences difficulties coping with the world sometimes but if an individual's abnormal behaviour, mood or thinking adversely affects their well being (e.g. ability to maintain employment, a bearable quality of life, normal social relations etc.) then the definition will draw attention to the fact that help is needed. On a more extreme level, if an individual's abnormal behaviour becomes a danger to their own safety (e.g. neglecting self care, self mutilation, suicidal etc.) or the safety of others (e.g. dangerous behaviour) then they may be defined as abnormal and institutionalised ('sectioned' under the Mental Health Act, 1983, for example).

Evaluation

Failure to function adequately may not be recognised (e.g. by those who are in a psychotic state) or cared about (e.g. those with anti-social personality disorder), so the definition may have to be applied by others in society. However difficulties in functioning adequately may be the result of social rejection and 'adequate' functioning is, to some extent, a social judgement which may be based more on threats perceived by the majority in society than actual threats or a genuine concern to help.

DEVIATION FROM IDEAL MENTAL HEALTH

The idea that a single characteristic can be used as the basis of a general definition of abnormality has been rejected by some in favour of a set of criterion characteristics of abnormality or normality. Jahoda (1958) has described several characteristics that mentally healthy people should possess, such as the ability to introspect, integration and balance of personality, self-actualisation, autonomy, ability to cope with stress and see the world as it really is, and environmental mastery.

Evaluation

Unfortunately this criterion approach has also had its problems as a definition, since just how many of these characteristics do you have to lack or possess, and to what degree, to be regarded as normal or abnormal? Jahoda's characteristics of mental health have been regarded as too idealistic, in fact it is 'normal' to fall short of such perfect standards, and humanistic psychologists such as Maslow would argue that very few people actually reach self-actualisation. Not everyone agrees with the ideal characteristics or that all are necessary for mental health, for example other cultures may disagree with the ideals of autonomy and independence, and view other characteristics as more important.

The medical model of abnormality

MEDICAL MODEL ASSUMPTIONS

Also known as the somatic, biological, or physiological approach.

NOTION OF NORMALITY

- Properly functioning physiology and nervous system and no genetic predispositions to inherit mental disorder.

NOTION OF ABNORMALITY

- Like physical illness, **mental illness** has an **underlying physical/bodily cause.**
- **Genetic, organic, or chemical disorders** cause mental illness, which gives rise to behavioural and psychological **symptoms.**
- These symptoms can be classified to **diagnose the psychopathology,** which can then be treated through **therapy** in psychiatric **hospitals** to **cure the patient.**
- Note the use of medical terminology which this approach has borrowed.

ETHICAL IMPLICATIONS

There are both positive and negative ethical implications of the medical model definition of abnormality:

1 Positively for the abnormal individual, the idea that they are mentally 'ill' means that the individual is **not** to be held **responsible** for their predicament - they are more likely to be seen as a **victim** of a disorder that is **beyond their control** and, therefore, they are **in need of care** and **treatment.** The medical model is, therefore, intended to be a more caring and humane approach to abnormality - especially given the blame, stigmatisation, and lack of care for abnormality that had been the norm before the approach.

2 Negatively, the medical model's assumptions have produced many unfavourable ethical consequences.

  a The assumption that abnormal people are mentally ill and, therefore, **not responsible** for their actions can lead to
- the **loss of rights,** such as the right to **consent** to treatment or institutionalisation, and even the right to vote if sectioned under the Mental Health Act.
- the **loss of an internal locus of control,** loss of self-care, and an abdication of responsibility to others.
- the assumption that **directive therapy** is needed for the benefit of the mentally ill individual. The concept of directive therapy may be less debatable with acute schizophrenia, where insight may be totally lacking, but becomes more controversial when we consider the rights of depressed patients to withdraw from electro-convulsive therapy which may prevent their suicide.

  b The assumption that there is always a **biological underlying cause** for mental disorder may be incorrect and, therefore, lead to the **wrong** diagnosis and/or treatment being given.
- There is not always a clearly identifiable underlying biological cause for disorders.
- Many disorders have a large psychological contribution to their cause, such as the learning theory explanations of phobia acquisition.
- Heather (1976) suggests that the basis of defining abnormality is often governed by social and moral considerations rather than biological - thus the inclusion of psychosexual disorders such as paedophilia.

  c The assumption that mentally ill people are **distinctly different** from mentally well people can lead to **labelling** and **prejudice** against those defined as abnormal under the medical model.

PRACTICAL IMPLICATIONS

The use of the medical model to define abnormality as mental illness can lead to:

1 **The use of sectioning** under the Mental Health Act (1983) - the compulsory detention and even treatment of those regarded as mentally ill, if they represent a danger to their own or others' safety. This is based on the medical model assumption that mental illness leads to a loss of self-control and responsibility; but note that a social worker is required to section somebody, in addition to a GP and a psychiatrist (implying that social as well as physical factors need to be taken into account).

Section 2 of the Act can be used to detain people for up to 28 days for observation and assessment of mental illness.
Section 3 of the Act involves the enforced application of treatment and loss of rights.

Power is firmly in the hands of society, since

  a Section 5 of the act can prevent the right of even the nearest relative to withdraw the sectioned individual from care.

  b Section 136 gives the police the right to arrest in a public place anybody deemed to show mental illness to maintain security.

  c Section 139 removes all responsibility for mistaken diagnosis from those involved in sectioning, providing the diagnosis was made in good faith and the legal procedures were carried out correctly.

2 **Institutionalisation** - which can have both positive and negative implications:
- **Positively,** institutionalisation allows the removal to a controlled environment of individuals who may represent a danger to themselves or others. The controlled environment allows the close monitoring, support, and treatment of those suffering from mental illness.
- **Negatively,** institutionalisation may worsen the condition of the patient, providing them with an abnormal environment and causing the internalisation of the passive and dependent role of 'mental inmate'. Rosenhan's study 'On Being Sane in Insane Places' revealed the often negative treatment received in mental institutions.

3 **Biological treatments** - which include the administering of drug treatment, electro-convulsive therapy, or even psychosurgery, all of which have their dangers and side effects as well as the possibility of beneficial effects.

Psychological models of abnormality

THE PSYCHOANALYTIC APPROACH

Notion of normality
Balance between id, ego, and superego. Sufficient ego control to allow the acceptable gratification of id impulses. No inconvenient fixations or repression of traumatic events.

Notion of abnormality
Emotional disturbance or neurosis is caused by thwarted id impulses, unresolved unconscious conflicts (e.g. Oedipus complex), or repressed traumatic events deriving from childhood. Psychological and physical symptoms are expressions of unconscious psychological causes. Conflict and neurosis is always present to some extent - the difference between the 'normal' and 'abnormal' is only quantitative.

ETHICAL IMPLICATIONS
- **Directive therapy** - due to the unconscious cause of psychological problems and the resistance patients put up to unconscious truths, the patient must trust the therapist's interpretation and instructions. However, psychoanalysis does occur under voluntary conditions.
- **Anxiety provoking** - psychoanalysis can reveal disturbing repressed experiences.
- **Humane** - psychoanalysts do not blame or judge the patient, who is not responsible for their problems.

PRACTICAL IMPLICATIONS
- **Expensive** - Freud argued you do not value what you do not pay for.
- **Long term** - several sessions a week for many months are usually required, although Mallan's Brief Focal Therapy is faster.
- **No institutionalisation** required.
- **Low success rates** - with many disorders, e.g. psychoses.

THE BEHAVIOURAL APPROACH
(Also known as the behaviourist or learning theory approach)

Notion of normality
A learning history that has provided an adequately large selection of adaptive responses.

Notion of abnormality
Maladaptive responses have been learnt or adaptive ones have not been learnt. Observable, behavioural disorder is all abnormality consists of. Abnormal behaviour is not a symptom of any underlying cause.

ETHICAL IMPLICATIONS
- **Directive therapy** - due to the environmental determinism of behavioural problems, patients need to be re-programmed with adaptive behaviour.
- **Stressful** - behaviour therapy can be painful and disturbing, e.g. flooding and aversion therapy.
- **Humane** - specific maladaptive behaviours are targeted, the whole person is not labelled.

PRACTICAL IMPLICATIONS
- **Relatively cheap** - due to the fairly quick nature of treatments.
- **High success rates** - with certain disorders.
- **Institutionalisation** - may be required to ensure environmental control with certain treatments, e.g. selective reinforcement for anorexia.

THE COGNITIVE APPROACH

Notion of normality
Properly functioning and rational cognitive thought processes that can be used to accurately perceive the world and control behaviour.

Notion of abnormality
Unrealistic, distorted, or irrational understanding and thoughts about the self, others, or the environment. Difficulty in controlling thought processes or using them to control actions.

ETHICAL IMPLICATIONS
- **Semi-directive therapy** - due to the client's problems controlling their thoughts, external aid has to be provided by the therapist, although this will vary in its directiveness depending on how forceful the persuasive techniques used by the therapist are.
- **Stressful** - rational emotive therapy can be disturbing although most cognitive therapy is humane.

PRACTICAL IMPLICATIONS
- **Relatively cheap** - depending on length of therapy.
- **Fairly high success rates** - with certain disorders and when combined with behavioural therapies.
- **No institutionalisation** is usually necessary.

THE HUMANISTIC APPROACH
(Also known as the phenomenological or existential approach)

Notion of normality
Positive self regard, ability to self actualise, healthy interpersonal relationships, and responsibility and control over life.

Notion of abnormality
It is wrong to talk of abnormality, since everyone is unique and experiences 'problems with living' occasionally. These problems stem from interpersonal relationships (which prevent healthy interpersonal relationships) and thwarting environmental circumstances (which prevent self actualisation). The client should not be labelled or directed.

ETHICAL IMPLICATIONS
- **Non-directive therapy** - clients have free will and, therefore, the responsibility and capability to change their thoughts and behaviour (with insightful help).
- **Humane** - the happiness of the client is of most importance. The client is given unconditional positive regard.
- **Non-labelling** - humanist therapists believe labelling is counter-productive and irrelevant, since each person is a unique individual.

PRACTICAL IMPLICATIONS
- **Fairly expensive** - based on length of therapy required.
- **No institutionalisation** - is completely since treatment is completely voluntary.
- **Low success rates** - with many disorders, e.g. psychoses. Better success with 'problems with living' in interpersonal areas.

'On being sane in insane places' Rosenhan (1973)

AIM

To illustrate experimentally the problems involved in determining normality and abnormality, in particular
* the poor reliability of the diagnostic classification system for mental disorder at the time (as well as general doubts over its validity)
* the negative consequences of being diagnosed as abnormal and the effects of institutionalisation

METHOD

Subjects: Eight sane people (3 women and 5 men from a small variety of occupational backgrounds), using only fake names and occupations, sought admission to a range of twelve hospitals (varying in age, resources, staff-patient ratios, degree of research conducted, etc.).

Procedure: Each pseudo-patient arranged an appointment at the hospital and complained that he or she had been hearing voices. The voices were unclear, unfamiliar, of the same sex and said single words like 'empty', 'hollow', and 'thud'. Apart from the aforementioned falsifying of name and occupation and this single symptom, the pseudo-patients did not change any aspect of their behaviour, personal history or circumstances. On admission to the hospital ward, every pseudo-patient immediately stopped simulating any symptoms and responded normally to all instructions (except they did not swallow medication) and said they were fine and experiencing no more symptoms. Their tasks were then to
* seek release by convincing the staff that they were sane (all but one pseudo-patient were very motivated to do this)
* observe and record the experience of the institutionalised mentally disordered patient (done covertly at first, although this was unnecessary)

RESULTS

Admission: Pseudo-patients were admitted to every hospital, in all cases except one with a diagnosis of schizophrenia, and their sanity was never detected by staff - only by other patients (35 out of 118 of whom voiced their suspicions in the first three hospitalisations). To check the poor reliability of diagnosis, and to see if the insane could be distinguished from the sane, a later study was conducted where a teaching hospital (who had been informed of Rosenhan's study) was told to expect pseudo-patients over a three month period. During that time 193 patients were rated for how likely they were to be pseudo-patients - 41 patients were suspected of being fakes, 19 of which were suspected by both a psychiatrist and one other staff member, even though no pseudo-patients were sent during that time.

Release: Length of stay ranged from 7 to 52 days, with an average of 19 days. All except one were released with a diagnosis of 'schizophrenia in remission', supporting the view that they had never been detected as sane.

Observation results:
* **Lack of monitoring** - very little contact with doctors was experienced, and a strong sense of segregation between staff and patients was noted.
* **Distortion of behaviour** - all (normal) behaviour became interpreted in the light of the 'label' of 'schizophrenia', for example:
  a A normal case history - became distorted to emphasise the ambivalence and emotional instability thought to be shown by schizophrenics.
  b Note taking - pseudo-patients were never asked why they were taking notes, but it was recorded by nurses as 'patient engages in writing behaviour', implying that it was a symptom of their disorder.
  c Pacing the corridors out of boredom - was seen as nervousness, again implying that it was a symptom of their disorder.
  d Waiting outside the cafeteria before lunch time - was interpreted as showing the 'oral-acquisitive nature of the syndrome' by a psychiatrist.

* **Lack of normal interaction** - for example, pseudo-patients courteously asked a staff member 'Pardon me, Mr (or Dr or Mrs) X, could you tell me when I will be presented at the staff meeting?' or 'When am I likely to be discharged?'. They found mostly a brief, not always relevant, answer was given, on the move, without even a normal turn of the head or eye-contact (psychiatrists moved on with their head averted 71% of the time and only stopped and talked normally on 4% of occasions).
* **Powerlessness and depersonalisation** - was produced in the institution through the lack of rights, constructive activity, choice, and privacy, plus frequent verbal and even physical abuse from the attendants.

EVALUATION

Methodological:

Lack of control groups - Only the experimental condition was conducted.

Data analysis - Was mostly qualitative rather than quantitative.

Ethical problems - The study involved deception, but it might be argued that the hospitals had the power not to be deceived and were in fact being tested in their jobs. In addition, the study's ends (its valuable contribution) outweighed its slightly unethical means, and kept data confidentiality.

Theoretical: Despite the fact that 'schizophrenia in remission' is an unusual diagnosis according to Spitzer (1976), the study is widely held to have fulfilled its aim of showing the deficiencies of the classification system for mental disorder at the time (the DSM II) and the negative consequences of being labelled and institutionalised for mental disorder. Studies like these led to pressure to revise and improve the accuracy of the classification systems.

Links: Problems with the diagnosis and classification of mental disorders. Stereotyping.

Eating disorders - symptoms and diagnosis

BACKGROUND
Eating disorders like anorexia and bulimia are fairly recent arrivals to the classification manuals - appearing for the first time in the DSM III in 1980. There is debate over whether these disorders have always existed, but what is certain is that they have increased in prevalence in recent years. This could be due to increasing media publicity drawing attention to the disorder and thus making referral and diagnosis more common, or due to the media actually influencing the increase in the frequency of the disorder (see theories). These disorders are ten times more common in women than men and often occur together in the same individual.

ANOREXIA NERVOSA
DIAGNOSIS: 'Anorexia' comes from the Greek term for 'loss of appetite' and involves problems maintaining a normal body weight. The DSM IV states that the four symptoms below must be shown for the classification to be made.
The DSM IV also suggests two sub-types:
The 'restricting type' maintains low body weight by refusing to eat and/or indulging in frequent exercise.
The 'binge-eating/purging type' maintains low body weight by refusing to eat in combination with bingeing and purging (like bulimia below but usually less frequently)
PREVALENCE - 0.5 - 1% of females in adolescence to early adulthood.

BEHAVIOURAL SYMPTOMS
1 A refusal to maintain a body weight normal for age and height (weight itself is less than 85% of that expected).

COGNITIVE SYMPTOMS
2 Distorted self-perception of body shape (over-estimation of body size) and over-emphasis of its importance for self-esteem. Denial of seriousness of weight loss.

EMOTIONAL SYMPTOMS
3 An intense fear of gaining weight even though obviously under-weight.

SOMATIC SYMPTOMS
4 Loss of body weight and absence of menstruation for 3 consecutive months.

BULIMIA NERVOSA

DIAGNOSIS: 'Bulimia' is derived from the Greek for 'ox appetite' and involves binge eating followed by compensatory behaviour to rid the body of what has just been consumed.
The DSM IV states that the symptoms opposite must be shown for the classification to be made, and includes a 'non-purging' subtype who binges but uses excessive physical exercise instead of purging to compensate.
PREVALENCE - Around 1 - 3% of females in adolescence to early adulthood.

BEHAVIOURAL SYMPTOMS
1 Recurring binge eating - excessive quantities consumed within a discrete period of time (e.g. 2 hours) without a sense of control over what or how much is consumed.
2 Recurring inappropriate compensatory behaviour to prevent weight gain - such as self-induced vomiting, misuse of laxatives or fasting.
3 Binge eating and compensatory behaviours occur on average at least twice a week for three months.

COGNITIVE SYMPTOMS
4 Self-image is overly influenced by body size and shape.

HOW SIMILAR ARE THE TWO DISORDERS?
• The main differences are that bulimia sufferers usually maintain their weight within the normal range (although bulimia causes much other damage to their bodies) and, despite some anorexia sufferers being obsessed with food and reporting hunger, bulimia involves an urge to overeat that often causes bingeing long before purging and other methods are used as compensations.
• However, some researchers think anorexia and bulimia should be thought of as two variants of the same disorder, since they have many features in common, are often both found in the same person (anorexia can progress to bulimia with age), and have similar theories provided to explain them.

Explanatory theories of eating disorders

BIOLOGICAL THEORIES

PSYCHOLOGICAL THEORIES

Genetics

Family studies have shown that there is a higher risk of developing anorexia or bulimia if a first-degree relative suffers from it, while monozygotic (MZ) twin concordance studies have suggested there may be a stronger genetic link with anorexia than bulimia.

Holland et al (1984) found the likelihood of one identical (MZ) twin also getting anorexia if the other developed it was 55%, compared to 7% for non-identical, dizygotic (DZ) twins.

Kendler et al (1991) reported concordance rates of 23% for MZ twins and 8.7% for DZ twins with bulimia however.

Physiology

Early research indicated that disruption to the ventromedial or lateral areas of the hypothalamus could severely affect eating behaviour - ablating the ventromedial hypothalamus in rats for example caused them to overeat until they became obese, while removal of the lateral hypothalamus caused them to refuse to eat. Set Point Theory suggests an imbalance in the relative influences of these areas of the hypothalamus may be involved in eating disorders.

Eating disorders have been linked to depression and some studies have found lower levels of the neurotransmitter serotonin in sufferers of bulimia. The neurotransmitter noradrenaline and the hormone CCK-8 may also be involved.

Evaluation

Some twin studies have not always controlled for the effect of similar shared environments (e.g. by using adoption studies) or have found more environmental than genetic influences in eating disorders. Since concordance rates are nowhere near 100% for MZ twins, environmental triggers do seem to be involved. It is also uncertain what is actually inherited to cause the eating disorder, some researchers suggest personality traits such as perfectionism, others a predisposition to inherit mental disorder in general.

The biological cause and effect of eating disorders is difficult to determine since the physical disorders found in anorexia and bulimia may be an effect of starvation and purging rather than a cause. Post mortem studies have not revealed damage in the hypothalamus of those with eating disorders, however anti-depressants that increase serotonin levels are also effective in treating bulimia.

Psychoanalytic theory

Psychoanalytic theory has produced various explanations for eating disorders.

The anorexic's refusal to eat has been interpreted as an unconscious denial of the adult role and wish to remain a child (in figure at least) provoked by the development of sexual characteristics in puberty. The timing of onset in anorexia and the loss of menstruation support this idea.

Another psychoanalytic interpretation is that anorexics are unconsciously rejecting their bodies as a reaction to sexual abuse in childhood.

Cognitive theory

Cognitive psychologists have suggested that irrational attitudes and beliefs, and distorted perception are involved in eating disorders. These beliefs may concern unrealistic ideals or perception of body shape, or irrational attitudes towards eating habits and dieting (e.g. the disinhibition hypothesis – once a diet has been broken, one might as well break it completely by bingeing).

Cognitive researchers have also proposed that sufferers of anorexia and bulimia may be seeking to assert control over their lives to an excessively idealistic extent - Dura and Bornstein (1989) found this drive for perfection in hospitalised anorexics extended to academic achievements which were at a much higher level than their IQ scores would predict.

Learning theory

Learning theory explains eating disorders in terms of reinforcement consequences for eating behaviour.

Social praise or respect from a society that places a high value on slim female appearance may reward weight loss or control. Alternatively, the attention and concern shown towards someone with an eating disorder may be reinforcing. Social learning theory would suggest that thin or dieting role models would be imitated, while some learning theorists have proposed that a weight gain phobia is involved in eating disorders.

Evaluation:

Psychological level theories gain more strength when integrated with the following, social, cultural and family research findings.

The idea that cultural exposure to socially desirable conceptions of body shape is responsible for eating disorders has received much support. For example, anorexia and bulimia occur most in:

- Cultures where thinness is socially desirable, e.g. North America, Western Europe and Japan. Indeed evidence suggests that immigrants to these countries show higher levels of eating disorder than their native countries.
- Western women - physical attractiveness is the best predictor of self-esteem in western girls.
- Groups where thinness is particularly valued, e.g. ballet dancers, models and gymnasts.

Many researchers have found that the families of children with eating disorders show the following characteristics:

- Less emotional and nurturing - this may lead to eating disorders developing as an attention-gaining tactic.
- Overly protective - restricting independence may force the child to assert its own control and autonomy through the eating disorder.
- Middle class, overachieving parents - whose high expectations of success may lead to overly idealistic notions of success in matters of weight control.

However, although anorexics may develop their symptoms at puberty and may have been sexually abused in some cases, the effects of these events are often more convincingly explained in non-psychoanalytic terms. While cultural and family experiences do seem correlated with eating disorders, it is difficult to always work out the cause and effect and not all people will react in the same way to these experiences - some under-eat, others over-eat.

'A case of multiple personality' Thigpen and Cleckley (1954)

AIM

To describe the case study of a 25-year-old married woman referred to two psychiatrists for severe headaches and blackouts, but soon discovered to have a multiple personality. The article presents evidence for the existence of this previously rare condition in the subject, in a cautious but convinced manner.

SUMMARY OF THE CASE

The first few interviews with the woman, Eve White, only found her to have 'several important emotional difficulties' and a 'set of marital conflicts and personal frustrations'. The first indication of multiple personality was when the psychiatrists received a letter from Eve that she did not remember sending and which contained a note at the end written in a different and childish handwriting. On her next visit, after a period of unusual agitation, she reported that she occasionally had the impression that she heard a voice in her head - and then suddenly and spontaneously showed a dramatic change in her behaviour, revealing the character (and answering to the name) of Eve Black.

Over a period of 14 months and around 100 hours of interview time, the two psychiatrists investigated the two Eves, first using hypnosis, but later without the need for it. Eve White was found not to have access to the awareness and memories of Eve Black (experiencing blackouts when Eve Black took over control) although the reverse was true for Eve Black (who often used the ability to disrupt Eve White's life by taking over and getting her into trouble or by giving her headaches).

Later during the course of therapy, a third personality emerged called Jane - again suddenly and with a different set of characteristics. Jane had access to the consciousness of both Eves, but incomplete access to their memories before her emergence, and could only emerge through Eve White.

The authors admit the possibility of fakery, although they think it highly unlikely, and argue for more research to answer some fundamental questions concerning the multiple personality phenomena.

EVIDENCE FOR THE EXISTENCE OF MULTIPLE PERSONALITY

Personality distinctions gained through interview:

• Character - Eve White - self-controlled, serious, matter of fact, and meticulously truthful.
  Eve Black - childish, carefree, shallow, mischievous, and a fluent liar.
• Attitudes - Eve White - distressed about failing marriage, warm love for daughter.
  Eve Black - thought Eve White's distress and love was silly, seemed 'immune to major affective events in human relationships'.
• Behaviour - Eve White - responsible and reserved.
  Eve Black - irresponsible, pleasure and excitement seeking, sought the company of strangers to avoid discovery.
• Mannerisms - 'A thousand minute alterations in manner, gesture, expression, posture, of nuances in reflex... of glance' between the two Eves.

Personality distinctions gained through independent psychological testing:

• Psychometric tests - IQ of Eve White was 110, IQ of Eve Black was 104, differences between the two were found in memory function.
• Projective testing - Rorschach revealed
  a Eve Black to show regression and hysterical tendencies, but to be far healthier than Eve White.

b Eve White to show repression, anxiety, obsessive-compulsive traits, and an inability to deal with her hostility. The psychologist was of the opinion that the tests revealed one personality at two stages of life - that Eve Black represented a regression to a carefree state, as a way of dealing with her dislike of marriage and maternal pressures.

Personality distinctions gained through physiological EEG testing:

Eve White and Jane were found to show similar Electroencephalograph readings, with Eve Black definitely distinguishable from the other two.

Evidence for multiple personality as a distinct and valid disorder:

• Clearly distinguishable from other disorders, such as schizophrenia, but with some similarities to disorders like dissociative fugue.
• Eve's behaviour showed such remarkable consistency within characters that two psychiatrists were persuaded she was not deliberately faking.
• Shows similarities of symptoms with other multiple personality cases such as patterns of amnesia between personalities and similar causal circumstances that provoke a denial of parts of the self.

EVALUATION

Methodological:

Case study method - Lack of objectivity when involved with the patient, especially when trying to help through therapy, rather than attempting rigorous experiments to test the possibility of fakery.

Unreliability of testing - Those tests that were conducted were of doubtful validity, because they could have been affected by deliberate attempts to fake (except perhaps the EEG test, although what the differences found represented is open to interpretation) and projective tests are also of doubtful reliability due to the subjective nature of their interpretation.

Theoretical: Doubts about the validity of this study are caused by Chris Sizeman (the real name of Eve) later revealing that she had other personalities before (and after) 1954, yet these were not detected or mentioned at the time. Doubts about the validity of multiple personality disorder in general are caused by the fact that they are often investigated through hypnosis and are becoming increasingly common in America but not other countries. There are ethical and legal implications involved in accepting multiple personality as a valid disorder, e.g. culpability.

Links: Abnormality (particularly problems in diagnosing), personality, freewill, case studies, hypnosis.

Variables

VARIABLES

A variable is any object, quality or event that changes or varies in some way. Examples include: aggression, intelligence, time, height, amount of alcohol, driving ability, attraction.

OPERATIONALISATION

Many of the variables that psychologists are interested in are **abstract concepts,** such as aggression or intelligence. Operationalisation refers to the process of making variables physically measurable or testable. This is done in psychology by recording some aspect of **observable behaviour** that is assumed to be indicative of the variable under consideration. For example:
Aggression - a psychologist may record the number of punches thrown.
Intelligence - a psychologist may record the number of puzzles solved in an hour, or calculate the score on an IQ test.

Reification (regarding hypothetical variables like intelligence as having a real physical existence) is a danger, however.

INVESTIGATING VARIABLES

OBSERVATIONS, CASE STUDIES, SURVEYS, ETC.

In these methods variables are precisely measured in varying amounts of detail.

CORRELATIONS

Variables are measured and compared to see how they co-vary with each other (what relationship they have together).

EXPERIMENTS

One variable (the **independent variable**) is **altered** to see what **effect** it has on another variable (the **dependent variable**).
The independent variable is the variable that is manipulated in two or more conditions to see what effect it has on the dependent variable.
The dependent variable is the main measured outcome of the experiment, hopefully due to the manipulation of the independent variable.
For example, the independent variable (IV) of alcohol could be manipulated to see what effect it had on the dependent variable (DV) of driving ability by testing in two conditions, one with no alcohol and the other with four pints of lager. However, many **extraneous variables** (other variables that could potentially influence the dependent variable apart from the independent variable), could spoil the experiment and so **controls** are employed to prevent extraneous variables from becoming confounding variables (those that actually affect the dependent variable strongly enough to distort the effect of the independent variable). Extraneous variables can be either **random** (unsystematic variables that can affect the dependent variable but should not affect one condition more than another) or **constant** (those that have a systematic effect on one condition more than another). While random errors will reduce the accuracy of the results, only constant errors usually truly confound the experimental results.

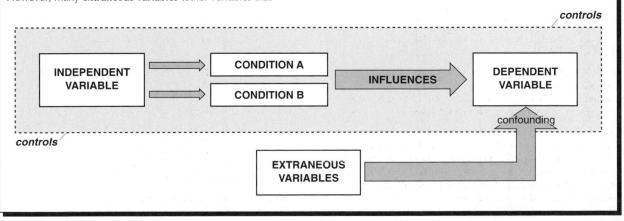

Hypotheses

HOW DO PSYCHOLOGISTS MAKE THEIR PREDICTIONS?

HYPOTHESES are *precise, testable statements*

THEY SHOULD BE

THEY CAN BE

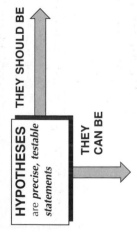

BOLD

2-tailed hypotheses simply predict an effect, such as a difference or correlation.

1-tailed hypotheses predict a particular direction in the effect, e.g. that one condition will do better than another, or that a positive correlation will occur.

PRECISE

Precise hypotheses should contain fully **operationalised variables** and the words 'statistically significant' if inferential statistics are to be conducted on the results.

REFUTABLE

To be scientific every hypothesis should be capable of being **shown to be wrong**. For this reason a **null hypothesis** is proposed that states that there will be **no significant effect** (either difference or correlation). Sometimes, however, it is the null hypothesis which researchers wish to study.

EXPERIMENTAL HYPOTHESES

Predict significant differences in the dependent variable [DV] between the various conditions of the independent variable [IV].

BOLD

2 - tailed
There will be a significant **difference in** [the DV] **between** [condition A of the IV] **and** [condition B of the IV].

1 - tailed
There will be a significant **increase in** [the DV] **in** [condition A of the IV] **compared to** [condition B of the IV].
or
There will be a significant **decrease in** [the DV] **in** [condition A of the IV] **compared to** [condition B of the IV].

PRECISE

2 - tailed example
There will be a **statistically significant** difference in **I.Q. scores** between **male subjects** and **female subjects**.

1 - tailed examples
There will be a **statistically significant** increase in **I.Q. scores in male subjects compared to female subjects**.
or
There will be a **statistically significant** decrease in **I.Q. scores in male subjects** compared to **female subjects**.

REFUTABLE

2 - tailed example
There will be **no** statistically significant difference in I.Q. scores between male subjects and female subjects.

1 - tailed examples
There will be **no** statistically significant increase in I.Q. scores in male subjects compared to female subjects.
or
There will be **no** statistically significant increase in I.Q. scores in female subjects compared to male subjects.

CORRELATIONAL HYPOTHESES

Predict significant patterns of relationship between two or more variables.

BOLD

2 - tailed
There will be a significant **correlation between** [variable 1] and [variable 2].

1 - tailed
There will be a significant **positive correlation between** [variable 1] and [variable 2].
or
There will be a significant **negative correlation between** [variable 1] and [variable 2].

PRECISE

2 - tailed example
There will be a **statistically significant** correlation between **hours of psychology revision conducted** and **A level grade gained in psychology.**

1 - tailed example
There will be a **statistically significant** positive correlation between **hours of psychology revision conducted** and **A level grade gained in psychology.**

REFUTABLE

2 - tailed example
There will be **no** statistically significant correlation between hours of psychology revision conducted and A level grade gained in psychology.

1 - tailed example
There will be **no** statistically significant positive correlation between hours of psychology revision conducted and A level grade gained in psychology.

Experimental methods

HOW DO PSYCHOLOGISTS INVESTIGATE THEIR HYPOTHESES?

EXPERIMENTS

An experiment involves the **manipulation of the independent variable** to see what effect it has on the dependent variable, while attempting to **control** the influence of all other **extraneous variables**.

TYPES

LABORATORY

The researcher **deliberately manipulates** the independent variable while maintaining **strict control** over extraneous variables through standardised procedures in a controlled environment.

FIELD

The researcher **deliberately manipulates** the independent variable, but does so in the subject's own **natural environment**.

NATURAL/QUASI

The independent variable is **changed by natural occurrence**; the researcher just records the effect on the dependent variable. Quasi experiments are any where control is lacking over the IV.

EXAMPLES

BANDURA ET AL (1961)

Bandura manipulated the independent variable of 'exposure to aggression' to see what effect it had on the dependent variable of 'imitation of aggression in children' under controlled laboratory conditions by randomly allocating children to either a condition where they saw
* an adult being violent towards a Bobo doll, or
* an adult showing no violence.

The number of aggressive acts shown by each child was later also measured in the laboratory.

FESHBACH AND SINGER (1971)

Feshbach and Singer manipulated the independent variable of 'exposure to aggression' to see what effect it had on the dependent variable of 'imitation of aggression' in children' by showing boys in a residential school either
* aggressive television or
* non-aggressive television.

This field study was conducted over 6 weeks, during which the boys' aggression was rated.

JOY ET AL (1977)

Joy et al investigated the independent variable of 'exposure to aggression' to see what effect it had on the dependent variable of 'imitation of aggression in children' by measuring levels of aggression in children of a small Canadian town
* before television was introduced to the town, and
* after television was introduced to the town.

STRENGTHS

The most scientific method because the
* manipulation of the independent variable indicates **cause and effect**.
* laboratory **increases control** and accurate measurement of variables thus more **objectivity**.
* laboratory standardisation means greater ability to replicate (repeat again) the study.

* Has **greater ecological validity** than laboratory experiments, since behaviour occurs in its own natural environment.
* **Less bias** from sampling (subjects do not have to be brought into the laboratory) and demand characteristics (if subjects are unaware of being tested).

* Has **great ecological validity**, since a 'natural' change (not induced directly by the experimenter) occurs in a natural environment.
* **Very little bias** from sampling or demand characteristics (if subjects are unaware of being observed by experimenters).

WEAKNESSES

* **Total control** over all variables is **not possible.**
* **Artificial** laboratory conditions may produce unnatural behaviour that **lacks ecological validity** (results do not generalise to real life).
* Results more likely to be **biased** by sampling, demand characteristics, experimenter expectancy.
* May raise ethical problems of deception, etc.

* **More bias** likely from extraneous variables, due to **greater difficulty of controlling** all aspects of experiment outside the laboratory.
* More **difficult to replicate** exactly.
* More **difficult to record data** accurately.
* **Ethical problems** of consent, deception, invasion of privacy, etc.

* **Hard to infer cause and effect** due to **little control** over extraneous variables and no direct manipulation of the independent variable.
* **Virtually impossible to replicate** exactly.
* Bias if subjects are aware of being studied.
* **Ethical problems** of consent, deception, invasion of privacy, etc.

Non-experimental methods 1. Observation

OBSERVATIONS

Observations involve the precise measurement of naturally occurring behaviour in an objective way.

NATURALISTIC

TYPES

Naturalistic observations involve the recording of spontaneously occurring behaviour in the subject's own natural environment.

EXAMPLES

- Fagot's (1973) naturalistic observation of parent-child interaction in gender socialisation in the home.
- Sylva et al's (1980) naturalistic observation of types of play in children's playgroups.
- Ethological observations of animal behaviour in the animal's natural habitat.

STRENGTHS

- **High ecological validity** (realism) of observed behaviour if observer is hidden.
- Can be used to **generate ideas** for or **validate findings** from experimental studies.
- Sometimes the only ethical or practical method.

WEAKNESSES

- **Cannot legitimately infer cause and effect** relationships between variables that are only observed but not manipulated.
- **Lack of control** over conditions makes **replication** more difficult.
- **Ethical problems** of invasion of privacy.

CONTROLLED

Controlled observation involves the recording of spontaneously occurring behaviour, but under conditions contrived by the researcher (e.g. in the laboratory).

- Sleep studies - laboratory equipment is needed to record eye movements and changes in brain activity as subjects naturally fall to sleep.
- Parent-child interaction - observed through one way mirrors.
- Human sexual response, e.g. Masters and Johnson's work.

- **More control** over environment which leads to **more accurate** observations.
- Greater control leads to **easier replication**.
- Usually avoids ethical problems of consent, unless research purpose and observer are hidden.

- **Participant reactivity** may distort the data if subject is aware of being observed, e.g. abnormal sleep patterns in unnatural laboratory conditions.
- **Lower ecological validity** than naturalistic observations, can cause demand characteristics.
- Cause and effect can not be inferred.

PARTICIPANT

Participant observations involve the researcher becoming involved in the everyday life of the subjects, either with or without their knowledge.

- Rosenhan (1973) used eight 'normal' undisclosed participant observers to gain admittance to psychiatric hospitals through faking symptoms and then record their experiences of being a psychiatric inpatient.
- Whyte's (1955) participant observation of Italian gang behaviour in the USA.

- Very **high ecological validity** if participant undisclosed, less if disclosed depending upon level of integration with subjects.
- Extremely **detailed** and **in depth knowledge** available, not gained from any other method.

- **Difficult** to record data promptly and **objectively**, and impossible to **replicate** exactly.
- Participant's behaviour may **influence subjects**.
- **Ethical problems** of deception with undisclosed participants.
- Cause and effect can not be inferred.

Data recording techniques

TECHNIQUE	ADVANTAGES	DISADVANTAGES
BEHAVIOUR SAMPLING METHODS		
• **Event sampling.** Key behavioural events are recorded every time they occur.	Limits the behaviours observed, thus reducing the chance that the behaviour of interest will be missed.	It is difficult to observe all incidents of key behaviour over large areas. Other important behaviour may be ignored.
• **Time sampling.** Behaviour is observed for discrete periods of time.	Reduces the amount of time spent in observation and thus may increase accuracy.	Behaviour may be missed if random time samples are not taken across the day.
• **Point sampling.** The behaviour of just one individual in a group at a time is recorded.	Increases the accuracy of observation and number of behaviours that can be recorded.	May miss behaviour in others that is important for an understanding of the individual.
DATA RECORDING TECHNIQUES		
• **Frequency grids.** Nominal data is scored as a tally chart for a variety of behaviours.	Quick and easy to use and can record a larger number of behaviours at a time.	Nominal data provides little information, e.g. it cannot say how long or intensely a behaviour was shown.
• **Rating scales.** Scores ordinal level data for a behaviour, indicating the degree to which it is shown.	Provides more information on the behaviour.	Rating using opinion rather than fixed scales, such as timing, introduces subjectivity.
• **Timing behaviour.**	High accuracy of data.	Loss of descriptive detail of behaviour.
DATA RECORDING EQUIPMENT		
• **Hand-written** notes or coding systems.	Less intimidating than more mechanical methods of recording.	Data may be missed or subjectively recorded.
• **Audio-tape** recording.	Accurately records all spoken data for later leisurely and accurate analysis.	Omits important gestures and non-verbal communication accompanying speech.
• **Video.**	Accurately records all data in view for later analysis - increases objectivity.	May produce participant reactivity and unnatural behaviour due to intimidation.
• **One way mirrors** in laboratories.	Reduces participant reactivity.	Unethical if subjects are not informed.
CONTENT ANALYSIS A **quantitative** method for analysing the **communication** of people and organisations, e.g. in their conversations, or media records. The researcher first decides what media they are going to sample and then devises the **coding units** they are interested in measuring, e.g. the frequency of, or amount of time and space devoted to, certain words or themes.	Content analysis is a useful tool for gathering data on a variety of topics, from rhetorical devices used in political speeches to the stereotyping or aggressive content of books and films. It can be used to assess what is omitted from speech, not just what is included. The data gained is usually of high ecological validity.	It is sometimes difficult to arrive at objectively operationalised coding units and the technique can be time consuming. Content analysis can be used to examine the function that a person's or organisation's communication serves, e.g. justifying or criticising, but the analyst's interpretations are also open to interpretation!
QUALITATIVE DATA ANALYSIS The analysis of qualitative data in its own right, without reducing it to quantitative numbers, can be very useful. Qualitative data can be gained from a variety of methods, such as observations, interviews, case studies and even experiments - for example in terms of **how** the subject **behaved** during testing and what they **said**.	Qualitative data is useful to describe information lost in the quantified and narrowed analysis of figures. Interviews with subjects after experiments can often reveal the causes of their behaviour and provide ideas for future research. However, qualitative analysis can be a useful research tool in its own right - arriving at an in-depth analysis and discussion of behaviour.	Qualitative analysis is often attacked for its lack of objectivity. However, • techniques exist to check its reliability and validity, e.g. triangulation (using more than one method of investigation) and repetition of the research cycle (to check previous data). • subjective opinion and participant consultation is regarded as a strength by many researchers, e.g. feminists.

Non-experimental methods 2. Questioning

HOW DO PSYCHOLOGISTS INVESTIGATE THEIR HYPOTHESES?

> **QUESTIONING PEOPLE**
> There are many techniques for gathering **self report** data, which can be employed in varying detail - from the superficial survey of many people to the in-depth assessment of individuals.

TECHNIQUES	EXAMPLES	STRENGTHS	WEAKNESSES
INTERVIEWS All interviews involve direct verbal questioning of the subject by the researcher, but differ in how structured the questions are:		Generally, interviews generate a large amount of detailed data, especially about internal mental states/beliefs.	Generally interviews rely on self report data which may be untrue. Cause and effect can not be inferred.
• **Structured interviews** - contain fixed predetermined questions and ways of replying (e.g. yes/no).	Usually used in large scale interview-based surveys, e.g. market research.	Easy to quantify and analyse. Reliable, replicable and generalisable.	Less validity - distorts/ignores data due to restricted answers or insensitivity.
• **Semi-structured interviews** - contain guidelines for questions to be asked, but phrasing and timing are left up to the interviewer and answers may be open-ended.	Schedule for affective disorders and schizophrenia – a diagnostic interview. Most employment interviews.	Fairly flexible and sensitive. Fairly reliable and easy to analyse.	Flexibility of phrasing and timing could lead to lower reliability. Open-ended answers are more tricky to analyse.
• **Clinical interview** - semi-structured guidelines but further questioning to elaborate upon answers.	Piaget's interviewing of his children. Freud's interviewing of his patients.	Very flexible, sensitive and valid. Fairly reliable and easy to analyse.	Flexibility leads to more difficulty in replication and bias from interviewer.
• **Unstructured interview** - may contain a topic area for discussion but no fixed questions or ways of answering. Interviewer helps and clarifies interview.	Often used in humanistic based therapy interviews.	Highly detailed and valid data. Extremely flexible, natural and un-constrained.	Very unstandardised, therefore, not very replicable, reliable or generalisable. Difficult to quantify and analyse.
QUESTIONNAIRES Questionnaires are written methods of gaining data from subjects that do not necessarily require the presence of a researcher. They include:		Generally questionnaires collect large amounts of standardised data relatively quickly and conveniently.	Generally questionnaires lack flexibility, are based on self report data and are biased by motivation levels.
• **Opinion surveys,** e.g. attitude scales and opinion polls. Questions can be closed or open-ended and should be precise, understandable and easy to answer.	Likert attitude scales.	Highly replicable and easy to score (unless open-ended answers).	Biased by socially desirable answers, acquiescence (agreeing with items) and response set (replying in the same way).
• **Psychological tests,** e.g. personality and I.Q. tests. Items need to be standardised for a population and tested to show reliability, validity and discriminatory power.	Eysenck's personality inventory (to measure extroversion for example) or Bem's sex role inventory (to assess gender role identity).	Highly replicable and standardised between individuals. Easy to score.	Difficult to construct highly reliable and valid tests.

Non-experimental methods 3. Case study and correlation

HOW DO PSYCHOLOGISTS INVESTIGATE THEIR HYPOTHESES?

TECHNIQUES AND EXAMPLES

CASE STUDY

An idiographic method involving the **in-depth** and **detailed** study of an **individual** or particular group. The case study method is often applied to unusual or valuable examples of behaviour which may provide important insights into psychological function or refutation of psychological theory.
Examples of case studies include: Freud's studies of his patients and Piaget's studies of his children.

CORRELATIONS

A method of data analysis which measures the relationship between two or more variables to see if a trend or systematic pattern exists between them. Inferential statistics can be used to arrive at a correlation coefficient which indicates the strength and type of correlation, ranging from:

−1 −.9 −.8 −.7 −.6 −.5 −.4 −.3 −.2 −.1 0 +.1 +.2 +.3 +.4 +.5 +.6 +.7 +.8 +.9 **+1**

| perfect negative correlation | strong negative correlation | weak negative correlation | NO correlation | weak positive correlation | strong positive correlation | perfect positive correlation |

STRENGTHS

Highly detailed and in depth data is provided which superficial methods might miss or ignore.

High ecological validity of data obtained.

Often the only method suitable for studying some forms of behaviour, e.g. investigating the acquisition of human language in primates.

Often the only method possible due to rarity of behaviour, e.g. natural cases of human environmental deprivation, such as the case of Genie.

Precise information on the degree of relationship between variables is available in the form of the correlation coefficient. It can readily quantify observational data.

No manipulation of behaviour is required.

Strong significant correlations can suggest ideas for experimental studies to determine cause and effect relationships.

WEAKNESSES

No cause and effect can legitimately be inferred.

Lack of generalisability to the population due to single cases being too small and unrepresentative a sample.

Low reliability due to
• many case studies involving recall of past events, which may be open to memory distortion.
• subject reactivity
• lack of observer objectivity

Difficult or impossible to replicate.

Time consuming and expensive.

No cause and effect can be inferred.

Correlations should be plotted out on scattergrams to properly illustrate the relationship between variables - a zero correlation coefficient may not form a random pattern.
For example, both of these patterns would not yield a significant correlational result.

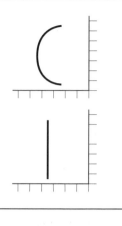

Sampling

HOW DO PSYCHOLOGISTS SELECT THEIR SUBJECTS?

SAMPLING

- Sampling is the process of selecting subjects to study from the **target population** (a specified section of humankind).
- Since the results of the study on the sample will be generalised back to the target population (through inference), samples should be as **representative** (typical) of the target population as possible.
- Samples should be of a sufficient size (e.g. 30) to represent the variety of individuals in a target population, but not so large as to make the study uneconomical in terms of time and resources.

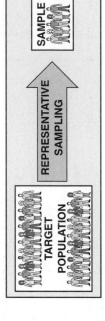

TARGET POPULATION

REPRESENTATIVE SAMPLING

SAMPLE

TYPES OF SAMPLING

RANDOM
Truly random sampling only occurs when **every member** of a target population has an **equal chance** of being selected.
For example:
Putting the names of every member of the target population into a hat and pulling a sample out (without looking!).

STRATIFIED
Involves **dividing** the target population into important **subcategories** (or strata) and then selecting members of these subcategories in the **proportion** that they occur in the target population.
For example:
If a target population consisted of 75% women and 25% men, a sample of 20 should include 15 women and 5 men.

OPPORTUNITY
Opportunity sampling simply involves selecting those subjects that are around and **available at the time.** An effort may be made to not be biased in selecting particular types of subject.
For example:
University psychologists may sample from their students.

SELF-SELECTING
Self-selecting samples consist of those individuals who have consciously or unconsciously **determined their own involvement** in a study.
For example:
Volunteers for studies or passers by who become involved in field studies, i.e. in bystander intervention studies.

STRENGTHS

Random sampling (in large numbers) provides the **best chance of an unbiased representative sample** of a target population.

A **deliberate effort** is made to identify the characteristics of a sample most important for it **to be representative** of the target population.

It is **quick, convenient** and often the most economical method of sampling.
It has, therefore, been the most common type of sampling.

Self-selecting samples are relatively convenient and, if volunteering is made on the basis of informed consent, ethical. The choice is not biased by the researcher.

WEAKNESSES

The larger the target population, the more difficult it is to sample randomly, since compiling a selection list of everyone becomes more impractical. True random sampling is, therefore, very rare.

Stratified sampling can be very **time consuming,** since the subcategories have to be identified and their proportions in the target population calculated.

Opportunity sampling gives very unrepresentative samples and is often **biased** on the part of the **researcher** who may choose subjects who will be 'helpful'.

Self-selecting samples are often unrepresentative - being **biased** on the part of the **subject**. Volunteers are unlike non-volunteers in many ways.

Experimental design

REPEATED MEASURES

INDEPENDENT MEASURES

MATCHED PAIRS

DESIGN

A repeated measures design involves using the **same subjects** in each condition of an experiment, e.g. giving a group of subjects a driving test with no alcohol, followed at a later time by the same test after a pint of lager.

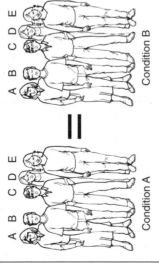

Condition A   =   Condition B

An independent measures design involves using **different subjects** in each condition of the experiment, e.g. giving one group of subjects a driving test with no alcohol, and a different group of subjects the same test after a pint of lager.

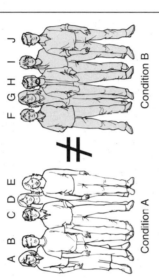

Condition A   ≠   Condition B

A matched pairs design involves using **different but similar subjects** in each condition of an experiment. An effort is made to match the subjects in each condition in any important characteristics that might affect performance,
e.g. in driving ability, alcohol tolerance, etc.

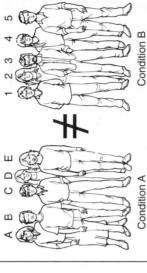

Condition A   ≠   Condition B

STRENGTHS

- **Subject variables** (individual differences shown by every subject, e.g. intelligence, motivation, past experience, etc.) which could become extraneous variables are **kept constant** between conditions.
- **Better statistical tests** can be used because of less variation between conditions.
- **Fewer subjects** are required (because each is used more than once) therefore more economical.

- **Order effects** such as learning, fatigue or boredom do not influence a second condition, since the subject only participates in one condition.
- **Demand characteristics** are less of a problem as the subject only participates in one condition so is naive to the test, and is less likely to guess the aim of the study and act differently.
- The **same test** can be used.

- **Subject variables** are kept **more constant** between conditions.
- **Better statistical tests** can be used because of less variation between conditions.
- **Order effects** do not occur since the subject only participates in one condition.
- **Demand characteristics** are less of a problem as the subject only participates in one condition.
- The **same test** can be used.

WEAKNESSES

- **Order effects** such as learning, fatigue or boredom may become constant errors when one condition is done after another, e.g. a subject given the same test may do better due to practice.
- **Demand characteristics** may become a problem - as the subject does both conditions of the experiment, they may guess the aim of the study and act differently.
- **Different tests** may be needed.

- **Subject variables differ,** which could become confouncing variables unless controlled for.
- **Worse statistical tests** can be used because of more variation between conditions.
- **More subjects** are required (because each is used only once) and is, therefore, less economical.

- **Subject variables** can never be perfectly matched in every respect.
- Matching subjects is very **time consuming** and **difficult.**
- **More subjects** are required (because each is used only once) and is, therefore, less economical.

Controlling extraneous variables and bias

HOW DO PSYCHOLOGISTS CONTROL EXTRANEOUS VARIABLES AND BIAS IN THEIR STUDIES?

TYPE OF PROBLEM	PROBLEM	METHOD OF CONTROL
SUBJECTS	**INDIVIDUAL DIFFERENCES** Subject variables can become a problem especially in an independent measures design, creating random or even constant confounding effects.	**Sample large** and **randomly** to gain a representative sample. Use a repeated measures or matched pairs design. **Allocate** subjects **randomly** to each condition of an independent measures experiment to balance out subject variables.
METHOD	**ARTIFICIALITY** Laboratory environments and operationalised variables may lack ecological validity.	Use a **non**-laboratory environment instead, e.g. field study. Broaden or increase the number of definitions for the operationalised variable.
DESIGN	**ORDER EFFECTS** Where learning, boredom or fatigue can influence the second condition of an experiment using a repeated measures design.	Use independent measures design instead. Delay or change the second test. **Counterbalance** the conditions, by getting half the subjects to perform condition A before condition B, and the other half to perform condition B before condition A, thereby balancing the order effects equally between conditions.
	DEMAND CHARACTERISTICS Working out the aim of the study and behaving differently (e.g. trying to please the researcher or spoil the study).	Use independent measures design to stop exposure to both conditions of the experiment, therefore reducing chances of guessing the aim of the study. Use **deception** to hide research aim. However, there are ethical problems with this. Use **single blind method** - the subject does not know which condition of the experiment they are in, e.g. whether they have been given placebo or real pills.
	EXPERIMENTER EXPECTANCY Where the expectations of the researcher influence the results either by consciously or unconsciously revealing the desired outcome or through unconscious procedural or recording bias.	Use **double blind method** - neither the subject nor the researcher carrying out the procedure and recording the results knows the hypothesis or which condition the subjects are in. Use **inter-observer reliability** measures to overcome biased observation. An observer with no vested interest in the result, simultaneously, but separately, rates the same piece of behaviour with the researcher. When results are compared, a high positive correlation should be expected.
PROCEDURE	**DISTRACTION AND CONFUSION** Both sources of extraneous variables which could confound studies unless controlled for.	Standardised instructions should be given in a clear and simple form and the subject should be asked if they have questions, so each participant receives equal information. Standardised procedures should be employed so each subject is tested under equal conditions with no distractions.

Reliability and validity of studies

HOW DO PSYCHOLOGISTS TEST THE QUALITY OF STUDIES?

RELIABILITY
The reliability of a method of measurement (whether it be an experimental test, questionnaire or observational procedure) refers to how **consistently** it measures.

INTERNAL RELIABILITY
Internal reliability refers to **how consistently a method measures within itself**. If methods of measurement were not **standardised** they would give distorted final scores.
For example, internal reliability would be lacking if
- a ruler consisted of variable centimetres,
- an I.Q. test was made up of half ridiculously easy questions and half ridiculously difficult questions (virtually everyone would score half marks and be equally intelligent!) or
- different observers using the same observational definitions simultaneously scored the same individual differently.

Internal reliability could be checked for test items by the **split half method** - correlating the results of half the items with the other half (e.g. the odd numbers with the even numbers of the test) and gaining a high positive correlation coefficient.

EXTERNAL RELIABILITY
External reliability refers to **how consistently a method measures over time when repeated**. Methods of measurement should give similar scores when repeated on the same people under similar conditions.
For example external reliability would be lacking if
- a ruler measured an unchanging object different lengths each time it was used,
- an I.Q. test scored the same person a genius one day but just average a week later.

External reliability could be checked for test items by the **test-, re-test method** - correlating the results of the test conducted on one occasion with the results of the test conducted on a later occasion (with the same subjects) and gaining a high positive correlation coefficient.

VALIDITY
The validity of a method of measurement (whether it be an experimental test, questionnaire or observational procedure) refers to whether it **measures what it is supposed to measure** - how realistically or truly variables have been operationalised.

INTERNAL VALIDITY - refers to whether the results of a study were really due to the variables the researchers suggest were tested by their methodology.

EXTERNAL VALIDITY refers to whether the results can be generalised if conducted in different environments or using different participants.

FACE/CONTENT VALIDITY
Face or content validity involves **examining** the content of the test to see if it **looks** like it measures what it is supposed to measure.
For example, examining the test items of an intelligence test to see if they seem to measure general intelligence, not just general knowledge or linguistic comprehension.

CONCURRENT VALIDITY
Concurrent validity involves **comparing** a **new** method or test **with** an already well **established** one that claims to measure the same variable(s). A high positive correlation should be gained between the results of the two tests.
For example, correlating the results from the same people tested by a new intelligence test and an older established one.

CONSTRUCT VALIDITY
Construct validity refers to whether the test or method can be used to **support** the **underlying theoretical constructs** concerning the variable that it is supposed to be measuring.
For example, if theory suggests the offspring of two highly intelligent parents raised in a stimulating environment should be intelligent, an IQ test should confirm this.

PREDICTIVE VALIDITY
Predictive validity refers to whether the test will **predict future performance** indicated by its results.
For example, high scorers on an I.Q. test at a young age should be predicted to later perform better in studies or jobs requiring intelligence.

ECOLOGICAL VALIDITY
Ecological validity refers to whether a test or method measures behaviour that is representative of naturally occurring behaviour. Too specifically operationalised tests or those conducted under contrived conditions may not reflect spontaneously occurring, natural behaviour. For example, do the items on an intelligence test represent all the types of behaviour we would describe as intelligent in everyday life?
However, since there is difficulty in saying what conditions are 'natural' or 'normal' (laboratories are human social situations too, while some field studies may be conducted under very unusual circumstances) ecological validity is perhaps best measured by the extent to which research findings can be generalised to other research settings.

'A nation of morons' Gould (1982)

AIM
To describe one part of the early history of intelligence testing as a way of discussing the following issues in psychology:
- The problematic nature of psychometric testing in general and the measurement of intelligence in particular.
- The problem of theoretical bias influencing research in psychology, in particular how psychological theories on the inherited nature of intelligence and the prejudice of a society can dramatically distort the objectivity of intelligence testing.
- The problem of the political and ethical implications of research, in this case the use of biased data to discriminate between people in suitability for occupation and even admission to a country.

THE HISTORY OF YERKES' TESTING OF INTELLIGENCE

What did Yerkes aim to do?
Yerkes aimed to
- show that psychology could prove itself as a respectable science by using intelligence testing to aid recruitment, and
- find support for the hereditarian view of intelligence (that intellectual ability was inherited through the genes).

How did Yerkes test intelligence?
Yerkes tested 1.75 million army recruits during the First World War, using three intelligence tests:
- Army alpha - a written exam for literate recruits
- Army beta - A pictorial exam for illiterate recruits and those who failed the alpha
- Individual exam - for those who failed the beta

Every individual was given a grade from A to E (with plus and minus signs), for example:

C- indicated a low average intelligence, suitable for the position of ordinary private in the army

D indicated a person rarely suited for tasks requiring special skill, forethought, resourcefulness or sustained alertness

What did Yerkes find?
- White American adults had an average mental age of 13, just above the level of moronity.
- Nations could be graded in their intelligence based on immigrants' intelligence test scores - people from Nordic countries scored higher than those from Latin or Slavic countries, with American 'Negroes' at the bottom of the scale.

What was wrong with Yerkes' findings?
Lots - they were a methodological, ethical, and practical disaster!

Methodological problems:	• Validity errors - the tests did not measure innate intelligence, since questions were often based on American general knowledge that recent immigrants would be unlikely to know e.g. 'The number of Kaffir's legs is - 2, 4, 6 or 8 ?' (Army alpha test) The Army beta asked often poor and illiterate immigrants to spot errors in pictures of things they had probably never seen before (e.g. a tennis match without a net) and then write their answer.
	• Reliability errors - unstandardised procedures were followed, with individuals being given the wrong test, being rushed, and not given the appropriate re-tests - especially during the testing of black subjects.
Interpretation of findings errors:	• Ignored experience issue - the finding that immigrants scored higher the longer they stayed in America
	• Ignored education issue - the finding that there was a positive correlation between number of years in education and the IQ test scores - Yerkes interpreted causation from this by arguing that intelligent people chose to stay longer in education.
Negative implications of faulty conclusions:	• Intelligence can be objectively measured - therefore, people were assigned military positions and tasks according to their scores.
	• Intelligence is inherited - therefore, providing illegitimate evidence for those who advocated eugenics (selective breeding in humans), racist politics, and immigration restriction (the tests were influential in denying the immigration into America of up to 6 million people from Southern, Central, and Eastern Europe, many seeking political refuge, from 1924 to 1939).
	• IQ tests can predict future performance - thus providing biased support for the argument that special educational measures were a waste of time and money.

EVALUATION

Methodological: Gould's criticism is based primarily on a methodological and theoretical critique of Yerkes' testing without presenting any empirical support for his own views.

Theoretical: Contributes to an evaluation of an area of psychology which has many important implications. IQ tests have improved in sophistication, although there is still debate over their validity.

Links: The ethics of socially sensitive research, the nature-nurture debate in intelligence, the validity and reliability of psychometric testing, bias in cross-cultural testing (see Deregowski).

Timing and location of investigations

WHEN SHOULD PSYCHOLOGISTS INVESTIGATE?

CROSS-SECTIONAL STUDIES

In cross-sectional studies subjects of **different** ages are investigated **at one particular point in time**. It is a form of independent measures design.

LONGITUDINAL STUDIES

In longitudinal studies the **same** subjects are investigated **over a long period of time**. It is a form of repeated measures design.

WHERE SHOULD PSYCHOLOGISTS INVESTIGATE?

CROSS-CULTURAL STUDIES

In cross-cultural studies subjects from **different cultures** are given the same test and their results are compared.

EXAMPLES

ASCH (1951)

Asch's findings on conformity were not replicated by some later researchers, indicating that his findings may have been influenced by factors present in his society *at that particular time*.
Kohlberg (1981) compared the moral development of three groups of boys aged 10, 13 and 16.

KOHLBERG (1971)

Kohlberg conducted a twenty year longitudinal study of moral reasoning.
Developmental psychologists concentrate on how abilities and behaviour may vary over time, from infancy to adulthood, and so may find that studying the same subjects over a long period of time is the most accurate way of discovering the principles and processes of development.

MEAD (1935)

Mead studied three different tribes in New Guinea and compared their gender role behaviours.
Cross-cultural studies have investigated whether variation occurs in different countries in conformity, obedience, intelligence, perception and attachment - to name just a few examples in psychology.

STRENGTHS

- Immediate results can be gained, therefore, they are convenient.
- Cheaper and less time consuming than longitudinal studies.
- Less likelihood of losing subjects between conditions.

- Less bias from subject variables.
- In some areas of psychology, such as mental illness, a longitudinal study may be the only way of determining how a disorder progresses.

- Combats an ethnocentric culturally biased view of human psychology.
- Widens the generalisability of results.
- Provides data on cultural differences or similarities which may increase understanding of psychological development.

WEAKNESSES

- Cross-sectional studies may be overly influenced by the social environment of the time, and therefore need to be regularly replicated.
- All disadvantages of independent measures design, e.g. subject confounding variables, greater number of subjects needed, etc.
- Cohort effect may bias data.

- Time consuming, expensive and high likelihood of losing subjects between conditions.
- Extremely difficult or impossible to replicate exactly.
- Longitudinal studies can be carried out retrospectively by examining the history of subjects, but this has many disadvantages, such as memory distortion and lack of objectivity.

- More time consuming, difficult (due to language barriers etc.) and expensive.
- Open to ethnocentric misinterpretation when researchers from one culture investigate another culture.
- Subject reactivity may increase with a cross-cultural observer, producing untypical behaviour.

Numerical descriptive statistics

HOW DO PSYCHOLOGISTS SUMMARIZE THEIR DATA NUMERICALLY?

LEVELS OF DATA

NOMINAL
Nominal data is a simple **frequency headcount** (the number of times something occurred) found in **discrete categories** (something can only belong to one category).

For example, the number of people who helped or did not help in an emergency.

Nominal data is the simplest data.

ORDINAL
Ordinal data is measurements that can be put in an **order**, **rank** or **position.**

For example, scores on unstandardised psychological scales (such as attractiveness out of 10) or who came 1st, 2nd, 3rd, etc. in a race.

The **intervals** between each rank, however, are **unknown,** i.e. how far ahead 1st was from 2nd.

INTERVAL AND RATIO
Both are measurements on a **scale**, the **intervals** of which are **known and equal**. **Ratio** data has a **true zero** point, whereas **interval** data can go into **negative** values.

For example, **temperature** for interval data (degrees centigrade can be minus) **length** or **time** for ratio data (no seconds is no time at all).

The most **precise** types of data.

MEASURES OF CENTRAL TENDENCY

MODE
The value or event that occurs the most frequently.
The most suitable measure of central tendency for nominal data.
Not influenced by extreme scores; useful to show most popular value.
Crude measure of central tendency; not useful if many equal modes.

MEDIAN
The middle value when all scores are placed in rank order.
The most suitable measure of central tendency for ordinal data.
Not distorted by extreme freak values, e.g. 2, 3, 3, 4, 4, 4, 4, 5, 5, 6, 42.
However, it can be distorted by small samples and is less sensitive.

MEAN
The average value of all scores.
The most suitable measure of central tendency for interval or ratio data.
The most sensitive measure of central tendency for all data.
However, can be distorted by extreme freak values.

MEASURES OF DISPERSION

RANGE	ADVANTAGE	DISADVANTAGE
the difference between the smallest and largest value, plus 1. For example, 3, 4, 7, 7, 8, 9, 12, 4, 17, 17, 18 **(18 - 3) +1 = Range of 16**	• Quick and easy to calculate.	• Distorted by extreme 'freak' values, an extra value of 43 would give a range of 41.

SEMI-INTERQUARTILE RANGE
 When data is put in order, find the first quartile (Q1) and third quartile (Q3) of the sample, subtract the Q1 value from the Q3 value and divide the result by two.
 For example,
 3, 4, 7, 7 8, 9, 12, 14, 17, 17, 18
    ↑   ↑   ↑
   Q1   Q2   Q3
    7   17
 17 - 7 = 10 10 ÷ 2 = **Semi-interquartile range of 5**
	• Less distorted by any extreme 'freak' values.	• Ignores extreme values.

STANDARD DEVIATION The average amount all scores deviate from the mean. The difference (deviation) between each score and the mean of those scores is calculated and then squared (to remove minus values). These squared deviations are then added up and their mean calculated to give a value known as the variance. The square root of the variance gives the standard deviation of the scores.	• The most sensitive measure of dispersion, using all the data available. • Can be used to relate the sample to the population's parameters.	• A little more time consuming to calculate but no important disadvantages.

Standard deviation worked example:

score	mean	d	d squared
6 –	10 =	−4	16
8 –	10 =	−2	4
10 –	10 =	0	0
12 –	10 =	+2	4
14 –	10 =	+4	16
			40

mean of 40 = 8 = variance
square root of variance
= standard deviation = 2.8

Graphical descriptive statistics

HOW DO PSYCHOLOGISTS SUMMARIZE THEIR DATA PICTORIALLY?

FREQUENCY POLYGON

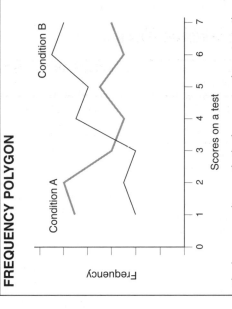

Also known as a line graph, the frequency polygon is similar to the histogram, except that it allows two or more sets of data to be shown on the same graph.

NORMAL DISTRIBUTION

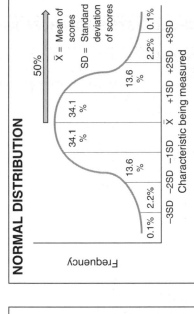

Normal distribution curves occur in the populations of many continuous psychological variables and are involved in parametric statistics. They are bell shaped and symmetrical at the midpoint where the mode, median and mean all fall.
The percentage of scores covered by the areas between the standard deviations of the curve are known.

HISTOGRAMS

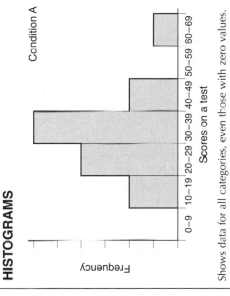

Shows data for all categories, even those with zero values.
The column width for each category interval is equal so the area of the column is proportional to the number of cases it contains of the sample.

SCATTERGRAMS

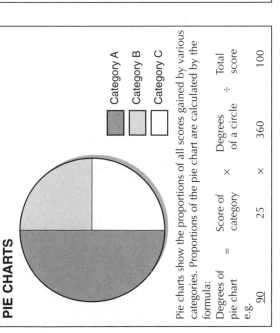

Scattergrams plot pairs of scores against each other to show their correlational relationship.
Emergent patterns or trends in the data can be calculated to show a line of best fit.

BAR CHARTS

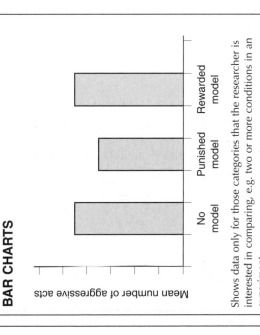

Shows data only for those categories that the researcher is interested in comparing, e.g. two or more conditions in an experiment.

PIE CHARTS

Pie charts show the proportions of all scores gained by various categories. Proportions of the pie chart are calculated by the formula:

Degrees of pie chart	=	Score of category	×	Degrees of a circle	÷	Total score
e.g.						
90		25	×	360		100

■ Category A
▨ Category B
□ Category C

Inferential statistics

HOW DO PSYCHOLOGISTS KNOW HOW SIGNIFICANT THEIR RESULTS ARE?

WHAT IS MEANT BY SIGNIFICANCE?

DEFINITION: A significant result is one where there is a **low probability that chance factors** were responsible for any observed difference, correlation or association in the variables tested.

FOR EXAMPLE

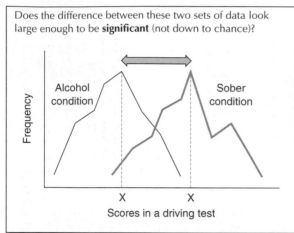

Does the difference between these two sets of data look large enough to be **significant** (not down to chance)?

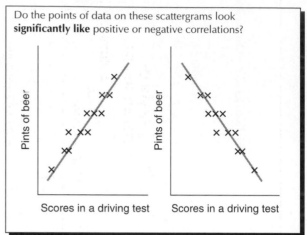

Do the points of data on these scattergrams look **significantly like** positive or negative correlations?

HOW SIGNIFICANT DO RESULTS HAVE TO BE?

LEVELS OF SIGNIFICANCE

How large an effect (difference or relationship) is required for psychologists to conclude that a result is significant (not probably due to chance factors)?

Significance levels are expressed as a decimal in the form **P < 0.00** where 'P' stands for probability that chance factors are responsible for results

Psychologists have concluded that for most purposes in psychology, the 5% level of significance (**P < 0.05**) is appropriate; a result that is significant at this level can be said to be less than 5% likely to be due to chance factors (a 1 in 20 chance it was a 'fluke' result).

There are many other possible levels of probability but the P < 0.05 seems reasonable since:

- Significance levels of: **P < 0.5** (a 50% or 50:50 probability that chance factors were responsible) or **P < 0.3** (a 30% or roughly 1 in 3 probability that chance factors were responsible)

  are regarded as **too lenient** - the effect (difference or correlation) is too likely to have happened by chance and a **type one error** is more likely to be made (the **null hypothesis may be falsely rejected** - the researcher may falsely claim an effect exists).

- Significance levels of: **P < 0.01** (a 1% or 1 in a 100 probability that chance factors were responsible) or **P < 0.001** (a 0.1% or 1 in a 1000 probability that chance factors were responsible)

  are regarded as **too strict or stringent** - a strong effect (difference or correlation) is too likely to be ignored because the level is overly demanding and a **type two error** is more likely to be made (the **null hypothesis may be falsely accepted** - the researcher may falsely claim an effect does not exist).

N.B. - Stringent levels are required when greater certainty of significance is needed, e.g. during safety tests.

WHAT DO INFERENTIAL STATISTICAL TESTS TELL PSYCHOLOGISTS?

INFERENTIAL STATISTICAL TESTS

Inferential statistical tests provide a calculated value based on the results of the investigation.

This value can then be compared to a critical value (a value that statisticians have estimated to represent a significant effect) to determine whether the results are significant.

The critical value depends upon the level of significance required (P < 0.05, P < 0.01, etc.) and other factors such as the number of subjects used in the test and whether the hypothesis is one or two tailed.

In the Chi squared, Sign test, Spearman's Rho, Pearson's product and Related or Unrelated T-tests, the **calculated** value has to **exceed** the **critical** value for a significant result.

Inferential statistics allow us to **infer** that the **effect gained from** the results on a **sample** of subjects is **probably typical of** the **target population** the sample was derived from.

Choosing inferential statistical tests

HOW DO PSYCHOLOGISTS CHOOSE AN APPROPRIATE STATISTICAL TEST?

1 TEST OF DIFFERENCE OR RELATIONSHIP REQUIRED?
2 WHAT EXPERIMENTAL DESIGN HAS BEEN USED?
3 WHAT LEVEL OF DATA IS BEING USED?
4 ARE ALL THREE PARAMETRIC CONDITIONS MET?
   a Interval or ratio data
   b Both sets of data normally
      distributed or from normally
      distributed populations
   c Both sets of data have
      similar variance.

1

TESTS OF RELATIONSHIP

CORRELATION   OR   ASSOCIATION

	TESTS OF DIFFERENCE		TESTS OF RELATIONSHIP
	INDEPENDENT MEASURES DESIGN	REPEATED MEASURES OR MATCHED PAIRS DESIGN	CORRELATION OR ASSOCIATION
NOMINAL DATA	CHI SQUARED TEST	SIGN TEST	CHI SQUARED TEST
ORDINAL DATA	MANN WHITNEY U TEST*	WILCOXON SIGNED RANKS TESTS*	SPEARMAN'S RHO CORRELATION
INTERVAL OR RATIO DATA	UNRELATED T-TEST	RELATED T-TEST	PEARSON'S PRODUCT MOMENT CORRELATION COEFFICIENT

2

3

4

PARAMETRIC TESTS
The most powerful
and sensitive tests.

* NB The two ordinal level tests of difference are the only ones where the calculated value of the test has to be LESS THAN the critical value.

Research methods 109

Ethical guidelines for conducting research

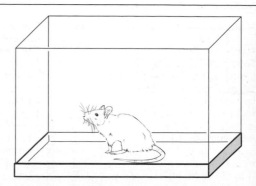

ETHICAL GUIDELINES FOR THE USE OF ANIMALS IN RESEARCH

The Experimental Psychology Society (1986) has issued guidelines to control animal experimentation based on the legislation of the 'Animals (Scientific Procedures) Act' (1986). In general all researchers should:

1. Avoid or minimise stress and suffering for all living animals.
2. Always consider the possibility of other options to animal research.
3. Be as economical as possible in the numbers of animals tested.

However, before any animal is tested a Home Office Licence to conduct animal research has to be acquired. The Home Office provides legislation for and monitors:

- **The conditions under which animals are kept** – cage sizes, food, lighting, temperature, care routine etc. all have to be suitable for the species and its habits.
- **The researchers conducting the research** – all involved have to demonstrate they have the necessary skills and experience to work with the particular species they wish to study in order to acquire their personal licences.
- **The research projects allowed** – applications must be submitted outlining the project's aims and possible benefits as well as the procedures involved (including the number of animals and the degree of distress they might experience). Projects are only approved if the three requirements above are met and the levels of distress caused to the animals are justified by the benefits of the research. The conditions of the licence have to be strictly adhered to regarding the numbers, species and procedures (e.g. limits on the maximum level of electric shock) allowed. Research on endangered species is prohibited unless the research has direct benefits for the species itself, e.g. conservation.

Bateson (1986) has specified some of the factors involved in deciding on the viability of animal research. Often the decision will involve a trade off between

a. The certainty of benefit from the research.
b. The quality of the research.
c. The amount of suffering involved for the animals.

Home Office licences are most likely to be awarded if factors 'a' and 'b' are high, and factor 'c' is low.

ETHICAL ISSUES IN HUMAN RESEARCH

The aim of Psychology is to provide us with a greater understanding of ourselves and, if required, to enable us to use that understanding to predict and control our behaviour for **human betterment**. To achieve this understanding psychologists often have no other choice but to investigate human subjects for valid results to be obtained. Humans, however, not only experience physical ***pain*** and ***anxiety*** but can also be affected mentally - in terms of ***embarrassment*** or ***loss of self-esteem*** for example. Humans also have **rights** of ***protection*** and ***privacy*** above the levels granted to other animals, and so this leads us to ethical dilemmas:

- How far should psychologists be allowed to go in pursuing their knowledge?
- Should humankind aim to improve itself by allowing people to be dehumanised in the process?
- Do the **ends** of psychological research **justify** the **means**?
- Can we ever know whether a piece of research will justify abusing the rights of individuals before we conduct it?

The existence of ethical constraints is clearly a serious but necessary limitation on the advancement of Psychology as a science and the major professional psychological bodies of many countries have published ethical guidelines for conducting research. In Britain, the British Psychological Society (1993) has published the "***Ethical Principles for Conducting Research with Human Participants***", which guides psychologists to consider the implications of their research (e.g. by asking members of the target population if they would take offence to the research) and deals with a number of methodological ethical issues such as:

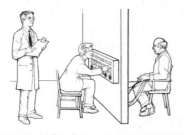

CONSENT - Researchers are obliged, whenever possible, to obtain the participants' ***informed*** consent - *all* aspects of the research that might affect their willingness to give consent should be revealed. Consent is especially an issue when testing involves children or those unable to give it themselves, e.g. people with serious brain damage. Authority or payment must not be used to pressure participants into consent.

DECEPTION - The BPS Ethical Principles (1993) states that "Participants should never be deliberately misled without extremely strong scientific or medical justification. Even then there should be strict controls and the disinterested approval of independent advisors". Many psychology studies would not achieve valid results due to demand characteristics if deception was not employed, and so a cost-benefit analysis of the gains vs. the discomfort of the participant must be considered.

DEBRIEFING - Involves clarifying the participants' understanding of the research afterwards and discussing or rectifying any consequences of the study to ensure that they leave the study in as similar a state as possible to when they entered it. This is especially important if deception has been employed and the procedures could cause long term upset.

WITHDRAWAL FROM THE INVESTIGATION - Any participant in a psychological study should be informed of their right to withdraw from testing whenever they wish.

CONFIDENTIALITY - Under the Data Protection Act (1984) participants and the data they provide should be kept anonymous unless they have given their full consent to make their data public. If participants are dissatisfied after debriefing they can demand their data is destroyed.

PROTECTION OF PARTICIPANTS - Participants should leave psychological studies in roughly the same condition in which they arrived, without suffering physical or psychological harm. The risk of harm should not be greater than that found in everyday life.

OBSERVATIONAL RESEARCH - Hidden observational studies produce the most ecologically valid data but inevitably raise the ethical issue of invasion of privacy.

INDEX

Bold type indicates main entries.